Play Time

FILM AND CULTURE SERIES

FILM AND CULTURE

A series of Columbia University Press

Edited by John Belton

For a complete list of titles, see page 283

Play Time

Jacques Tati

and Comedic

Modernism

MALCOLM TURVEY

Columbia University Press

New York

Columbia University Press

Publishers Since 1893

New York   Chichester, West Sussex

cup.columbia.edu

Library of Congress Cataloging-in-Publication Data

Names: Turvey, Malcolm, 1969– author.

Title: Play time : Jacques Tati and comedic modernism / Malcolm Turvey.

Description: New York : Columbia University Press, [2019] |

Series: Film and culture | Includes bibliographical references and index.

Identifiers: LCCN 2019013487 | ISBN 9780231193023 (cloth : alk. paper) |

ISBN 9780231193030 (paperback : alk. paper) | ISBN 9780231550116 (ebook)

Subjects: LCSH: Tati, Jacques—Criticism and interpretation. |

Comedy films—France—20th century—History and criticism.

Classification: LCC PN1998.3.T374 T87 2019 | DDC 791.4302/8092—dc23

LC record available at https://lccn.loc.gov/2019013487

Columbia University Press books are printed

on permanent and durable acid-free paper.

Printed in the United States of America

COVER DESIGN: Julia Kushnirsky

COVER IMAGE: *Mon Oncle* (Jacques Tati, 1958)

© Les Films de Mon Oncle

—Specta Films C.E.P.E.C.

For Will

CONTENTS

PREFACE AND ACKNOWLEDGMENTS

When I was thirteen years old, my parents took me to see my first Jacques Tati film, *Jour de fête* (1949). It was the summer of 1982, the year Tati died, and *Jour de fête* was enjoying one of its many revivals at the recently opened Barbican cinema in the City of London. I wish I could report that I was a precocious teenager who experienced an epiphany while watching the film. Sadly, for the most part, all I remember is being mildly bored by it (although I vividly recall the boy skipping behind the cart of merry-go-round horses as the fair leaves town at the end). I mention my first encounter with Tati not because it made a huge impression on me, but because my *parents* knew and admired Tati's films enough to want me to see them. Although my father and mother loved the arts and independently pursued music and painting later in life, neither went to university nor received any formal training in arts appreciation. My dad came from a working-class family badly scarred, like so many others, by World War II. He left school at fifteen and took a number of low-wage jobs before completing his national service and working his way into a white-collar profession by attending night school. My mum hailed from a slightly higher class, but only stayed at school until she was sixteen. However, they were lucky enough to come of age in England in the late 1950s, the "never-had-it-so-good" years of social mobility and prosperity recounted in exhaustive detail in David Kynaston's *Modernity Britain*, and by the time they took me to see *Jour de fête*, they were firmly middle class, if perhaps on the lower end.[1] In later years they would often fondly reminisce about the jazz clubs they had frequented and the movies—one of which may have been Tati's *Mon Oncle* (1958), which played in the UK in 1959—they had seen when going out in London in their twenties.

Tati is widely revered as one of the most innovative and challenging film-makers in the history of cinema. In "Fifteen Years of French Cinema," André Bazin's retrospective essay which he first delivered as a lecture in 1957, the great French film critic referred to Tati and Robert Bresson as "the two most original, and therefore unclassifiable, talents of postwar French cinema,"[2] and Tati is frequently included among the film modernists such as Bergman and Antonioni.[3] "Like Godard, Tati is among the few filmmakers who attempt both to criticize social conditions and to create films that force us into new film-viewing skills," writes Kristin Thompson in her seminal essay on *Play Time* (1967).[4] Yet unlike these other postwar modernist directors (and indeed unlike modernists in general), Tati's films won a popular audience and were box office successes until the commercial disaster of *Play Time*.[5] When I, as a beneficiary of my parents' hard work and entry into the middle classes, began learning about the cinema at repertory theaters and then at the University of Kent in my late teens, I would often ask them if they had heard of filmmakers such as Godard, and their answer was invariably no. But Tati's films they knew and loved, and after they died, I discovered a videocassette of *Jour de fête* among their remaining possessions.

In this book, I try to explain how it was that Tati's films appealed to people like my parents—lovers of cinema, to be sure, but not educated cinephiles with any knowledge of elite film culture—while being almost universally hailed as "among the most original and audacious experiments in film construction of the postwar period" by critics.[6] How was Tati, perhaps alone among art cinema directors of the postwar period, able to craft a genuinely popular *and* radically innovative modernism? My answer, in brief, is that he systematically combined a modern-ist aesthetic with slapstick, sight gags, and other conventions of the mainstream tradition of comedian-centered comedy that had flowered in the silent era in the films of Charlie Chaplin and many others, thereby modernizing this tradition without ever abandoning it. His films, as I show in detail in chapters 2 and 3, struck a careful balance between avant-garde innovation and the established norms of comedian comedy, thereby capturing elite and mass audiences alike. Another way of saying this is that Tati mined the modernist potential of come-dian comedy, something avant-gardists had been doing since at least the 1910s. Of all the genres of mainstream cinema, modernists possibly felt the closest affinity for comedian comedy, and starting with the films of Chaplin, avant-gardists drew on the genre's conventions as I demonstrate in chapter 1. Tati's postwar films therefore continue an already established prewar tradition I call comedic modernism, although Tati inflected this tradition with the distinct concerns of postwar modernism, particularly the desire to democratize art.

The synthesis of modernism and comedian comedy in Tati's films is not the only reason for their widespread appeal. They also vividly express an attitude shared by many toward the rapid modernization that occurred in Western European societies after World War II as a result of renewed prosperity. This is not an antimodern or reactionary attitude, which has often erroneously been ascribed to Tati. Rather, it is much closer to what Alvin Toffler famously called future shock, which he defined as "the shattering stress and disorientation that we induce in individuals by subjecting them to too much change in too short a time."[7] My father, who experienced first-hand the British version of the modernization satirized in Tati's films, often remarked to me that it wasn't change he and others of his generation found hard, but the *rate* of change. I suspect that part of the appeal of Tati's films to him and others was that, through the character of Monsieur Hulot and the confusion he experiences in modern environments, they offered a concrete and humorous representation of the disorientation caused by the pace of postwar transformation, as I claim in chapter 4.

In writing this book, I have been standing on the shoulders of giants. Some of the greatest film critics and scholars have written about Tati, including Bazin, Jean-Luc Godard, Noël Burch, Jonathan Rosenbaum, Roy Armes, Michel Chion, and David Bordwell, and I often draw on their insights in what follows. In particular, I owe a huge debt to Lucy Fischer and Kristin Thompson, who both, in very different ways, have explored the connections between Tati's films and modernism. Fischer's dissertation on Tati is one of the best dissertations I have ever read, and it is a great shame it was never published in full. Thompson's articles on Tati, two of which are collected in her essential *Breaking the Glass Armor*, are indispensable in understanding Tati's style. Even though I disagree with them sometimes, I would not have been able to write this book without their pioneering work. The same is true of Noël Carroll's groundbreaking article "Notes on the Sight Gag," to which I repeatedly turn in the pages that follow. It is a cliché that comedy is hard to analyze, but Carroll's article incisively identifies and elucidates the gag structures in classical comedian comedy. I use it to show that Tati drew on these structures while modifying, radicalizing, and adding to them in pursuit of his modernist goals. It is also a cliché that, in analyzing comedy, one inevitably destroys it. I have never found this to be true, and it certainly isn't the case with Tati, at least for me. My deep dive into his comic style has only increased my appreciation for the enormity of his comic achievement, and my sincerest hope is that readers will come to share this appreciation.

This book originated in a paper I delivered at the annual conference of the Society for the Cognitive Study of the Moving Image (SCSMI) in 2010.

The enthusiastic response from audience members, especially David Bordwell and Kristin Thompson, encouraged me to develop the paper into a book-length project. Although I consider myself more of a fellow traveler than card-carrying member of SCSMI, the society has been the closest thing I have to an intellectual home for twenty years, and I am grateful for the friends I have made through it, particularly Johannes Riis.

Much of the initial research for the book was undertaken while I spent a blissful year in 2011–2012 with my family in Palo Alto as an external faculty fellow at the Humanities Center at Stanford University. One could not ask for an environment more conducive to thinking and writing than the center, and I thank its staff, especially Katja Zelljadt and Robert Barrick, for their help, as well as the other fellows, particularly Martin Blumenthal-Barby, for many stimulating conversations. Marie-Pierre Ullola, who was senior executive officer for international programs at the center that year, kindly arranged for me to give a master class on Tati at the 55th San Francisco International Film Festival in 2012, and the illuminating exchanges with participants showed me that Tati remains beloved by cinephiles.

Talks at a number of institutions helped me develop and clarify my ideas. I am especially grateful to Pavle Levi at Stanford, Johannes von Moltke at the University of Michigan, and Sarah Keller at Colby College for their invitations and feedback. An invitation from Christine Poggi and Anna Vallye to speak in 2013 at the fifth annual Anne d'Harnoncourt Symposium at the Philadelphia Museum of Art, titled Reconsidering Paris in the 1920s: Fernand Léger in an Expanded Context, gave me a welcome opportunity to begin formulating my thesis about comedic modernism.

While writing this book, I was appointed Sol Gittleman professor in the department of art and art history at Tufts University and was charged with launching and directing Tufts' new film and media studies program. Although this task slowed down my writing for several years, it would have ground to a halt without the help of my wonderful colleagues in the program: Nancy Bauer, Amahl Bishara, Jennifer Burton, Alessandra Campana, Lee Edelman, Nina Gerass-Navarro, Leslie Goldberg, Vida Johnson, Khary Jones, Natalie Minik, Gina O'Connor, Tasha Oren, Joel Rosenberg, Laurence Senelick, and Stephen White. The faculty in art and art history—Cristell Baskins, Eva Hoffman, Ikumi Kaminishi, Christina Maranci, Diana Martinez, Andrew McClellan, Jeremy Mellius, Karen Overby, Peter Probst, Eric Rosenberg, Jacob Stewart-Halevy, and Adriana Zavala—warmly welcomed me into the department, and they haven't complained (yet!) about the amount of time I spend directing the film and media studies program. In particular, I owe a huge debt to

Howard Woolf, who is a fount of knowledge and wisdom about all things Tufts, and to whom I have turned again and again for advice; and Susan Napier, whose world-renowned scholarship on Japanese anime remains a source of inspiration, and who generously read the final version of the manuscript. I have been particularly fortunate to have Hesamedin Sharifian as my teaching assistant since arriving at Tufts. Without him, the last few years would have been immeasurably harder, and I will miss him when he moves on to what I am sure will be a stellar academic career. I am also grateful for a Grant-in-Aid award from Tufts, which helped defray the cost of the color images.

I have benefited enormously from discussing my ideas about Tati's films with a number of brilliant scholars, including Richard Allen, Alessandra Campana, Patrick Keating, Brian Price, Murray Smith, and Federico Windhausen. Ted Nannicelli and Todd Berliner gave helpful feedback on earlier drafts of several chapters while David Bordwell and Kristin Thompson read the entire manuscript and offered copious suggestions for improvement. David's friendship and encouragement over the past two decades has meant more to me than he knows, and the shining example of his work was always in my mind as I wrote this book. Two anonymous readers at Columbia University Press provided excellent recommendations for revisions, and I thank my editors at the press, Philip Leventhal and John Belton, as well as Jennifer Crewe, for their interest in my work on Tati. I also thank Monique Briones and Kathryn Jorge at Columbia, and Ben Kolstad at Cenveo, for the terrific job they have done copyediting and producing the book. Sadly, my mentor and friend, Annette Michelson, passed away just as I was completing the manuscript. As with so much else, Annette's classes in the Department of Cinema Studies at New York University—and especially her seminal article, "Dr. Crase and Mr. Clair"—first alerted me to the connections between comedy and modernism, and she was unswervingly enthusiastic as I embarked on this project. Annette's (sometimes wicked) sense of humor is not the least of the many things I will miss about her.

I will always be grateful for the friendship of Mary-Karen Zeugner, and I thank my sister, Alison, and nephew, Fintan, for our fun family vacations—I hope we will have many more. Tony and Susan Pasquariello are unfailingly generous and amusing to boot—what more could one ask for from parents-in-law? My wife, Lisa, who is a gifted writer, meticulously copyedited the manuscript, saving me from many awkward turns of phrase and embarrassing grammatical lapses. More importantly, she is a constant source of support and inspiration. Without her advice and encouragement, let alone the many hours she looked after our son while I worked on it, I wouldn't have been able to complete this project, and I thank her for her love.

This book is inextricably bound up in my mind with my son, William. I started it the year he was born, and he has taught me more than anyone or anything else about play and humor. Watching films with him has become a highlight, and I look forward to introducing him to Tati's work, just as my parents did me. I love him more than words can say, and I dedicate this book to him.

Play Time

INTRODUCTION

TATI'S STYLE

One of the best known and most beloved of Tati's gags occurs at the beginning of *Play Time* (1967), and it encapsulates pretty much everything about Tati's style, comic and otherwise.[1] Following the film's opening credits, which are projected on a background of clouds, we see a low-angle long shot of a gray, modern building, the cloudy sky visible behind it. A closer shot, presumably through the windows of the building shown in the previous one, reveals two nuns dressed in habits walking along an interior corridor. In the first comic moment of the film, the "horns" of their *cornettes* flap up and down in time with their movements, and their shoes make a squelching sound on the tiled floor. While perhaps amusing, neither the flapping nor the squelching is particularly funny, and they do not constitute full-blown gags. Rather, they are typical of Tati's predilection for slightly unusual or absurd details of costume, behavior, and setting, and they recur throughout his feature films for reasons explored in chapter 3.

A cut to a high angle discloses the nuns entering a waiting area with black seats on one side, gray cubicles on the other, and a lighter gray passageway in between, which stretches into the background and ends in large glass windows. A couple sits to the left in the foreground and three figures stand motionless in front of the windows at the back. All, like the nuns, are dressed in white, gray, and black. Other similarly attired people start entering the passageway while the woman in the foreground fusses over her companion, telling him to button his collar, take his vitamins, and look after himself. Because he appears sick, it is easy to assume they are in a hospital, an impression reinforced by the polished, antiseptic environment, the nuns, and the arrival of other characters who might be

FIGURE 0.1 *Play Time* (Jacques Tati, 1967).

hospital workers and visitors (although most have their backs to us and walk away from the camera). A man dressed in what look like scrubs pushes a trolley of what might be medical instruments. Another costumed in blue overalls holding a broom searches in vain for trash to clean up. A woman who appears to be a nurse carries an infant swaddled in towels, and we hear the sounds of a crying baby (fig. 0.1). A second woman seems to be pushing someone in a wheelchair.

The next shot provides a reverse angle of the passageway, into which more people emerge, the couple now barely visible in the top right corner. On the far left, the woman who had looked like a nurse in the previous shot enters to change the towels in a bathroom in one of the cubicles, and we begin to suspect that she and the other characters are perhaps not in a hospital after all (fig. 0.2). This is soon confirmed by an announcement on a loudspeaker about the arrival of a flight, and in the following shot the tail of a plane can be seen through the window as it pulls up to a gate and we hear the roaring of its engines (fig. 0.3).

By tricking us into thinking that the film opens in a hospital rather than an airport, Tati has created one of the most elaborate examples in film history of a type of gag Noël Carroll calls the "switch image."[2] Found occasionally in classical comedian comedy of the silent era and beyond, switch images typically occur at the beginnings of films or scenes when a shot, due to framing and mise-en-scène, suggests an interpretation of its subject that is then revealed to be wrong. The incongruity between the spectator's initial, incorrect interpretation of an event and the correct interpretation, of which he or she is subsequently informed,

FIGURE 0.2 *Play Time.*

is the source of the humor.[3] Probably the most well-known example of this technique, thanks to Rudolf Arnheim's discussion of it in *Film as Art* (1932), occurs at the start of Chaplin's *The Immigrant* (1917) when, following several shots of seasick passengers on a ship, the Tramp is shown from behind bending over the ship's side, his body apparently convulsing as if he were vomiting (fig. 0.4).[4]

FIGURE 0.3 *Play Time.*

FIGURE 0.4 *The Immigrant* (Charlie Chaplin, 1917).

But when he turns around to face the camera, we see that he has been happily fishing (fig. 0.5), and subsequent shots show him enjoying the lurching movements of the boat. Another well-known example can be found near the beginning of Buster Keaton's *Three Ages* (1923). It is the Stone Age, and we first see Keaton's caveman character lounging on what appears to be a ledge jutting out from a large rock. Suddenly, he strikes the ledge with a branch; it begins to move, and an extreme long shot reveals that he is sitting atop a dinosaur. In switch images, the film audience is, in effect, forced to experience the misunderstandings and confusions that are normally the lot of the characters, thereby participating in the creation of comedy. The viewer is the butt of the joke, as it is her own misinterpretation of onscreen events she finds amusing along with the film's deception. Because Tati fervently desired his viewers to play a role in his humor for reasons we will discover in chapter 2, he frequently resorted to switch images.

The gag also illustrates other distinctive features of Tati's comic style to be examined in detail in later chapters. By the time *Play Time* was released, Monsieur Hulot, the character played by Tati who was pivotal to the success of his two previous feature films, *Les Vacances de Monsieur Hulot* (1953) and

FIGURE 0.5 *The Immigrant.*

Mon Oncle (1958), was well known and much loved, and audiences would have come to *Play Time* expecting to see him. But he is nowhere to be found in this opening gag, and in fact he does not appear until more than eleven minutes into the film (although a Hulot lookalike is glimpsed several times at the airport and is mistaken by a woman for Hulot [fig. 2.26]). Instead, it is minor characters and extras, many of whom we never see again, who participate in the gag, although inadvertently. There is little of the slapstick, pantomiming, or eccentric behavior of the sort routinely found in classical comedian comedy to make us laugh. Instead, the characters are engaged in quotidian, if slightly exaggerated, activities in an everyday setting, which is why I often refer to Tati's humor in this book as a comedy of everyday life. In addition, the environment around the characters, in its similarity to both a hospital and an airport, is integral to this gag, as it is in much of Tati's humor. Tati's pronounced tendency to devolve comedy away from himself and Hulot to other characters and their settings is one reason his comic style has been described by critics as democratic.

Even though Tati is often thought of as a visual comedian, sound plays a crucial role in this gag as it does in his comedy more generally. The dialogue between the couple indicates the man is sick and they may be in a hospital, while it is the flight announcement on the loudspeaker that first confirms their actual location. The loud, hard noise of the characters' shoes on the floor helps convey the sterility of their environment, and the baby's cries, which commence just as the woman holding the towels enters the shot and end just as she leaves it, deceive us into thinking that she is holding an infant. Color also aids in the deception. Tati delighted in equating disparate objects and environments using color, and it is their gray surroundings coupled with the colors of the costumes worn by the would-be hospital workers that suggest they are in a hospital (color figure 1). The uniformity of modern environments represented in this gag is a major target of Tati's satire of modern life.

The visual style of this gag is typical of Tati's films too. It is filmed in long shots taken some distance from the action, so that the entirety of the characters' bodies and some of their surrounding environment are visible. Deep staging is used, and everything is in focus, no matter how near to or far away from the camera. The first shot of the passageway is a long take lasting one minute, forty seconds and the camera is motionless, as it is in the subsequent shot. At times, multiple characters are engaged in independent activities *simultaneously*, meaning there are numerous points of interest in each densely packed shot, and we cannot keep track of all of them. Nor are there close-ups or other variants of mobile framing to direct our attention to important information. These are standard techniques in Tati's films—although he perhaps takes them further in *Play Time* than in his other works—and they have led critics such as Jonathan Rosenbaum to suggest that Tati's visual style is, like his comedy, "to some extent . . . democratic," because it allows viewers the freedom to choose what to look at in the image.[5] This is no doubt true, but Rosenbaum's often-overlooked qualifier "to some extent" is important. As Lucy Fischer has shown, Tati uses many time-honored devices such as character movement, the power of the center, the gazes of characters, and sound to direct the spectator's attention to relevant parts of the frame at moments of his choosing.[6] In particular, Tati viewed color as an attention-grabbing device, stating that in *Play Time* he had "put the color where I want the people to watch."[7] Nor was this use confined to *Play Time*, as he hand-colored parts of the black-and-white image in the version of *Jour de fête* he released in 1964 to make aspects of the mise-en-scène stand out to the viewer. In the opening switch image in *Play Time*, we shift our gaze from the middle-aged couple to the man pushing the cart in part because his costume is white and stands out against the gray background, his cart makes a loud rattling sound, and he moves vigorously through the center of the image while everyone else on its edges is still; and the couple look intently at the cleaner in blue, thereby cuing us to do the same.[8]

More important for our purposes, Tati also employs these and other devices to mask certain parts of another switch image gag involving the couple. In front of them, just above the bottom edge of the frame and partly obscured by the black seats, is a baby carriage that is almost the same shade of gray as the airport floor, making it blend into its surroundings and exceedingly difficult to notice (color figure 1). The child we hear crying on the soundtrack, it turns out, is in that carriage and belongs to the couple. The woman who appears to be a nurse is not carrying a baby but rather the towels she places in the bathroom dispenser. Moreover, the only time in the shot that the couple acknowledges their infant, which is when it begins crying and the wife bends down to comfort it, occurs when the woman with the towels enters the scene. Because her high heels make a loud clicking sound, she is moving, she is near the center of the shot, *and* the couple glance at her before turning to their infant (color figure 1), our gaze is drawn to her and we may fail to spot the couple subsequently soothing their child. When our attention is brought back to them by the wife's comment to her husband that the baby is "cute," she appears to be referring to the infant seemingly being carried by the woman who looks like a nurse. The wife immediately resumes pampering her husband, and they do not look at their child again. Not only are we easily tricked into believing that a nurse in a hospital is carrying the baby we heard, we overlook the fact that it actually belongs to the couple.

Once it is revealed that we are in an airport, the couple make their way toward the departure gate holding the baby carriage between them. It remains difficult to discern the carriage, however, because its color blends with the background and because a woman in front of them in the center of the image is pushing a luggage cart with a red blanket over it, which against the gray monochrome background distracts the viewer's attention, as do other characters around the couple (color figure 2). Two shots later, the couple are again barely visible as they walk toward the departure gate in the top right of a long shot dominated in the center by an army officer berating a subordinate (fig. 3.56). Finally, we pick up the fragmented gag with the couple in a medium-long shot in which the wife bids farewell to her husband and hurries through the departure gate while an airline attendant takes the baby carriage. In a second switch image, what we had initially assumed was a wife comforting her sick husband in a hospital turns out to be a wife going on a trip with her baby while the husband stays behind. The pampering we had witnessed previously was an expression of the wife's concern that her husband will cope in her absence. Yet, although this payoff is staged in the right foreground of the shot, it occurs while a party of loud American tourists dressed in light gray and white (with the occasional red flower in their hats) arrives through the gate to the left, and their brighter clothes as well as the commotion they cause easily

FIGURE 0.6 *Play Time.*

draw our attention away from the couple, who are dressed in dark gray and make almost no audible sound. Furthermore, the baby carriage is positioned in such a way that it looks like a travel bag, once again making it easy to overlook the fact that it contains a baby (fig. 0.6). Tati has systematically staged this gag so that even if viewers grasp one part of it—say, the couple bidding farewell to each other—our attention is distracted from others—such as the baby carriage they are holding—meaning that the gag will appear incomplete or incomprehensible, or will not be perceived at all.

The two gags involving the couple with the baby span three zones of percepti-bility. The first, the switch image from hospital to airport, is fairly easy for view-ers to discern, and most, in my experience, do. The second, the switch image from a wife comforting her husband in a hospital to a wife expressing concern that her husband will manage on his own while she is away, is harder to notice because Tati diverts our attention from the gag's resolution. The fact that they have an infant and the wife is leaving with it on the trip, however, is almost impossible to perceive because of the color of the baby carriage and the other techniques used to mask it. Indeed, even seasoned viewers of Tati's films often miss it.[9] This is an example of what I call in chapter 3 a hidden gag, and it is illustrative of Tati's tendency to deliberately obscure aspects of his comedy. In such cases, rather than allowing his audiences to choose what to look at by democratically giving equal weight to comic moments in his shots, Tati intentionally diverts the viewer's attention away from them. This comic opacity is the most innovative, challenging, and modernist dimension of Tati's humor, and it is one of the ways he departs markedly from his classical forebears. Unlike any film comedian before him, Tati tries to conceal, rather than foreground, parts of his comedy, and much of this book is taken up with explaining why. Nevertheless, in this opening sequence, as in his films in general, Tati effects a balance between this hidden gag and the more accessible switch image from hospital to airport, and this is one way, I suggest, he attempted to capture both popular and elite audiences. While he may not have fully achieved this goal in *Play Time*, thereby perhaps contributing to its commercial failure, his comedy typically interweaves easily recognizable, conventional gag structures with less discernible, more avant-garde ones. This is one reason for his success in crafting a popular comedic modernism.

THIS BOOK

As noted in the preface, Tati is widely regarded as one of the greatest postwar European filmmakers, and his films still generate considerable interest some thirty-five years after his death. There are frequent exhibitions and retrospectives of his work, such as the Cinémathèque Française's *Jacques Tati, Deux Temps, Trois Mouvements* in the spring of 2009, and all six of Tati's features, along with his surviving shorts, have been released on DVD and Blu-Ray in Europe and the United States. Documentaries continue to be made about the director, such as *The Magnificent Tati* (Michael House, 2009), and one of Tati's unrealized scripts was recently made into a feature-length animated film called *The Illusionist* (Sylvain Chomet, 2010). Most importantly, a number of Tati's films have been restored and rereleased, including *Play Time*, a glorious 70 mm restoration of which premiered at the Cannes Film Festival in 2002. Yet no book-length study of the director's oeuvre has been published in English in almost twenty years.[10] Meanwhile, older books by English-language authors are out of print and suffer from various limitations, including their reliance on deficient versions of Tati's films.[11]

Play Time: Jacques Tati and Comedic Modernism is intended to help fill this gap, but there is much I don't discuss, such as the industrial and economic conditions in which Tati made his films, the biographical events affecting them, and his production process.[12] Rather, taking advantage of the restored and rereleased versions of Tati's films, I focus almost exclusively on the comic style manifest in them, which, unlike Tati's filmmaking style, has not, for the most part, been thoroughly analyzed. I closely study his gags and other aspects of his humor along with his techniques for filming them. While others have identified some of these, I provide a comprehensive, in-depth examination of Tati's style of comedy in its totality. I also show how Tati drew on the rich legacy of classical comedian comedy of the silent period while modernizing its conventions and adding an innovative use of sound, thereby fashioning a modernist form of comedy. In doing so, I demonstrate that Tati both satirized aspects of modern life and attempted to inculcate in his viewers a playful, participatory attitude toward the modern world in order to overcome what he saw as passivity characteristic of modernity. He thereby produced a body of work unlike anything else in cinematic modernism or, indeed, the history of film.

Despite my title, I don't privilege *Play Time*, which is widely (and with some justification) viewed as Tati's masterpiece. While *Play Time* in certain respects challenges spectators to a greater extent than Tati's other films, all its comic techniques can be found in *Jour de fête* (1949), *Les Vacances de Monsieur Hulot*, *Mon Oncle*, and *Trafic* (1971). Where appropriate, I therefore provide at least one example from each of these five films of the gags and other comedic devices under consideration in order to establish the continuity of Tati's comic style. Nor do I have much to say about Tati's surviving early short films which, while interesting, display little of the avant-garde innovation evident in his features starting with his first, *Jour de fête*, in 1949. Although *L'école de facteurs* (1946) introduces the theme of modernization that was to preoccupy Tati for the rest of his career and serves as a template for *Jour de fête*, to my eyes and ears it mainly consists of routine slapstick and gags while showcasing Tati's considerable skill as a mime, as do the three extant shorts preceding it. I also postpone discussion of *Parade* (1974), Tati's idiosyncratic final feature, until the afterword. *Parade* has much in common with Tati's other feature-length films and is in many ways a fitting summation of his career. But it captures an ostensibly live performance by Tati and a troupe of circus entertainers, thereby setting it apart from his fictional features.

COMEDIC MODERNISM

Tati, I maintain throughout this book, was a comedic modernist, bringing together the popular genre of comedian comedy with modernism. Modernism is a vague and contested notion over which a great deal of ink has been spilled. However, as András Kovács has pointed out in his indispensable analysis of cinematic modernism, "the common ground in all definitions of artistic modernism is that modern art is an aesthetic reflection on and a critique of its own traditional forms."[13] As P. Adams Sitney puts it:

> Innovation is the sole legitimate means of guaranteeing a link to tradition. Typically the modernist artist mines the greatest works of the tradition for irreducible structures which can be made to support new works. . . . At the same time the modernist artist defends a position in history and stakes claims for creative freedom by making works that aggressively assert their autonomy. These works bear signs of rupture from the successful achievements of the immediate past and stylistically distinguish themselves from the works of contemporaries so as to make the authorial signature immediately apparent.[14]

All of this applies to Tati, which is *one* reason I claim him as a modernist. As we shall see, he reflected in depth on his relation to classical comedian comedy of the silent era and drew on its gag structures, such as switch images. However, he asserted his connection to that tradition by departing from it, sometimes radically—for example, by obscuring his comedy and de-emphasizing his comic character, Monsieur Hulot. These inventions and many others in turn became hallmarks of his authorship and individuality. Kovács also suggests that the narrative and stylistic innovations of cinematic modernists did not occur in a vacuum but rather arose in response to "the disconnection of human actions from traditional routines or patterns of human relationships . . . what is commonly referred to as modern 'alienation.'"[15] While one might question whether this was true of all modernists, Tati's updating of comedian comedy certainly was motivated by his belief that people in the modern world are increasingly alienated and his hope that his films could at least in part overcome, or provide respite from, this alienation. His comic style was very much a response to the rapid modernization he witnessed occurring in France after the war and the social conditions modernization gave rise to, particularly what he viewed as the increasing passivity of modern people.

Comedian comedy, as defined by Steve Seidman, is a genre that coalesced in Hollywood and elsewhere in the silent era in the films of Chaplin, Keaton, Mabel Norman, Harold Lloyd, Laurel and Hardy, and so on and persisted after the coming of sound in the work of the Marx Brothers, Mae West, Crosby and Hope, Abbott and Costello, Danny Kaye, and many others, continuing to the present in Sacha Baron Cohen's Borat and the slapstick characters played by Melissa McCarthy. It centers on one or more eccentric characters who are often childlike or animalistic, and comedy is generated by their unwillingness or inability to conform to social and other norms. The eccentric character is usually performed by a well-known and highly skilled comedian whose:

> talents are translated into the counter-cultural drives of the comic figure. . . . Certain aspects of these performing talents, such as adaptability to disguise, verbal manipulation (impressions, dialects), and physical dexterity become the personality traits of the comic figure. These traits allow the comic figure to be different from those of his culture; he is shown as more creative and playful. Yet, this difference is also translated into aberrant kinds of behavior, manifested by either identity confusion . . . and/or the maintenance of childishness.[16]

Crucially, "because of the comedian's virtuosity . . . aberrant behavior is made 'entertaining'" and therefore attractive.[17] Often, as in the films of Keaton and Lloyd, comic characters begin films unable to fit in due to their eccentricity, but the imaginativeness and creativity that set them apart become the means through which they finally manage to integrate into society. In other cases, as in many of the films of Chaplin, the comedian remains an outcast throughout. Either way, it is the clown's lack of conformity to norms of behavior—his or her inability to fit into society—that is the source of humor.

Tati, I claim, brought comedian comedy and modernism together, but he was not the first to do so, and another contribution of this book is to demonstrate that Tati was part of a broader tradition of comedic modernism. Comedy is usually overlooked in accounts of modernism, which tend to stress its serious, pessimistic manifestations.[18] Yet, as I demonstrate in chapter 1, many modernists before Tati made use of the figure of the clown in advancing their avant-garde agendas. This strain within modernism—what I call comedic modernism—is bookended, perhaps, by Gustave Flaubert's unfinished novel *Bouvard et Pécuchet*, which Flaubert began writing in the mid-1860s; and, along with Tati's films, Samuel Beckett's *Film* (1964), starring Buster Keaton, made a century later. As the latter example makes clear, by comedic modernism I do not mean humorous modernism but rather the employment of the comedian as a subject and/or model in modernist theory and practice.[19] In chapter 1, I account for the pervasive appeal of the clown to modernists by examining the European avant-garde's appropriation of film comics in the interwar period. Numerous scholars have explored the attraction of specific avant-gardists to particular film comedians, such as the Soviets' zeal for Charlie Chaplin.[20] However, it is often not recognized that the affinity for slapstick film on the part of the interwar European avant-garde was one instance of a much broader phenomenon; and in chapter 1 I trace the major forms of assimilation of the cinematic clown by modernists, which transcended any particular comic or avant-garde group.

In chapter 2, I show how many of the variants of comedic modernism that arose in Europe before World War II re-emerge in Tati's films after the war. However, Tati developed his comic style within a social and artistic context that had changed dramatically since the 1920s. In particular, postwar artists were concerned with fashioning more democratic and participatory forms of art in the face of what they perceived to be an increasingly hegemonic and alienating mass culture and society. Tati shared this concern, and it had a major impact on his humor, which I explore in depth in chapter 2. Tati especially wanted his viewers to *participate* in his comedy, and in chapter 3 I explore his ingenious techniques for involving them. This involvement is why I titled this book *Play Time*. Playing is an activity, something one *does* rather than passively consumes, and of all Tati's films, *Play Time* is the title that best reflects his participatory goal for his spectators. He also hoped his films would encourage his audiences to pay attention to the humor putatively occurring all around them in their daily lives outside the movie theater, and some of his most original comic inventions are designed to cultivate this more active mode of observation. In chapter 4, I turn to the frequent target of Tati's comedy, the rapid modernization that occurred in postwar Europe. Tati's interpreters have often perceived in his films an unrelenting hostility toward the modern world, but his stated position was more nuanced than one might expect, and his satire of modernity is, on close inspection, complex and multifaceted. I elucidate it by examining the depiction of modern environments in his films, especially in *Mon Oncle* and *Play Time*. Finally, in the afterword, I consider how *Parade* exemplifies Tati's democratic comic style. While an anomaly in certain respects, *Parade* is the film that most clearly illustrates the concerns motivating Tati's comedy. In general, I suggest, Tati's films demonstrate that the goal of creating a participatory culture, which commentators such as Henry Jenkins see as a hallmark of contemporary media, long predates the current moment.

Those readers conversant in contemporary film theory might be wondering why I haven't used other terms to describe Tati's work, particularly Miriam Hansen's *vernacular modernism* and David Bordwell and Kristin Thompson's *parametric narration*, given that they seem to fit Tati's films well. In the remainder of this introduction, I explain why I haven't turned to these categories. I also justify why I conceive of Tati as a single author, and my frequent appeal to his stated intentions. Aren't I thereby committing the so-called intentional fallacy, some might worry, and isn't cinema a collaborative art, meaning that films lack single authors? My answer to both questions is a qualified no.

TATI AND VERNACULAR MODERNISM

Tati's films exemplify Miriam Hansen's well-known and influential concept of vernacular modernism. For starters, they "register, respond to, and reflect upon processes of modernization and the experience of modernity," which, for Hansen, makes them quintessentially modernist.[21] Jettisoning the widespread notion of modernism as "an aesthetic reflection on and a critique of . . . traditional forms," Hansen defines modernism much more broadly than other scholars, arguing that it consists of:

> cultural practices that both articulated and mediated the experience of modernity, such as the mass-produced and mass-consumed phenomena of fashion, design, advertising, architecture, and urban environment, of photography, radio, and cinema. I am referring to this kind of modernism as "vernacular" . . . because [it] combines the dimension of the quotidian, of everyday usage, with connotations of discourse, idiom, and dialect, with circulation, promiscuity, and translatability.[22]

For Hansen, any form of culture that "articulated and mediated the experience of modernity" counts as modernist, although she privileges cinema, claiming it was "the single, most inclusive cultural horizon in which the traumatic effects of modernity were reflected, rejected, or disavowed, transmuted or negotiated."[23] As we shall see, Tati's films address modernization, including what might be thought of as its traumatic aspects, and they do so by way of a comedy of everyday life, making them seem particularly vernacular. In addition, they are rooted in the genre of comedian comedy, which is Hansen's primary example of vernacular modernism. According to Hansen, following Walter Banjamin, Siegfried Kracauer, and others, the cinema "engaged the contradictions of modernity at the level of the senses."[24] It enabled viewers to reflect on modernization not just cognitively but through the sensory-affective experiences it afforded. This is especially true of slapstick. "The reason slapstick comedy hit home and flourished worldwide was not critical reason but that the films propelled their viewers' bodies into laughter," writes Hansen.[25] Although Hansen never explains how laughing at the antics of slapstick comedians occasions or consists of nonrational reflection on modernization, in Tati's films, it is often Hulot's failure to successfully navigate modern environments and gadgets that generates humor. This would seem to make his variant of comedian comedy a good vehicle for reflection on modernity. Of course,

Hansen originally developed her concept of vernacular modernism in relation to Hollywood cinema of the 1920s through the 1950s, contending that it could explain the global appeal of Hollywood's films of this period better than the notion of Hollywood classicism proposed by David Bordwell, Janet Staiger, and Kristin Thompson in their monumental study *The Classical Hollywood Cinema*.[26] "American movies of the classical period offered something like the first global vernacular," she maintained. "If this vernacular has a transnational and translatable resonance it was not just because of its optimal mobilization of biologically hardwired structures and universal [classical] narrative templates but, more important, because it played a key role in mediating competing cultural discourses on modernity and modernization, because it articulated, multiplied and globalized a particular historical experience."[27] Yet, Hansen herself suggested that the concept of vernacular modernism was not confined to Hollywood of the classical period, applying it to Shanghai cinema of the 1920s and 1930s.[28] That Tati's films are French therefore doesn't appear to be an impediment to classifying them as vernacular modernist.

However, that Tati's films fit Hansen's definition so well, along with all Hollywood films of the 1920s through the 1950s, Shanghai films of the 1920s and 1930s, and, presumably, many if not all modernist films, points to the limitations of the concept of vernacular modernism. It is defined so broadly by Hansen as to be almost meaningless, and it doesn't allow us to discriminate between Tati's films and those of Chaplin, Keaton, and other classical Hollywood comedians, let alone classical Hollywood cinema in general. All would seem to fall within Hansen's definition of vernacular modernism. Part of the problem is that Hansen never spells out criteria for determining whether a film is articulating, mediating, or reflecting modernity, with the result that almost any film can be yoked to her concept, given that a creative interpreter could always find some way to connect a film to modernity. In fact, at times Hansen writes as if vernacular modernism applies to all cinema rather than to a particular kind of film: "*The cinema* not only traded in the mass production of the senses but also provided an aesthetic horizon for the experience of industrial mass society."[29] But if this is so, then Hansen's concept, which she proposed in order to counter what she saw as the "totalizing,"[30] "universalist"[31] account of classical Hollywood cinema offered by Bordwell, Staiger, and Thompson, is far more totalizing than theirs. As Charlie Keil puts it, "Although Hansen presents her model of vernacular modernism as improving on the ahistorical obsession with stability she perceives in the dominant conception of classicism, one finds little evidence of the vaunted historical specificity."[32] By classicism, Bordwell, Staiger, and Thompson mean the narrative and stylistic norms governing Hollywood filmmaking since about 1917. These are conventions that most Hollywood films follow to a greater or lesser extent, but not all do, or do so equally, and the authors acknowledge that there are plenty of outliers and exceptions. Moreover, identifying these norms allows them to distinguish between Hollywood films and other traditions of filmmaking that utilize different conventions, such as cinematic modernism. Art historical analysis requires robust categories to classify different kinds of works, the disparate traditions to which they belong, and the varying effects and functions of their properties. Classicism and modernism, like genre categories, allow us to do this, even though, as with all art historical categories, there is debate about their precise meanings, prototypes, borderline cases, and institutional contexts. Hansen's theory, however, equates classicism and modernism as if there were no differences between them, and unlike Bordwell, Staiger, and Thompson's concept of classicism, it seems to apply equally to all Hollywood films from 1920 to 1950 along with many other films. This does not mean there weren't popular or vernacular versions of modernism. In fact, Tati's films, I argue in this book, provide a salient example of popular modernism in their box office success (until *Play Time*). But unless we want to deny that Tati's films are very different from classical comedian comedy, vernacular modernism won't help us identify what is distinctive about them and the tradition to which they belong because it levels the distinction between classicism and modernism.

TATI AND PARAMETRIC NARRATION

A far more precise, discriminating, and well-defined category has been proposed by David Bordwell to describe the work of Tati and a select few other filmmakers, and Kristin Thompson has applied it in detail to Tati's films. Bordwell calls this category parametric narration, introducing it in his seminal *Narration in the Fiction Film* (1985) as one of four modes of narration historically present in fiction film alongside classical, art cinema, and historical-materialist. In parametric narration, unlike in the other modes, overarching stylistic patterns are present in a film for their own sake rather than to serve narrational, thematic, or other purposes. They are noninstrumental. Four criteria determine whether a film belongs to the parametric-narrational mode. First, it must contain *systematic* stylistic patterning. It is not enough for there to be occasional stylistic flourishes that stand out. Instead, "in parametric narration, style is organized across the film."[33] Bordwell continues, "For style to come forward across the whole film, it must possess internal coherence."[34] Second, stylistic patterns must be independent of narrative rather than serving "the *syuzhet* [plot]'s process of cueing us to construct the *fabula* [story]."[35] "Stylistic features can create patterns independent of immediate narrative needs," writes Bordwell.[36] They don't take part in the narration, and nor should they function thematically, which is Bordwell's third criterion. "If a film's stylistic devices achieve prominence, and they are organized according to more or less rigorous principles, independent of syuzhet needs, then we need not motivate style by appealing to thematic considerations."[37] Finally, because they are independent of narrative and thematic meanings and functions, the presence of these stylistic patterns must be motivated "artistically." "A film's stylistic patterning splits away from the *syuzhet* when only artistic motivation can account for it," Bordwell maintains,[38] thereby achieving "a structural prominence that is more than simply ornamental."[39] By artistic motivation, Bordwell means an element in a film, such as a stylistic pattern, that is "present simply for its own sake" because it does not serve any purpose.[40] Parametric narration therefore consists of stylistic patterning across a film that is independent of the film's narrative and themes, and that, in Thompson's words, "exists solely to call attention to itself."[41] Bordwell gives the example of Jean-Luc Godard's *Vivre sa vie* (1962) which "moves through a paradigm of alternatives to orthodox shot/reverse shot" that, according to Bordwell, serve no narrative or thematic ends.[42] These alternatives are therefore present for their own sake, he maintains. While Bordwell acknowledges that the parametric mode of narration is hardly widespread, he suggests that some "significant filmmakers have employed it,"[43] among them Tati.[44]

In developing his concept of parametric narration, Bordwell is, I believe, pointing to something true and important about certain films, namely, that their style seems to exceed any narrative or thematic function. It is orchestrated into patterns that go beyond what is needed to communicate the film's story and themes, thereby drawing attention to itself. Tati's employment of long shots and avoidance of close-ups isn't necessitated by his narratives, which could unfold using a mixture of closer and longer shots. And while an interpreter might alight upon some thematic meaning for them—that they express the emotional distance between people in modern life, for instance—this would not explain their *systematic* deployment. They are used even when characters are close in Tati's films, such as when Hulot looks after his beloved nephew in *Mon Oncle*. Nevertheless, the category of parametric narration faces some hurdles. First, it is not clear why parametric stylistic patterns constitute a distinct mode of narration, given that, by definition, they are independent of the narrative. Nor does Bordwell identify any narrational conventions definitive of parametric narration as he does with the classical, art cinema, and historical-materialist modes of narration. This is perhaps why parametric style can be found in these other modes too. Ozu, for example, is normally thought of as belonging to the classical and Bresson to art cinema, yet both also count as examples of parametric filmmakers according to Bordwell. Parametric narration therefore seems less a mode of narration than a distinctive stylistic option that can be used in the other modes.

Second, and more importantly, the independence of systematic stylistic patterning from narrative and theme does not entail that stylistic patterning exists exclusively for its own sake. While a stylistic pattern may not have a narrational or thematic function, this does not preclude it from serving some other purpose, as is the case with Tati's use of long shots. Thompson argues that Tati's "alternative filmic system" makes use of "parametric form,"[45] and she gives as an example the fact that "Tati does not always center and foreground comic gags for us."[46] Instead, he "creates scenes in which multiple comic actions compete for our attention."[47] "The dense *mise-en-scène*," she suggests, is one of Tati's "main parametric structures."[48] However, Tati stated that he did not direct the viewer's attention to gags and other comic elements for a reason: he wanted his audiences to participate in his comedy by searching for it themselves. "The trouble with today's audiences," he complained, "is that they're not used to participation, they're used to television which makes no demands on the part of the viewer. I do not make close-ups of people so the audience must see what they see with their own eyes, not what the camera tells them."[49] In an interview in the documentary, *In the Footsteps of Monsieur Hulot* (1989), made by his daughter, Sophie Tatischeff, Tati remarks that "I like when the audience—I give them an image. I don't spell it out for them. I like them to look. I make them participate." Tati, in other words, used long shots and a dense mise-en-scène with a clear purpose, to make his spectators search for gags and other important information in his images, and in fact Thompson agrees that this is their function, claiming that "we must seek out the potential funny elements."[50] But if this is the case, then these stylistic patterns are not present purely for their own sake. They do not exist "solely to call attention" to themselves because they also serve the purpose of making viewers look for humor, and are therefore not an instance of parametric narration.[51]

Bordwell and Thompson might allow this in the case of Tati, yet still maintain that there are other films in which style is noninstrumental and therefore present for its own sake. However, it is hard to conceive of a stylistic pattern in a narrative film that is completely independent of narration. At the very least, most stylistic devices communicate information about the diegesis even if they exceed that purpose. The alternatives to orthodox shot/reverse shot in *Vivre sa vie* doubtless draw attention to themselves by going well beyond what is necessary to convey in the conversations they depict. Nevertheless, they do communicate discussions between Nana and the other characters, and we learn much about the characters and their narrative world through them; the narration does not come to a halt when these stylistic devices are employed. Similarly, Tati's long shots and dense mise-en-scène are not necessary for, and to some extent interfere with, his representation of the narrative worlds in *Play Time* and his other films. Yet by virtue of these and other stylistic techniques, we still receive information about their narratives. This does not mean that noninstrumental style is impossible. One can imagine a lighthearted romance in which, say, five seconds of black leader is inserted every five minutes for no reason other than that the filmmaker likes black leader and wants his audiences to appreciate it too. In this example, the black leader would serve no narrational purpose (other than perhaps pausing the narrative) and, given the film's pleasant subject matter, even the most creative interpreter would have trouble linking it to a theme. This perhaps would constitute an example of parametric style in Bordwell and Thompson's sense. However, even here an unintentional function or effect might be found for the black leader (such as Brechtian alienation). And this example, in its aberrancy, suggests that stylistic patterns nearly always contribute to the narration even if they go well beyond what is necessary to convey narrative information.

The problem with his theory of parametric narration, I suspect, is that Bordwell separates artistic motivation from the other forms of motivation he identifies: compositional, realistic, and transtextual. While he allows that these three "often cooperate with one another"—as when we justify the presence of an element because it advances the narrative (compositional), it could occur in reality (realistic), and it usually occurs in the genre to which the film belongs (transtextual)—he argues that artistic motivation "remains distinct from the others: the spectator has recourse to it only when the other sorts do not apply."[52] For him, artistic motivation only obtains when no purpose can be found for the element in question and it is therefore present purely for its own sake. However, if I am correct, this sets the bar too high, as it is rare to find a completely noninstrumental stylistic pattern in a film. Consider, for example, the timing of cuts that Bordwell views as an instance of parametric style in Bresson's *Pickpocket* (1959). After characters exit a shot, Bordwell astutely points out, Bresson holds "the empty framing for a noticeable interval before cutting away."[53] There seems to be no narrative or thematic reason for doing this, which is why Bordwell counts it as parametric. Nevertheless, such empty shots are not completely independent of the narrative because they depict narrative space, even if redundantly. I conjecture that parametric stylistic patterns are in most cases only *in part* present for their own sake while serving other purposes too, such as conveying narrative information. The filmmakers Bordwell calls parametric design their stylistic patterns to stand out from their narratives and themes, but these patterns are rarely completely independent of them. Certainly this is true of Tati. While his stylistic choices perhaps exceed their narrational and other functions, and therefore seem partially arbitrary, they still perform these functions.

SINGLE AUTHORSHIP

In responding to Bordwell and Thompson's concept of parametric narration, I have referred to Tati's stated intention in using long shots and a dense mise-en-scène in his films. I have also maintained that it was Tati's intention that explains why these techniques were used rather than, say, the intention of one of his collaborator's, and throughout this book, I argue that Tati was the single author of his films and that his intentions matter in understanding their design. Some readers might object that, given the collaborative nature of filmmaking, films typically do not have single authors, and that even if they did, "the design or intention of the author is neither available nor desirable as a standard for judging the success of a work."[54] Such objections are commonplace in film and media theorizing. For example, the claim that, excepting those made entirely by one person, films are always multiply authored has been robustly defended recently by the analytic philosopher Bery Gaut, who argues that any film with two or more people in "key production roles" (what Gaut calls a "mainstream" film) is multiply authored.[55] Gaut maintains that whoever occupies a key production role contributes artistic properties to a film and is therefore its coauthor. In the case of actors, even if, say, the director exercises a great deal of control over an actor's performance, this control cannot be total. The actor will "inevitably bring something of his own personality and training" to his performance and therefore contribute artistic properties to it, thereby making him a coauthor of the film, and the same is true of other production roles such as the composer.[56] In those cases in which a director can totally control a production role—by specifying, for example, exactly where a film should be edited—the director effectively occupies the production role. Our concept of a production role, Gaut believes, "requires some discretion to be exercisable by a person to count as her fulfilling" the role.[57] If a person in a key production role is exercising discretion, then she is contributing artistic properties to a film and counts as its coauthor.

The multiple author thesis is important and deserves to be taken seriously, but one wonders whether Gaut is correct to argue that, just because an actor's performance is his, he necessarily contributes *artistic* properties to it, for the actor's performance may be artless. It is at least conceivable that only one person contributes an artistic property to a mainstream film and therefore, according to Gaut's definition of authorship, counts as its single author. More importantly, Gaut could be accused of conflating artists with authors. He defines an artist as "someone who produces a work of art by non-accidentally making a work with some artistic properties," and claims that "this account of the author as artist naturally generalizes to an account of authors in general."[58] This is why he thinks that anyone who helps create a work by contributing artistic properties to it, such as a film actor or an assistant in a painting studio, is necessarily the work's coauthor. But this seems to overlook something essential about authorship. According to Gaut's argument, if an extra is hired for one day to appear in one shot of a film and contributes an artistic property to that shot, she is both an artist and a coauthor of the film in which the shot is included. But what if, as is often the case, the extra not only makes no contribution to the rest of the film but knows nothing about it, perhaps because it has been kept secret by the filmmakers to prevent leaks about the narrative to the general public? One can grant that the extra is an artist who cocreates her performance in the film, but how can she be a coauthor of the film as a whole when she knows nothing about it and contributes nothing else to it? Gaut may object that an extra is not a key production role. But even lead actors often don't know which takes of their performances will be used in the final film, whether any scenes in which they appeared will be deleted, how shots of them will be edited, what music (if any) will accompany these shots, which version of a scene will be used if multiple versions have been filmed, and so on. In fact, on occasion, they are given only the pages of the script that pertain to their characters, and they shoot their scenes in ignorance of what happens in the rest of the film or TV show, as was reportedly the case with the actors (excepting Kyle MacLachlan) in David Lynch's revival of *Twin Peaks* (2017).[59] Even in more normal circumstances, because of the strict division of labor in industrial filmmaking, few individuals have knowledge of all aspects of the production, and the need for someone to control and coordinate them is the reason the film director exists.[60]

Gaut might allow this but contend that there can be different degrees of authorship of a multiply authored work. "The multiple authorship view," he writes, "is not that the contribution of all authors must be of equal importance. Just because the director's is the most important 'voice' in the film does not mean that others' contributions do not entitle them to count as authors too."[61]

Perhaps the extra is a less important coauthor than the director but a coauthor all the same. However, it is still not clear how somebody can be a nonaccidental producer of a work, which is Gaut's definition of an author, if she has no knowledge of the work itself, as in the case of the extra. This suggests that it is not enough to make a creative or artistic contribution to a work to be the work's author, for one can do this without having any knowledge of the overall work to which one is contributing. Rather, as the philosopher Paisley Livingston has argued, authorship requires control over the work as a whole.[62] Such control need not be total, and Livingston follows Victor Perkins in suggesting that only "sufficient control" is necessary for authorship; others can make artistic and other contributions to a work.[63] However, the author is the person who has sufficient control over these contributions in the sense of requesting and directing them; approving, rejecting, or asking for changes to them once they are completed; coordinating them with the contributions of others and making sure they mesh with the overall design of the work; and taking responsibility for the work once it is finished.[64] Moreover, while necessary to authorship, sufficient control alone is not adequate. It is not enough to be in charge of the creative and artistic contributions of others to be the work's author. Rather, one must make a contribution oneself, which for Livingston consists of trying to realize artistic and expressive intentions in the work. The film author typically controls the contributions of others in trying to ensure they express the attitudes she wishes to convey in the work as well as accomplish her other artistic goals. More than one person can exercise sufficient control and express attitudes in a work, and this is often the case in industrial filmmaking. Hence many, perhaps even most, mainstream films are multiply authored. But this is not because lots of people contribute artistic properties to them, as Gaut would have it, but because two or more people (say, the producer and the director, as in the case of the Coen brothers) control the filmmaking in the process of attempting to realize their expressive and artistic intentions. However, one person can also exercise sufficient control, making single authorship a possibility, and Livingston cites the director Ingmar Bergman as an example.

> In such cases the author supervises and guides the contributions made by others and decides which results will be used in the function of his or her preferences regarding the final design of the work. Although various collaborators make artistic contributions, only the author is responsible for the work as a finished whole, and the work is taken to be a fallible expression of that person's attitudes.[65]

There is ample evidence that Tati was a single author in Livingston's sense of an individual who exercises sufficient control over a whole work in the realization of his expressive and artistic intentions. Not only did Tati write or cowrite all his features, but he directed and starred in them too, and he had a controlling stake in the production companies, Cady and Specta, that made the first four. Notoriously, he dictated to his actors the precise movements he wished them to make, as behind-the-scenes footage of the making of *Play Time* confirms. This footage also shows him telling his crew exactly where to position the camera and admitting that the shooting script is all "in his head," meaning that nobody else had access to it. Tati's stated intentions for the most part mesh with the audio-visual evidence in his films, suggesting he had a great deal of control over their design, and there is a remarkable stylistic, comic, and thematic consistency to them regardless of who his collaborators were. This does not mean he had total control. He cut *Play Time* as its commercial failure became imminent, and his final two features, *Trafic* and *Parade*, were made in reduced financial circumstances following his bankruptcy. However, as Livingston notes, "coercion comes in degrees. . . . Authorship is, then, a scalar concept with respect to coercion."[66] It is only when coercion is severe that it vitiates authorship, and there is no evidence that financial considerations dramatically curtailed his plans in his final two films.

INTENTION

As for the issue of appealing to Tati's intentions, the theoretical difficulties underpinning the appropriate role authors' intentions should play in understanding and evaluating their works are enormously complex, and there is little consensus about how to resolve them. Philosophers have proposed a bewildering array of theories about the subject, ranging from varieties of so-called actualist intentionalism to hypothetical intentionalism, conditionalist intentionalism, and anti-intentionalism.[67] Rather than dive into these muddy waters, I will make three points about the importance of an author's intentions that I hope are relatively uncontroversial. First, even the most rabid anti-intentionalist, I assume, would grant that an author's intentions must be considered, if only to identify and individuate their works. How do we know that the work we are analyzing is the author's, or that it is complete, without referring to the author's intentions? To be sure, there are times when we are interested in altered versions of an author's work, as when we are studying the role of censorship in the exhibition of Hollywood films and the extent to which they were changed to meet the demands of local censorship boards. However, the only way to determine that a work has been altered is if we can compare it to the original version, and this requires knowing what, according to its author's intentions, constituted the original version. This criterion pertains to Tati's films because when English-language film scholars first started writing about them in the 1970s, they often only had access to mutilated prints of them. That they were altered was established by reference to the original versions Tati intended. Moreover, Tati himself deliberately created multiple versions of his films, such as the French and international releases of *Mon Oncle*, which differ in important ways, and the 1964 reissue of *Jour de fête*, which in addition to the hand-coloring, included new footage of a painter painting the scenes depicted in the original. Without knowing that Tati himself intentionally created these alternate versions, one might worry that others had and discount them. Authors' intentions matter, then, if only in individuating their works.

Second, while it may be that authors' intentions do not determine the *meanings* of their works, as anti-intentionalists tend to argue, their intentions might still play a crucial role in *evaluating* them.[68] For example, features of a work that could seem aesthetically flawed in the absence of knowledge about the author's goals can appear very different once we are apprised of these goals. Tati's films, like Jean Renoir's, were sometimes accused of being muddled and confusing in the press because of his use of long shots and a dense mise-en-scène. Tati, reviewers complained, failed to draw the viewer's attention to his humor. However, once one learns that Tati intentionally did this to encourage his audiences to actively search for comedy in his images and soundtracks in order to counter what he viewed as the passivity of modern life, it can no longer be described as a failure given that Tati wasn't always trying to alert his spectators to his gags in the first place. This does not mean we have to appreciate and enjoy these aesthetic choices, for one might still wish that Tati had highlighted his comedy. But it does mean that we can no longer judge him to have failed in achieving the aesthetic goal of drawing our attention to his humor, as this was not usually his aim. Furthermore, these aesthetic choices are grounded in a philosophical rationale—the belief that people in the modern world are too passive—rather than being arbitrary or based on a whim. That they have an intellectual justification might further increase their value in our eyes, especially if we agree with it.

In this book, I appeal to Tati's intentions *not* because I believe they necessarily determine the meanings of his works, but because I want readers to understand what may otherwise seem like perplexing and perhaps defective features of his films. One of the reasons that the intentions of authors matter in art historical analysis is that we value, appreciate, and seek to understand the design of art works. We want to know why they have been executed in a particular way, especially if they are innovative and unusual, which is why we appeal to or make conjectures about the intentions of those who made them. Tati designed his films the way that he did in order to realize certain expressive and artistic intentions, and one has to grasp these intentions in order to understand the distinctive design of his films. In addition, he did so with considerable skill and ingenuity, which only becomes apparent if one comprehends his intentions. While the opening scene of *Play Time* might look to some like a chaotic mess, in fact Tati carefully controls the viewer's attention using techniques such as sound, color, and the gazes of characters in order to disguise the airport as a hospital and divert the spectator's gaze away from the couple's baby carriage. It is only if one understands that Tati deliberately sought to hide the baby carriage that one can appreciate that he is drawing our attention away from it using an arsenal of meticulously orchestrated techniques. Without this knowledge, the scene might appear like a free-for-all rather than the painstakingly wrought switch image that it is. Livingston makes the crucial point that "part of what we admire in works is the skill with which worthwhile goals have been realized."[69] But we can only appreciate the realization of a goal as skillful if we grasp the goal that is being realized.

Finally, while authors' intentions might not determine the meanings of their works, they surely offer good, if imperfect, guides to them. We often discern meanings in films and other artworks we would not otherwise have noticed upon learning their authors' communicative intentions. Films that might seem to mean one thing often come to mean something quite different in the light of their authors' goals. Authors can alert us to details and patterns of their works pertaining to their meanings that we might not have noticed otherwise. They can also place their more readily apparent features in an interpretive context we might not have considered. I leave it to philosophers to decide whether authors' indications about the meanings of their works should override other interpretations, but at the very least I think their intentions should be taken into consideration. After all, it is their intentionally created works we are trying to understand and evaluate! While the meaning of the conventions used by the work and the interpretive norms of the community interpreting it, may, ultimately, defeat the author's communicative intentions, it is still the case that the work in some respects might mean what its author says that it does and do so in surprising ways. Of course, authors can fail to successfully realize their communicative intentions in their works, which is why their intentions are defeasible. A character who a filmmaker intended to be completely unsympathetic might come across as partially appealing as a result of the actor's portrayal, which is intentionally (or unintentionally) contrary to the director's wishes. Nevertheless, when we learn about a filmmaker's intentions, we typically look to see if they mesh, to use Livingston's word, with the audio-visual evidence of their film, and in many cases they do.[70] Because their intentions sometimes reveal meanings we would not otherwise have discerned, our experience is all the richer and more complete for knowing them. In Tati's case, I will argue in chapter 4 that, with respect to the attitude toward modernity he wished to convey, his stated intentions alert us to the presence of greater nuance and complexity in his films than might otherwise be apparent, making them all the more interesting and provocative. Yet his films do not always conform to his stated intentions, and they suggest meanings he did not explicitly endorse, which is why authors' stated intentions can never completely determine the meanings of their works.

Nothing I have said in the preceding paragraphs is likely to change the mind of a committed anti-intentionalist or proponent of the multiple authorship thesis. I hope merely to have provided prima facie plausible reasons for why I refer to Tati's intentions and conceive of him as a single author. But before further considering these intentions and analyzing his comic style in depth, we must understand the tradition of comedic modernism out of which he emerged.

CHAPTER 1

COMEDIC MODERNISM

J acques Tati was not the first to synthesize modernism with the popular tradition of comedian comedy. Although no filmmaker did so as systematically and completely as he, modern artists had long been fascinated with the pantomime, circus, and other comic entertainments; and since the late nineteenth century, many modernists have used the figure of the clown in their work.[1]

Like so much else in modernism, the roots of this affinity lie in Romanticism, which established many of the forms of assimilation of the slapstick comedian that recur throughout modern art. The confusion of identities and use of masks that are leitmotifs of commedia dell'arte as it was translated into pantomime in the early nineteenth century appealed to French Romantics uncertain of the role of artists in the new, postrevolutionary social order.[2] Drawn to the grotesque, they were captivated by the comic's liberating animality and subversion of hierarchy. They also identified with what they perceived to be his alienation from society, propagating the archetype of the sad clown, even while viewing him as a satirical double of the mythical bourgeois they detested.[3] Of the many comic types to be found in popular entertainment of the era, they celebrated in particular the mute version of Pierrot created by Jean-Gaspard Deburau in *pantomime-féeries* at the Funambules Theater in Paris beginning in the 1820s. The incoherence of the féerie's oneiric plot, with its abrupt transformations and supernatural characters, satisfied their desire for enchantment, and they saw in the libidinous, cruel, and cunning behavior of Deburau's egotistical Pierrot a heroic version of the revitalizing child-man they idealized.[4]

In the second half of the nineteenth century, as the pantomime and circus became more popular and modernism started to take root, writers and visual

artists frequently drew on the figure of the clown. Gustave Flaubert, who might
have seen Deburau perform in Paris in the early 1840s, collaborated in 1854 with
friend Louis Bouilhet on a pantomime, *Pierrot au serial*, in which the eponymous
hero retains many of the traits of Deburau's Pierrot.[5] In his last novel, *Bouvard
et Pécuchet*, left unfinished on his death in 1880, Flaubert used two clown-like
characters to satirize the extreme stupidity (*la bêtise*) he feared was engulfing
modern civilization. In cultivating *fumisme*, an attitude of irreverent skepticism
toward all values, the Hydropathes, Incohérents, and other avant-garde groups
that congregated in cabarets such as the Chat Noir in Montmartre from the
1880s onward parodied serious art and mocked social norms using sexual humor.
For Incohérent Adolphe Willette, who illustrated the *Chat Noir* journal, Pierrot
was the quintessential *fumiste*, and Willette used the clown's image in a series of
illustrations beginning with "Pierrot fumiste" in 1882.[6] Slapstick and licentious
humor also featured prominently in the puppet shows and shadow plays staged
at the Chat Noir, such as Louis Morin's *Pierrot pornographe* (1894), which in turn
set the scene (along with the Symbolists' passion for mimes and shadow plays)
for Alfred Jarry's infamous *Ubu Roi*, first performed with live actors in Paris in
1896. The character of Ubu, with his primitive, murderous appetite for power,
his scatological language, and his buffoonish incompetence, was indebted to the
slapstick tradition as filtered through guignol. Indeed, Jarry preferred using mar-
ionettes to stage the play. In introducing the live action version, he reportedly
discussed its debt to the puppet theater as well as its use of masks,[7] and in 1901 it
was performed as a puppet show at Les Quat'z'Arts, another avant-garde cabaret
in Montmartre.

Jarry was a hero for younger avant-gardists, such as Picasso, who lived in
Montmartre in the early 1900s. In selecting saltimbanques, Harlequins, and
fools as subjects, especially in his Rose Period, Picasso was also following in the
footsteps of Renoir, Degas, Cézanne, Toulouse-Lautrec, and other impression-
ists and postimpressionists who had painted these and related figures in depicting the popular culture of their time.[8] Picasso frequented the Cirque Medrano
in Paris, and he reportedly derived great pleasure from clowns and their slapstick antics.[9] Yet his portraits of circus entertainers perpetuated the archetype
of the sad clown by representing them as melancholic and exhausted (fig. 1.1).
According to Theodore Reff, Picasso viewed these performers as alter egos, as
highly skilled artists who, like himself, were estranged from society due to their
nonconformism and creativity, and he even went so far as to give several of his
harlequins his own features.[10] Picasso was also a devotee, like the futurist F. T.
Marinetti, of the music hall, where, in addition to comic acts such as the mimicry
of sporting activities that Tati would excel at on stage in the 1930s, films were

FIGURE 1.1 Pablo Picasso, *Family of Saltimbanques (Familia de saltimbanquis)*, 1905.

© 2019 Estate of Pablo Picasso / Artists Rights Society (ARS), New York. Photo credit: Album/Art Resource, NY.

projected.[11] As Richard Abel has shown, it was in the late 1900s that the French avant-garde, many of who were Picasso's friends, began embracing the cinema.[12] But it wasn't until World War I that they became captivated by slapstick film, due largely to Charlie Chaplin's international success from 1915 onward.[13] Comedic modernism began to encompass cinematic clowns, and first Chaplin, then other slapstick film comedians, entered the writings and visual works of a number of avant-gardists—including Picasso, Jean Cocteau, and Erik Satie's 1917 ballet *Parade*, in which the character of the Little American Girl walks like Chaplin.

The standard explanation for the modernist attraction to film comedians in Europe beginning in World War I argues that the avant-garde turned to popular culture, especially of the American variety, to modernize the arts and thereby break with nineteenth-century bourgeois artistic traditions and taste. "The principal foe of the modernists was not mass entertainment but an older version of 'high' culture," writes Richard Pells. "Their objective instead was to use the techniques and content of popular culture to reinvigorate novels, painting, and music."[14] Beginning with Cendrars, Apollinaire, and others in the late 1900s, cinema became a privileged example of popular culture for European modernists precisely because, as a new medium, it appeared to them to lack traditions. Hence, they vociferously protested any attempt to import what they perceived to be outmoded artistic forms from the other arts into film, particularly the psychological drama found in nineteenth-century bourgeois literature and theater, and they embraced instead low film genres such as comedian comedy.[15] American popular cinema in particular was lionized because of *américanisme*, the avant-garde's worship of what they viewed as "America's wild and primitive modernity" in contrast to "Europe's tradition-bound character,"[16] and because the action-oriented narrative with minimal depth of character psychology that had become the norm of Hollywood filmmaking by the late 1910s was seen as a revitalizing, energetic force that could be emulated in order to breathe new life into European art.[17] "For the Americans are primitive and at the same time barbarous, which accounts for the strength and vitality which they infuse into the cinema," wrote Elie Faure in the early 1920s.[18]

Like many standard stories, this one is not wrong, as it is true that modernists of the period were drawn to slapstick film for what they perceived to be the rejuvenating, modernizing potential of its American primitivism. However, as noted, the affinity of modern artists for clowns long predates (and survives) early twentieth-century *américanisme*, suggesting it was more fundamental and enduring than the European avant-garde's reveling in all things American in the first decades of the twentieth century. Furthermore, most of the forms of assimilation of the slapstick comedian by modernists were already established by the time they turned toward American popular cinema in the 1910s. The identification of the avant-garde artist with the clown's alienation from society (the sad clown) and fluid identity, the use of slapstick to satirize the detested bourgeois, the reveling in the comedian's primitive behavior, and the delight taken in the fantastical, illogical narratives of comedian comedy—all of these points of attraction, which resurface in Dada, surrealism, and other interwar avant-garde movements, can be traced back to the nineteenth century. Moreover, despite its often extreme rhetoric, it was rarely the case that the avant-garde adopted, or for that matter rejected, anything unequivocally, including American popular culture. Nor did it repudiate every artistic tradition, slapstick comedy with its venerable history stretching back to commedia dell'arte and earlier being an obvious example. The positions of modernists toward mainstream film were more nuanced, complex, and even ambivalent than the standard story suggests, with different artists drawing on divergent aspects of popular filmmaking in line with their own agendas. Indeed, it was often what they saw as the largely unrealized *potential* of film, glimpsed only occasionally in mainstream movies, that avant-gardists celebrated. The filmmaker René Clair, who worked at the intersection of comedian comedy and modernism in the 1920s and is Tati's most important precursor, wrote in 1923 that "we like the cinema not so much for what it is as for what it will be."[19]

Nor was comedian comedy admired simply because it was a low genre that, as some have suggested, otherwise bore no relation to the modernist appropriation of it. In discussing Ywan Goll's film poem *The Chaplinade* (1920), Yuri Tsivian maintains that "Goll's Chaplin has little to do with either Chaplin or Chaplin's art," and he characterizes the Soviet avant-garde's view of Chaplin as "nonsense."[20] In fact, as I will demonstrate, comedian comedy's major conventions accorded with, and sometimes shaped, modernist innovations. To be sure, avant-gardists were highly selective in borrowing from the genre, and they tended to fixate on and exaggerate the modernist potential of only those properties that suited their purposes, ignoring others. Nevertheless, the features of comedian comedy they fastened on to were real. Moreover, the genre's richness informed a number of different, even antithetical, avant-garde practices. There is, in other words, no single reason that modern artists were drawn to comedian comedy, as I will show in this chapter by untangling the principal uses of the slapstick film comedian by interwar modernists, which often overlapped in practice. Instead of summarizing every avant-garde citation of a cinematic clown, an impossible task given their sheer variety and number, I will delineate the major types of comedic modernism running through the period using salient examples from the work of those who were involved with film. I will then conclude by showing how Clair synthesized some of these variants in *Entr'acte* (1924), the celebrated avant-garde short he made with Dadaist Francis Picabia, as well as in some of his other more popular modernist films of the 1920s, before moving on in subsequent chapters to consider which strains resurfaced in Tati's films in the post–World War II period.[21]

COMEDIAN AS OBJECT

One of Chaplin's most fervent admirers among the interwar European avant-garde was Fernand Léger. Chaplin was the subject of Léger's marionette, *Charlot Cubiste* (1924), which appears at the beginning and end of his film

Ballet mécanique (1924) (fig. 1.2); some illustrations and drawings; several articles; and an unrealized film project that, according to Carolyn Lanchner, Léger still had hopes of making well into the 1930s with Chaplin's cooperation.[22] Léger championed Chaplin not for his comedy, however, but because the comedian seemed to Léger to comport with his view of film as a medium for revealing the

FIGURE 1.2 Fernand Léger, *Charlot cubiste*, 1924.

plastic properties of objects rather than the psychological ones of subjects. In common with other European modernists of the period, Léger argued that cinema should not imitate theater by narrating stories, claiming that "the dramatic effect of a living person, speaking with emotion, cannot be equaled by its direct, silent projection in black and white on a screen. The film is beaten in advance; it will always be bad theater."[23] Instead, Léger believed that, like modern painting, film should be a visual art dedicated to revealing "the intrinsic plastic value of the object," which it is able to exhibit with particular force and clarity, he felt, owing to movement, the size of the screen, and techniques such as editing and the close-up.[24] "Subject, literature and sentimentality are all negative qualities which weigh down the current cinema—in sum, qualities which bring it into competition with the theater," he stated in his text "Painting and Cinema."[25] "True cinema involves *the image of the object* which is totally unfamiliar to our eyes and which is in itself moving."[26] He therefore rejected as misguided the vast majority of both popular and elite filmmaking, and in his own film *Ballet mécanique*, made after he had come under the influence of Purism and its concern with type-objects that manifest what he saw as the geometrical order and beauty of modernity, Léger dispensed with narrative and made extensive use of editing, close-ups, and other techniques to focus the viewer's attention on the plastic features of a variety of manufactured objects as well as the human face and body.

Léger argued that Chaplin had "ceased" to be a subject—his character the "little fellow"—and had "instead become a sort of living object. . . . Just imagine him moving without any 'comical expressiveness' and he will certainly arouse your interest. There is a plastic aspect there, an image in itself."[27] Anyone with knowledge of comedian comedy in general and Chaplin's films in particular from this period might wonder what precisely Léger is referring to in comments such as these. The depsychologization and objectification of the comedian, whose stock character functions as a pretext for the comedian's subjection to all manner of physical indignities for the sake of humor, was central to the slapstick tradition in film and on stage and was by no means specific to Chaplin. After all the word *slapstick*, as Alan Dale reminds us,

> derives from an implement—"the double paddles formerly used by circus clowns to beat each other. The loud crack of the two paddle blades as they crashed together could always be depended upon to produce the laughter and applause." . . . For comedy to register as slapstick, you need only the fall, and its flipside, the blow. . . . The essence of a slapstick gag is a physical assault on, or collapse of, the hero's dignity.[28]

Moreover, unlike most other slapstick film comedians, Chaplin was already, in his Essanay Studio films of 1915, according to Walter Kerr and others, moving toward the combination of slapstick with pathos that was fully developed by the time of his first feature, *The Kid*, released in 1921, five years before the publication of the text by Léger on Chaplin I have just quoted.[29] Far from being a slapstick object, in other words, Chaplin was in the second half of the 1910s, when Léger first encountered him, already crafting a subject, an expressive character with a psychology, with mental states viewers are supposed to take seriously. Was Léger actually paying attention to Chaplin's films, one might ask?

In fact, by "living object," Léger meant something more than the reduction of the comedian to a depsychologized object in the slapstick tradition. He goes on to state that Chaplin's "power lies in knowing how to transform himself. Charlot [Chaplin's character or persona in film] and Charlie Chaplin are two different things. . . . Without seeming to, Charlot revives a great, ancient tradition of transformation on stage. . . . The art of invention is Charlot's alone," and Léger compared Chaplin to the "ancients" who "invented the Mask."[30] In emphasizing the great comedian's power of transformation and distinguishing between Chaplin and his characters, Léger is astutely drawing attention to a dimension of the clown's persona that has since become widely acknowledged by Chaplin scholars and critics. As Alan Dale describes it, Chaplin is "protean," "many-sided," "incoherent," "unresolvable," or as Kerr puts it, "he can be anyone."[31] These writers mean not only that Chaplin played contrasting characters in his short films but also that, even when he had settled on the "little fellow" or Tramp character, the Tramp, too, assumes a wide variety of identities and displays divergent, even incoherent character traits.

Kerr describes Chaplin as capable of being anyone following a consideration of his 1915 Essanay short *A Night in the Show*, which, according to Jennifer Wild, may well have been the first Chaplin film Léger saw with Apollinaire during World War I when on leave from the front in 1916.[32] In this film, Chaplin plays two drunks, one a gentleman, the other a commoner, who are watching a play and causing mayhem. The costume, make-up, and behavior of the two characters differ to such an extent that an uninformed viewer might not realize that the same actor plays both of them (figs. 1.3 and 1.4). But even if Léger did not see this particular film, he is pointing to Chaplin's (and the Tramp's) capacity to assume a range of personas and the resulting impression that he is putting on a mask or impersonating someone rather than being someone.[33] Masks proliferate, for instance, in *The Idle Class* (1921). Once again Chaplin plays two characters from opposite ends of the social spectrum—a wealthy alcoholic staying at a luxury summer resort and the Tramp who sneaks onto the resort's golf course to try his

FIGURE 1.3   In *A Night in the Show* (Charlie Chaplin, 1915), Chaplin plays both a gentleman . . .

FIGURE 1.4   . . . and a commoner.

hand at the game. This time, however, they look alike, and at a costume ball held at the resort, the alcoholic's estranged wife mistakes the Tramp for her husband dressed as a hobo for the ball. The husband, meanwhile, is outfitted in a suit of armor, his face masked by the vizor, which is stuck shut.

Léger was by no means alone among the avant-garde in his fascination with this dimension of Chaplin's persona. The Dadaists were entranced by Chaplin's skill both at blurring multiple, shifting identities in his films and at crafting a star image using the mass media.[34] This skill corresponded with their desire for freedom, specifically the freedom to create, play with, and perform their own labile, fragmentary identities (exemplified by Marcel Duchamp's alter ego Rrose Sélavy), and Dadaists therefore often compared themselves to Chaplin. In the film-poem *The Chaplinade* (1920), which Léger illustrated with drawings of Chaplin, Yvan Goll—who associated with a number of avant-garde groups, including the Dadaists in Zurich during the war—echoed the Dadaists' association of Chaplin with multiple identity-formation and the mass media by having all the posters of Chaplin in a city detached from their mounts and chased by its inhabitants. "Chaplin in every imaginable costume, in full dress, as a cook's apprentice, as a soldier, as king, as salesclerk, as a violinist, group together so that the pursued soon outnumber the pursuers," wrote Goll.[35] The crowd then "becomes confused and doesn't know which one to chase."[36]

Léger, however, was not interested in Chaplin's construction of personas so much as its attendant depersonalization and objectification. As Kerr points out, a man "who can instantly transform himself into absolutely anyone is a man who must, in his heart, remain no one."[37] He is just a body who, lacking his own psychology, temporarily assumes other peoples' identities. Chaplin's persona therefore harmonized with Léger's interest in depsychologizing the human body and treating it as a purely plastic object, especially when he turned to figure painting in the early 1920s. In his nudes and other works from this period, Léger fused the mechanical subject matter of his earlier paintings with a classical conception of the human body, depicting "classically and mechanically perfect" figures almost entirely devoid of individuality and subjectivity (fig. 1.5).[38] Chaplin might also have suggested to Léger a method for turning a person into an object in his own film *Ballet mécanique*. Throughout much of the film, close-ups show Kiki de Montparnasse switching rapidly between facial expressions, just as Chaplin does with characters and traits. Her face is thereby transformed into a mask, a pure plastic surface that performs expression and lacks psychological depth, much in the same way that Léger saw Chaplin (figs. 1.6 and 1.7).

FIGURE 1.5 Fernand Léger, *Three Women (Le Grand Dejeuner)*, 1921.

The fascination with Chaplin's distinctive version of the objectification of the comedian in slapstick film was broadly shared by those avant-garde movements that rejected the exploration of psychological interiority as bourgeois and theatrical and which instead sought to treat the human body as a plastic object, although each group inflected it with specific concerns. In the Soviet Union, for instance, futurists, Constructivists, and other avant-gardists who idolized the machine as both blueprint and tool for building a socialist utopia began appropriating Chaplin's image in the early 1920s, seeing in his plasticity a harbinger of the machine man of the future.[39] Writing in 1923, Viktor Shklovsky, echoing Léger, expressed the hope that "the high-society psychological film, where the action takes place in the drawing-room, will die out."[40] Proclaiming Chaplin "the first film actor" for his putative break with conventional theatrical acting and his use of purely physical movement as "raw material," he further suggested that Chaplin's performance is "mechanical" in the sense that it is constructed out of "a series of 'constant movements' repeated from film to film . . . Chaplin walks

FIGURE 1.6 *Ballet mécanique* (Fernand Léger and Dudley Murphy, 1924).

FIGURE 1.7 *Ballet mécanique.*

(laughter provokes the actual moment he moves from the spot), Chaplin on a staircase, Chaplin falls off a chair (head over heels and then he stays like that), Chaplin smiles (for three beats), Chaplin is shaken by the collar, and so on."[41] As Yuri Tsivian in particular has noted, it was Chaplin's control over his body, and the skill with which he manipulated it, that Soviet avant-gardists so admired as it accorded with their desire to organize physical labor scientifically by teaching Soviet citizens to move in disciplined and precise ways. "Not many people have Chaplin's mastery of their bodies," wrote filmmaker Lev Kuleshov in 1922, two years before he released his own foray into comedic modernism, the American-style slapstick comedy *The Extraordinary Adventures of Mr. West in the Land of the Bolsheviks* (1924). "Chaplin has studied the mechanism of his body and treats it as a mechanism. . . . We [at the state Cinema Institute] study the human body on the basis of exact calculations and scientific experiments. And Charlie Chaplin is our first teacher."[42]

While Chaplin may have exemplified the ideal of a living object for many avant-gardists, some perceived similar traits in other slapstick film comedians, especially as Chaplin became increasingly associated with sentimentality as the 1920s progressed. In the period leading up to the making of *Un chien Andalou* (1929), both Salvador Dalí and Luis Buñuel fastened on to what they saw as Buster Keaton's battle against "sentimental infections of all kinds" and his "monotonous expression."[43] Although Dalí transferred his affections to Harry Langdon and then the Marx Brothers once he had fully embraced surrealism, in 1927, while still under the influence of the Purism of Le Corbusier and *L'Esprit nouveau*, he described Keaton as "pure poetry," and two years earlier, he included stills from Keaton's films in his collage *The Marriage of Buster Keaton* (1925).[44] Both Buñuel and Dalí advocated a pure, objective antiart free of what they saw as the subjective, psychological distortions of traditional art, which, they believed, prevented reality from being perceived in all its irrational, brutal strangeness; and Dalí in particular applauded the products of modern machines and industry for their anonymity and standardization. "Telephone, pedal-sink, refrigerators white and shining with ripolin, bidet, little phonograph . . . objects of authentic and very pure poetry," he wrote in 1928, and he included popular Hollywood film, especially comedian comedies, among such impersonal, mass-produced objects.[45] It was Keaton's relative lack of expression that endeared him to Dalí and Buñuel, and for this reason Buñuel compared him to an object, calling his "expression . . . as modest as . . . a bottle's."[46] It wasn't just Keaton's emotional reticence that Buñuel viewed as object-like, however; it was also his facility with objects. As numerous critics since the 1920s have noted, one of the distinctive features of Keaton's comic style is his imaginative repurposing of objects to serve ends for which they are not designed. Such objects include his own body, which he often treats as an object that he manipulates in unexpected but ingenious ways to achieve his goals. In *The Navigator* (1924), a film beloved by Dalí, Keaton turns himself into a raft that his companion can paddle to safety by lying on his back in the water in his deep-sea diving suit.[47] As Buñuel noted approvingly in his review of *College* (1927), "Keaton achieves comic effect through direct harmony with the tools, situations and other means of production,"[48] and there is some evidence that Pierre Batcheff imitated Keaton in his performance as the major protagonist in Dalí and Buñuel's *Un chien Andalou*.[49] I will return to the important influence of the distinctive role of objects in comedian comedy on the avant-garde toward the end of this chapter.

COMEDIAN AS OUTCAST

I have spent some time delineating the comedian-as-object strain of comedic modernism because it has fewer precedents in the nineteenth century and is very much the product of the interwar European avant-garde's distinctive preoccupation with the human body as depsychologized object and machine. It also shows that at least one form of the modernist attraction to the slapstick film comedian resulted not just from the allure of American popular culture's modernizing primitivism but a recurring formal feature of comedian comedy: the clown's object-like nature, whether this resulted from the slapstick tradition of objectifying the comic's body, Chaplin (or Charlot's) protean identity, or Keaton's emotional reserve and skill at manipulating objects. The other major types of comedic modernism of the period can all be traced back to the nineteenth century, if not before, and have their roots in the most obvious reason that modernists, like the Romantics and post-Romantics before them, were drawn to comedian comedy: the comic's *freedom* from social norms as manifest in his aberrant behavior, and his concomitant alienation from society. Modern artists have long viewed themselves as social outcasts because of their creative nonconformity in both art and life. For them, the comic's imaginative flouting of society's norms was a pleasurable analogue of their own desire to break with convention, and as noted in the case of Picasso, some accordingly even likened themselves to clowns. In the words of Jean Starobinski in his classic work *Portrait de l'artiste en saltimbanque* (1970):

> Since the Romantic era . . . the buffoon, the *saltimbanque*, and the clown have served as the hyperbolic and deliberately *deforming* images that artists have

taken pleasure in presenting of themselves and of the state of art. What they have offered is a distorted self-portrait that is far more than just a sarcastic or mournful caricature. Musset picturing himself as Fantasio; Flaubert declaring "My basic character, whatever people say, is that of a saltimbanque (letter dated 8 August 1846); Jarry, on his deathbed, identifying himself with his parodic creature, "Father Ubu will try to sleep"; Joyce claiming "I am only an Irish clown, a great joker at the universe"; Rouault painting his self-portrait again and again in the guise of Pierrot or a sad clown; Picasso surrounded by his inexhaustible collection of costumes and masks; Henry Miller meditating on the clown he was and had always been.[50]

Of course not all modern artists have identified personally with the figure of the comic in the manner described by Starbonski. But the comedian's independence from, if not revolt against, society by means of his eccentric behavior, and the skill, whether physical or verbal, with which it is achieved has been a primary source of the clown's attraction for modernists. So too has the critique of society implicit, and sometimes explicit, in this estrangement. For if the comic is an outsider who does not cleave to society's rules, it is for many of the same putative reasons as the avant-garde artist is: the stultifying conventionality and philistinism of the bourgeoisie who are unable to appreciate the creativity and skill of the artist-clown; the utilitarianism, commercialism, mechanism, and hyperrationalism of modern life which leave no room for anything, such as art and slapstick, that defies means–end rationality; the oppressiveness of the family, police, law, and other institutions that brook no dissent; and so on. In other words, the slapstick film comedian, like the modern artist, may be a fool because he is unable to fit into society. But in his foolishness he is superior to those who *do* fit, because it is the abhorrent aspects of his culture to which he cannot, or will not, conform. Comedian comedy therefore also appealed to modernists because they perceived the comic's alienation to be the result of many of the same forces that marginalized them or that they criticized in their own work.[51] Sergei Eisenstein's famous essay "Charlie the Kid" exemplifies this perspective in attributing what Eisenstein calls Chaplin's "child's eye view," his "infantilism," to Chaplin's desire to "escape to freedom from the fetters of" America's excessive rationalism and instrumentalism.[52] "The short hop into infantilism serves even Chaplin himself as a psychological escape from the bounds of the measured, planned and calculated world of activity that surrounds him," Eisenstein averred.[53]

Some avant-gardists focused on the pathos and loneliness caused by the comedian's estrangement from the fallen modern world, thereby furthering, if often ironically, the tradition of the sad clown, and it is no surprise that Chaplin figured prominently in their work given that Chaplin famously (some would say shamelessly) exploited precisely this aspect of the Tramp's predicament in his films. As Louis Aragon and other surrealists noted:

> What [the Statue of Liberty's] torch casts in Charlot's films is the menacing shadow of the cops, those bounty hunters of the poor, the cops who pop up at every street corner and are instantly suspicious of the tramp's miserable suit. . . . Make no mistake, despite several happy endings, next time we shall rediscover him in misery. This awesome pessimist who today, in English and in French, has given new meaning to the saying: *une vie de chien*, a dog's life.[54]

In Goll's film-poem *The Chaplinade*, Chaplin escapes the poster in which he is imprisoned only to be pursued by various representatives of commercial culture, such as the billposter, who tries to return him to his poster so he can continue to turn a profit from Chaplin's image; and the public, who utter clichés and want him to go on entertaining them. After traveling on a train into the countryside and meeting a lady, who only seems interested in whether he has his checkbook, he journeys to the center of the earth with the lady's deer, where he listens to the "voices of the globe" through a telephone. However, the impoverished conversations he overhears lead him to condemn the inanity of mass communication: "The center of the earth is roaring / With a tumult of lies, stupidity of telephones, insanity of telegrams. How poverty-stricken man is."[55] Finally, after eluding the masses who attempt to appropriate him to lead their political movement, he walks with the deer in a dark forest and composes poetry. But the deer turns into a girl, who tells him she no longer loves him and runs away with a hunter, and he is left alone, sighing that "even the nymphs are bourgeoises."[56] "And that is Chaplin / Lonelier than all the others," he concludes, before he is surrounded by posters and is glued back into one by the billposter.[57]

Most modernists, however, gravitated to the liberating dimension of the slapstick film comedian's nonconformism as well as its rejuvenating powers. This took two principal forms. Those who waged war on rationality, whether because they sought to attack bourgeois values as did the Dadaists, or wished to free the mind from the artificial control of reason like the surrealists, were drawn to the relative absence of logical and rational constraints in comedian comedy. The dominant theory of humor, the so-called incongruity theory, argues that we find funny things that are "surprising, peculiar, unusual, or different from what we normally expect," and it was this aspect of the genre that captivated those artists interested in escaping the bounds of reason.[58] Some focused on the incongruity of the comic's gags. As Robert Knopf has shown, the surrealists

FIGURE 1.8 Buster Keaton as Rollo uses a lobster as a wirecutter in *The Navigator* (Donald Crisp and Buster Keaton, 1924).

particularly admired Keaton's use of objects "in an inappropriate or unusual manner" to achieve his goals, as when he repurposes a lobster as a wire-cutter in the underwater scene in *The Navigator* (fig. 1.8).[59] Such gags accorded with their own technique of juxtaposing incongruous objects to circumvent rational norms and elicit the marvelous. Furthermore, by embedding these implausible gags within a realistic environment in his films, Keaton effected the synthesis of dream and reality that the surrealists desired. For the surrealists, Keaton's imaginative and unconventional use of objects constituted a freedom from rational constraints. Others, as we shall see in the case of Clair, found this freedom in the incongruous narratives and editing of comedian comedy films.

The other major form of attraction exerted by the clown's freedom from social norms centered on the expression of repressed or forbidden impulses that this freedom permits. This, too, accords with a well-known theory of humor, the release theory, which asserts that humor derives from the release of tension, such as the tension created by having to obey social norms that prevent us from expressing our true feelings and desires.[60] In characterizing Chaplin's infantilism,

Eisenstein noted that "the misfortunes of others" are often the object of children's cruel humor before they learn as adults that this is socially proscribed.[61] "The collection of gags in *Modern Times* are in exactly the same spirit," he maintained, referring to the "amoral savagery of a child's approach to phenomena from Chaplin's point of view."[62] But it is probably Antonin Artaud in his response to the Marx Brothers who best exemplifies this particular modernist approach to comedian comedy. For Artaud, the Brothers' feature film, *Animal Crackers* (1930), exemplified humor in its truest sense: "The poetic quality of a film like *Animal Crackers* might correspond to the definition of humor, if this word had not long since lost its meaning of total liberation, of the destruction of all reality in the mind."[63] This was due, in part, to the unfettered, primitive behavior of its characters:

> In *Animal Crackers* when a woman suddenly falls over backward on a sofa with her legs in the air and for a split second shows us everything we might want to see, when a man suddenly grabs a woman in a drawing room, does a few dance steps with her, and slaps her on the behind in time to the music, a kind of intellectual freedom is exercised in which the unconscious of each character, repressed by customs and conventions, avenges itself and our unconscious at the same time.[64]

The same was true, according to Artaud, of the finale of the Brothers' *Monkey Business* (1931), which he described as a "hymn to anarchy and total rebellion" in part because "two lecherous servants happily paw the bare shoulders of their master's daughter, and chat casually with their helpless master, all this amid the intoxication, also intellectual, of the pirouettes of the Marx Brothers."[65] Artaud's use of the word *intoxication* here is crucial. For whether they were attracted to its incongruity or baseness (and these often overlapped in practice), avant-gardists found in the comedian's liberating humor a revivifying energy, a palliative vitality that they saw as combatting the excessive rationalism and conformity of modern life. Certainly this was true for Artaud:

> The films that are the most successful in this sense are those dominated by a certain kind of humor, like the early Buster Keatons or the less human Chaplins. A cinema which is studded with dreams, and which gives you the physical sensation of pure life, finds its triumph in the most excessive sort of humor. A certain excitement of objects, forms, and expressions can only be translated into the convulsions and surprises of a reality that seems to destroy itself with an irony in which you can hear a scream from the extremities of the mind.[66]

RENÉ CLAIR AND COMEDIC MODERNISM

For René Clair, too, Chaplin was a hero, and Charlot (performed by a Chaplin imitator) even appears in his third feature film, *Le Voyage Imaginaire*, made in 1925. In this comic fantasy, Jean, an office clerk played by Jean Borlin of Ballet Suedois fame, falls asleep at his desk and dreams that he and his beloved, Lucie, travel underground to fairyland, where they are given a magic ring. Their happiness is disrupted by two of Jean's fellow office clerks, Albert and August, who are rivals for Lucie's affections and who turn Jean into a dog using the magic ring. Jean, as a dog, pursues Albert and August, and they end up inside the Musée Grévin with Lucie. The waxworks of historical figures come to life, and Lucie and the canine Jean find themselves in the middle of a French Revolution trial. Jean, still a dog, is sentenced to the guillotine, and is about to be beheaded when the wax statue of Charlot helps save the day.

Clair's attachment to Chaplin was rooted in what Clair saw as Chaplin's ability, along with a select few others, to induce what he called "lyricism," an affect he believed to be central to cinema's distinctiveness as an art.

> I know of nothing which conjures up the idea of heroi-comic lyricism, or just plain lyricism, as well as the madcap dashes of Douglas Fairbanks, the implausible flights of Mack Sennett's bathing beauties or Charlie Chaplin's enormous sprints in no particular direction when pursued by a policeman or fate; these sprints continue simply because they have begun. Many effusions of lyric poets have no other reason for existing.[67]

In his writings of the 1920s, Clair, like Léger, decried the influence of the older, verbal arts of literature and theater on cinema, claiming that film was a visual art "created to record motion."[68] While he did not call for the abandonment of narrative, he routinely described a film's story as a mere pretext for the filmmaker to introduce the "greatest number of purely visual themes,"[69] and by "lyricism," he meant, in part, the cinema's capacity to impart the sensation of motion to the viewer, to make the viewer *feel* movement.

By lyricism, however, Clair also meant *mental* movement. "Thought emulates speed in the flow of images," he argued in 1925, echoing Dadaist Francis Picabia's contention that the juxtaposition of moving images in a film can be "as rapid as the thought in our brain."[70] Like Picabia, Clair extolled film's capacity to combine, through editing, a variety of moving images that have little or no logical connection, and he believed such combinations both imitate and encourage in the viewer the free movement of thought unconstrained by reason: "this series of images which is not bound up with the old tricks of thought and to which no absolute meaning is attached, why should it be burdened by logic?"[71] By movement, therefore, Clair not only meant the motion of physical things recorded in a shot but the movement of both the film and the viewer's mind from one incongruous image to another through editing: "Motion. I do not mean motion recorded by the image itself, but motion of the images in relation to one another. Motion, the primary basis of cinematic lyricism."[72] Hence, he praised films containing little physical movement, claiming that they were nevertheless "endowed with intense motion" in the form of the "incessant motion of [the] inner life."[73] And he often listed unrelated shots in an appositional fashion in an effort to convey to his reader how one "can be swept along by a torrent of images. . . . When we cease to care about a ridiculous plot and surrender ourselves instead to the charm of a series of images, forgetting the pretext for their appearance on the screen, we can taste a new pleasure. Images: a landscape in motion passes by. A hand appears. The bow of a boat. A woman's smile. Three trees outlined against the sky. Images."[74]

Clair claimed that cinema should not only be a visual art of physical movement, but that, through the combination of incongruous moving images via editing, it should give rise to an intense, revitalizing, highly pleasurable sensation of mental motion, which he likened to the experience of freedom occasioned by lyric poetry and music: "I feel a pleasure at the sight of these images which is, too infrequently, what I seek to awaken in myself—a sensation of musical liberty."[75] Moreover, while he doubted the possibility of achieving "pure psychic automatism" in film, by 1925, following the publication of André Breton's first manifesto of surrealism, he expressed agreement with the surrealists' emphasis "on the hallucinatory nature of the cinema and the uselessness of any logical commentary on the events which the screen shows," and likened the film viewer to a dreamer.[76] For these reasons, Clair argued in the 1920s that comedian comedy had "furnished the best expression of the cinema" to date, and he drew on it extensively in his attempt to craft a popular modernism in his films. Its lack of concern for unified, realistic narrative, he felt, "permits all sorts of implausibilities, the most poetic illogicalities," in contrast to the dramatic film genres, which had not yet won their "freedom."[77] Clair's love of illogical stories is a modernist version of the Romantics' enchantment with the incoherence and absurdity of the plots of *pantomime-féeries* from a century earlier.

In *Entr'acte*, Clair attempted to elicit a lyrical sensation of motion in the viewer through physical movement. It has long been recognized that the film's second half, in which a high society funeral procession devolves into a slapstick chase, is modeled on the one- and two-reel comic chase films of the 1900s and

1910s.[78] Clair greatly admired these films for exploiting the movement that he saw as the essence of film art, and in the chase, he increases the speed of editing and employs superimposition, upside-down shots, and graphic contrasts to create a powerful sense of motion. Less often noted is that *Entr'acte* illustrates some of the other forms of comedic modernism examined in this chapter. The first half of the film consists of a torrent of images with little or no logical connection of the kind that, Clair and others believed, could be found in comedian comedy and that unleashed revivifying mental mobility. For instance, following the prologue, we see upside-down rooftops, balloon heads being inflated and deflated on a moving platform, a dancing ballerina viewed from below through a glass floor, city lights moving in and out of focus, boxing gloves superimposed over a busy city intersection, and matchsticks superimposed on a man's head. These subjects are edited together in a fast-moving sequence with an average shot length of just over three seconds, and in their anarchic incongruity, they assault bourgeois rationality in the manner desired by the Dadaists. The film also revels in the release of socially prohibited impulses. Violence abounds, as when Picabia suddenly shoots a hunter for no discernible reason, and the matches superimposed on the man's head alight. Even the viewer is not spared, as throughout the film various weapons are aggressively discharged in the direction of the camera. This infantile delight in violence extends to sex through the shots of the ballerina from below, her groin and bottom visible. The ballerina is also the source of identity confusion when the camera reveals that she has a beard.

Entr'acte also exemplifies another type of comedic modernism present throughout much of the European avant-garde of the period, namely, the satire of the bourgeoisie (fig. 1.9). Film comedians, including Chaplin, often lampooned

FIGURE 1.9 The bourgeois funeral procession running after the hearse in *Entr'acte* (René Clair and Francis Picabia, 1924).

high society using slapstick to embarrass and humiliate stock bourgeois characters. In Chaplin's Mutual short *The Adventurer* (1917), Chaplin's character, an
escaped convict, saves a lady and her mother from drowning. He pretends to be
wealthy and is invited to stay at their mansion, where he pursues the lady. While
eating together on a terrace, Chaplin accidentally drops his ice cream down the
dress of a bourgeois woman seated beneath him, and she shivers and gasps in
shock as a man tries to retrieve the cold substance from her dress. As Chaplin
famously explained, "If I had dropped the ice cream, for example, on a scrub
woman's neck, instead of getting laughs, sympathy would have been aroused for
the woman. Also, because a scrub woman has no dignity to lose, that point would
not have been funny. Dropping ice cream down a rich woman's neck, however, is,
in the minds of the audience, just giving the rich what they deserve."[79] Chaplin's
account corresponds with another well-known theory of humor, the superiority
theory, which claims that comic amusement results "from a sense of superiority derived from the disparagement of another person."[80] Dadaists in particular
emulated this slapstick convention of making prosperous people look ridiculous,
including Picabia and Clair in the chase sequence of *Entr'acte*. In doing so, they
drew on what is, according to Louisa Jones, one of the major approaches to the
figure of the clown bequeathed to the twentieth century by nineteenth-century
artists, which "promotes the leveling of carnival in its most positive aspects as the
loss of difference between social classes in such a manner that *la blague* unites all
equally in a community of feeling."[81] Picabia and Clair erase social distinctions by
bringing the high down low, making the bourgeois mourners look increasingly
absurd as they first walk and then run ever faster after the coffin. Moreover, they
are joined by others in speeding vehicles, making it appear that the entire city of
Paris is united in the same madcap, carnivalesque pursuit of the hearse, thereby
creating a community of happy fools.

Clair also drew on the variant of comedic modernism of depsychologizing and
objectifying the comedian that we discovered in Léger's work, combining it to
varying degrees in his films of the 1920s with surrealist incongruity and Dadaist
ridiculing of the bourgeoisie. This is perhaps why, although Léger differentiated
his film *Ballet mécanique* from what he called *Entr'acte*'s "burlesque fantasy,"[82] he
nevertheless referred to Clair along with Marcel L'Herbier as one of the few contemporary filmmakers possessing a true, "plastic understanding" of cinema akin to
his own.[83] In addition to Chaplin, Clair idolized Mack Sennett, whose slapstick
films he described as "poems of the imagination in which clowns, bathing beau-
ties, an automobile, a little dog, a jug of milk, the sky, the sea and some explosive
are the interchangeable elements every combination of which arouses laughter
and amazement."[84] Like Sennett's and unlike Chaplin's, Clair's films of the 1920s

are very much comedies about *groups* of people, and they evince little interest in individual characters, let alone their psychologies. Léger, it should be noted, criticized Chaplin for "sacrificing the whole troupe [of his actors] to his personality," and he expressed regret that Chaplin was not a "director of an ensemble rather than an 'individual case.' "[85] It is precisely ensembles that one finds in Clair's films, which is why Charlot disappears into the crowd when saving the canine Jean in *Le Voyage Imaginaire*, something that would never happen in Chaplin's own films given his predilection for mise-en-scène and other techniques that separate the Tramp from groups and mark him as an exceptional individual.

Clair's characters are further depersonalized by his use of farce. Humor in his films is largely created by absurd, embarrassing, or ironic situations, and stock characters function to inadvertently create these situations and react improbably to them. In addition, Clair often employs doubling in his narratives, accentuating the impression that his characters are, like Sennett's, interchangeable elements to be moved around like pieces on a chessboard for comic effect. In his silent masterpiece *The Italian Straw Hat* (1927), there are two Italian straw hats, two romantic couples, two older men with sore feet and ill-fitting shoes, two clocks, and two almost identical bourgeois apartments, and the humor arises from the chance interaction and confusion of these doubles.

While Léger might well have found Clair's use of farcical tales about groups appealing because of its depsychologization of character, it is doubtless one of its other characteristics that led him to praise Clair for his plastic understanding. As a result of his situational comedy and lack of interest in the individual or psychology, settings play a crucial role in Clair's films.[86] And as numerous critics have noted, objects in these settings are often as important as the characters, who they come to define and even control.[87] This is true to a greater or lesser extent in all of Clair's films of this period, but it is in *The Italian Straw Hat* that Clair most perfectly combines his privileging of objects with Dadaist satire of the bourgeoisie and surrealist incongruity.

The film centers on the search of a wealthy young man, Fadinard, for a rare Italian straw hat to replace the one that his horse chewed while he was riding through the Bois de Vincennes on the way to his wedding. The original hat had been left behind by a lady, Madame Beauperthuis, on a tree in the woods while meeting her lover, a Lieutenant Tavernier, and Tavernier demands that Fadinard replace it before she returns to her husband that evening or her honor will be compromised. Tavernier holes up with Madame Beauperthuis in Fadinard's apartment, threatening to destroy his home if Fadinard does not return with a replacement, and Fadinard must repeatedly leave his wedding party, much to the annoyance of his new father-in-law, to search for a hat. During the wedding festivities, Fadinard imagines Tavernier destroying his possessions and apartment in a sequence that satirizes his concern for his belongings. Fadinard visualizes Tavernier, shown in slow motion, throwing his chairs out of his apartment window onto the street below and breaking his mirror (fig. 1.10). Stop-motion footage of Fadinard's bed and furniture emerging of their own accord onto the street below follows. In fast motion, bourgeois men dressed in suits and top hats appear and take the furniture away. Finally, having prized off Fadinard's window shutters, Tavernier, still in fast motion, gestures for the furniture removers to enter the apartment to dismantle it, and Fadinard's apartment building, clearly a miniature model, collapses. Following a convoluted sequence of absurd events resulting in Madame Beauperthuis gaining a new hat, the film ends with a series of close-ups of incongruous objects that have defined otherwise indistinguishable characters throughout: a necktie on one of the bride's cousins that keeps coming undone; the ear trumpet used by the deaf uncle; a missing glove belonging to another cousin; the boots that have plagued Fadinard's father-in-law because they are too small; and of course the straw hat and the bride's bouquet, a shot of which, incidentally, begins the film.

Juxtapositions of incongruous objects such as these recur throughout surrealist art and film. In a sequence reminiscent of Fadinard's fantasy about the destruction of his belongings, Gaston Modot's character in Buñuel and Dalí's *L'Age d'or* (1930) throws a burning tree, a bishop, his ceremonial staff, a plough, and then a giraffe out of a window (fig. 1.11). The latter is a miniature tossed from what is clearly a model window, much like the model apartment building that is

FIGURE 1.10 A chair is thrown out of Fadinard's window in *The Italian Straw Hat* (René Clair, 1927).

FIGURE 1.11 A giraffe is tossed from the window in *L'Age d'or* (Luis Buñuel and Salvador Dalí, 1930).

destroyed at the end of Fadinard's daydream. Objects like Fadinard's furniture that move on their own and rebel against their bourgeois owners, meanwhile, are a leitmotif of Dadaist film. The prologue to *Entr'acte* shows a canon moving around in fast motion on a rooftop in Paris before firing at the audience, and the hearse escapes the mourners in the funeral procession and proceeds to careen through the city streets on its own. In Hans Richter's *Ghosts Before Breakfast* (1928), men try to catch bowler hats that have escaped their grasp and are flying above them (fig. 1.12). It is surely Clair's use of such actor-objects, often filmed in close-up as at the end of *The Italian Straw Hat*, that would have struck Léger as clear evidence of Clair's plastic understanding. Either way, this privileging of the object, so important for Léger and other European avant-gardists of the 1920s, also had its antecedents in comedian comedy. As Dale has eloquently argued, slapstick is a genre in which, to use Frank Capra's memorable phrase, bewilderment and exasperation at the "intransigence of inanimate objects" is central, and much slapstick revolves around objects that defy human understanding and control.[88] In his writings, Clair celebrated in particular Chaplin's use of rebellious objects such as a folding chair on the deck of a pleasure cruiser in *A Day's Pleasure* (1919), which Chaplin struggles for several minutes to assemble before throwing in exasperation over the side of the boat (fig. 1.13).[89] In doing so, Clair was echoing other avant-gardists, such as Louis Aragon, who remarked in 1918 on how the "decor" in Chaplin's films "haunts the hero to such an extent that by an inversion of values, each inanimate object becomes a living thing for him, each human person a dummy whose starting-handle must be found."[90]

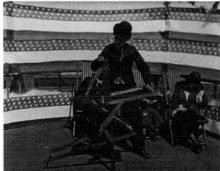

FIGURE 1.12 A man tries to capture an escaped bowler hat in *Ghosts Before Breakfast* (Hans Richter, 1928).

FIGURE 1.13 Chaplin's character struggles to assemble a deck chair in *A Day's Pleasure* (Charlie Chaplin, 1919).

The avant-garde appropriation of rebellious objects from slapstick shows once again what a rich resource the genre of comedian comedy has been for modernists. To be sure, it was attractive to them because it was a low, popular genre perfected by the Americans, as the standard story argues. But as we have seen, it also accorded with, and even influenced, avant-garde innovations through the depsychologization and objectification of the comedian; the figure of the alienated, sad clown; incongruity in gags and narrative structures; the satire of the bourgeoisie and the carnivalesque leveling of social distinctions; the release of primitive, instinctual behavior; and the privileging of often rebellious objects. A variety of modernists with antithetical commitments found inspiration in these myriad features, which perhaps accounts for the pervasiveness of comedic modernism. It is time, now, to turn to Tati to see which of these strains of comedic modernism resurfaced in his work and how he adapted them to the distinctive concerns of the post-World War II era.

CHAPTER 2

COMEDY OF EVERYDAY LIFE

Most of the prewar forms of comedic modernism surveyed in chapter 1 resurface in Tati's postwar films. However, the avant-garde had changed since the 1920s, and Tati's comic style emerged within a much-altered artistic context, one in which the putative authoritarian-ism of mass culture and the attempt to develop more democratic alternatives had become an overriding concern. Tati embraced this concern, and it had a profound effect on his comedy, motivating many of his innovations.

Tati's humor has long been associated with the concept of democracy because of the central role played by subsidiary characters in it. Whereas in classical comedian comedy the clown as performed by the star is the source of most of the humor, in Tati's films other characters participate in the comedy to a much greater degree. Michel Chion, for example, writes of Tati's comic democracy in which "every one of his numerous characters [is] a potential comic,"[1] while Stéphane Goudet, under the heading the "Democracy of the Gag," asserts that Tati's films "acknowledge the right of everyone who appears on the screen to be funny."[2] Jonathan Rosenbaum titled his seminal introduction to his 1973 inter-view with the director "Tati's Democracy," and Tati himself, in the interview, describes *Play Time* as a "democracy of gags and comics."[3] Tati did not confine this argument to *Play Time*, however. In a 1958 interview with André Bazin and François Truffaut for *Cahiers du cinéma* about his just-released third feature, *Mon Oncle*, we find him expressing the wish to make a film without his comic character, Monsieur Hulot, based solely on "people I see, I observe, I meet in the street." "In *Mon Oncle*, the maid is a comic character, the Italian merchant too, and so is the neighbor—she does much more than Hulot," he continued.[4]

In this chapter, I explore in detail what Tati meant by *democracy* and how it informed his comedic modernism. But first, why was he so concerned to democratize comedy? Tati was not an intellectual or a theorist, and he did not leave behind a manifesto or other detailed statement about his intentions. But it is clear from his remarks in interviews, and especially from his films (as we shall discover in chapter 4), that he shared with the post–World War II European intelligentsia *some* of its concerns about mass culture, especially American mass culture. In contrast to the *américanisme* of the avant-garde of the 1920s, which celebrated the primitivism of the popular culture of the United States as a revitalizing, modernizing force, postwar European intellectuals and artists of Tati's generation were more inclined to perceive American mass culture as hegemonic and totalitarian, engendering passivity and annihilating individuality. Already by the 1930s American society was widely viewed by Europeans as "mechanized and monotonous," and this only intensified after the war.[5] Richard Pells has claimed in his history of the European reception of American culture that this was in part the result of the pervasiveness of American movies, advertisements, books, popular music, fashion, and eventually television in Europe following World War II. As European countries enjoyed greater prosperity and personal incomes rose in the 1950s, the general public had more disposable income to spend on "such 'luxuries' as new furniture, electrical appliances, crystal and china, high-fidelity phonographs and records, television sets, and leisure wear—most of these made in America."[6] The emergence of mass consumption in Europe, and the popularity of American consumer items, in turn undermined "the power and prestige of the European intellectual elite," which reacted by accusing American mass culture of imperialism, of leveling cultural differences through uniform products that pacified consumers by bewitching them with ultimately meaningless forms of pleasure.[7] As Pells puts it, "Behind these beliefs lay the suspicion that mass culture was weakening the democratic ethos by reducing citizens to spectators, no longer capable of participating actively in decisions about political or social policy."[8] Avant-garde artist and theorist Guy Debord famously referred to this condition as the "society of the spectacle," a new "social relation among people, mediated by images," in which "everything that was directly lived has moved away into a representation."[9] Debord continued, "The alienation of the spectator to the profit of the contemplated object (which is the result of his own unconscious activity) is expressed in the following way: the more he contemplates the less he lives."[10]

Others, however, went further, viewing mass culture's extinguishing of individuality as an inevitable outcome not just of Americanization but of modernization in general. An influential example is Max Horkheimer and Theodor Adorno's *Dialectic of Enlightenment* (1944). The progress enabled by the increasing

dominance of human beings over nature through instrumental reason and technology, they insisted, inevitably results in greater control over humans themselves.
"The fallen nature of modern man cannot be separated from social progress,"
they lamented. "Even though the individual disappears before the apparatus he
serves, the apparatus provides for him as never before."[11] Mass culture instantiates
this dialectic. While it results from the prosperity occasioned by instrumental
reason and technology, it makes use of means-end reasoning and technology
to preprogram the consumer's response to its products, thereby eradicating her
autonomy: "No independent thinking must be expected from the audience: the
product prescribes each reaction."[12] The result is the liquidation of the individual:
"The most intimate reactions of human beings have become so entirely reified,
even to themselves, that the idea of anything peculiar to them survives only in
extreme abstraction: personality means hardly more than dazzling white teeth
and freedom from body odor and emotions."[13]

While it is unlikely that Tati read the German philosophers or Debord, many
held similar views to theirs after World War II, and one finds echoes of them in
Tati's remarks. "What I condemn in the 'new' life is precisely the disappearance
of any respect for the individual," he told Bazin and Truffaut in 1958, and he
repeatedly complained that modern technologies discourage participation and
beget passivity.[14] When discussing modern cars in the same interview, he opined:
"I believe it's important that children once used to shine the hubcaps, that their
mother made the seat covers herself, that the whole family participated together
in something. Now people don't participate in anything anymore; there is nothing to do, nothing left to work at."[15] Almost fifteen years later, after the release of
Trafic, he made the same point in relation to cars to Jonathan Rosenbaum: "The
more the engineers work for us, the less we have to do when we drive a car . . .
before, people *participated* in the driving; they knew by the sound of the motor
how to change gears—rmrmrm, into second, and so forth. You participated,
and you had to be a good driver. Now, with the new American car, it doesn't
make any difference whether you're a bad or good driver."[16] Moreover, among
modern technologies that putatively pacify people, Tati included mass media,
particularly television: "The trouble with today's audiences is that they're not
used to participation, they're used to television which makes no demands on the
part of the viewer."[17] The key term here, one that Tati repeats again and again
throughout his career, is *participation*: "You see, in *Play Time*, what I want is
participation," he stated.[18] It is for this reason that Tati described *Play Time* as a
"democracy of gags and comics." For him, democracy primarily meant dethron-
ing the star comedian and involving as many people as possible in comedy in
order to counter what he and others saw as the increasing passivity occasioned

by modern life, including mass media such as television. As we shall see, his efforts to democratize comedy went well beyond simply including subsidiary characters in it.

The goal of counteracting the supposedly pacifying effects of mass culture and restoring agency and autonomy to its users was widely shared by the avant-garde of the period, and it took many different forms. Kaira Cabañas has demonstrated how the Lettrists in France used "dissociative strategies in their films—disjunctures between speech and sound, sound and image, screen and space" because they "were committed to a cinema that implied spectators' active participation."[19] The Lettrists and the situationists who followed them, as well as Bruce Conner in the United States, employed the technique of what the situationists called *détournement*, or the "excision of an item of culture (whether image, text, or object) from its normative context and its subsequent juxtaposition with another fragment."[20] By appropriating elements from a variety of cultural sources, and organizing them into assemblages to create new meanings very different from their original ones, artists took control over them while inviting audiences to actively find their own connections among their parts. A number of films were created that put this assemblage aesthetic into practice, such as Conner's *A Movie* (1958) and Debord's *Critique de la séparation* (1961). Others, as Fred Turner has shown, "advocated a turn away from single-source mass media and toward multi-image, multi-sound-source media environments," what Turner aptly terms "democratic surrounds."[21] Influenced by the composer John Cage, who shifted in the 1940s and early 1950s "from an expressive sender–message–receiver model of music-making and toward an environmental, surround-based mode that simultaneously denied his own agency as composer and aimed to enhance the agency of his listeners,"[22] artists such as Stan VanDerBeek in his *Movie-Drome* (1962–1966) started constructing multimedia environments in which multiple images and sounds were exhibited simultaneously. Such environments allowed viewers to attend to those elements they were interested in and discover relationships among them for themselves, thereby actively constructing their own individualized experiences and meanings.

As someone interested in crafting a popular modernism, Tati chose a different route. Rather than attempting to dismantle and reconstruct mass culture, as did the situationists, or devise alternative forms of audio-visual experience such as democratic surrounds, Tati sought to make the mass medium of mainstream film *itself* more democratic and thereby empower his viewer. Moreover, he did so within the genre of comedian comedy, which was very much associated with Hollywood. Like most of his contemporaries, Tati did not reject American mass culture even while he was critical of it, and as I show in chapter 4, his films evince an ambivalent stance toward Americanization. However, Pells makes the crucial point that "even when Europeans did borrow American ideas or imitate American patterns of behavior, the ideas and the behavior were modified to suit the special requirements of France."[23] Tati, as did New Wave filmmakers such as Jean-Luc Godard and Truffaut with other Hollywood genres, appropriated the genre of comedian comedy but adapted it in light of his culturally specific concerns, especially his fear that modernization was making people more passive and his concomitant wish for a comic democracy. How did he go about doing this?

MONSIEUR HULOT AND REALISM

One method Tati used was to create in Monsieur Hulot a comic character that, he felt, was more realistic than classical slapstick comedians. As he put it, "I would like people to feel that the character of Hulot the uncle [in *Mon Oncle*] is not a circus character, to believe that he is really an uncle."[24] A number of critics have pointed to Tati's employment of realist conventions in his films such as dedramatization, which putatively emulates the ordinariness and arbitrariness of quotidian reality. The narrative structures of the first three Hulot films, as in many neorealist works, consist of events that aren't for the most part linked by character goals, as they typically are in classical narratives. Instead, incident follows incident without much connection between them, and there is a certain amount of dead time lacking dramatic action. What unifies the events in Tati's films isn't so much the characters and their goals, but rather, as Kristin Thompson incisively puts it:

> the set length of a time taken by a special event. . . . *Jour de fête*, for example, begins with the arrival of the travelling fair and ends with its departure. . . . The action of *Les Vacances* spans the seven days of Hulot's seaside vacation, from arrival to departure; no specific goal or line of action focuses the plot. *Play Time* covers the brief period of another visit—by a group of American tourists to Paris.[25]

Characters typically encounter each other by chance because they take part in these events.

André Bazin, for example, early on remarked on the antidramatic representation of time in *Les Vacances de Monsieur Hulot*:

> This is why Hulot could never be scripted. A story confers meaning; it leads from cause to effect, from beginning to end. *Monsieur Hulot's Holiday*, on the

contrary, can only be a series of events with both coherent meaning and dramatic independence. Each of the hero's adventures and misadventures begins as if we were being told "Another time, Monsieur Hulot . . ."[26]

The film is about Monsieur Hulot and other guests vacationing at a seaside hotel for a week, and it follows their daily routines and interactions in and around the hotel, only some of which are humorous. As Noël Burch noted, it alternates "between strong and weak moments, between deliberately action-packed, screamingly funny passages, and others just as deliberately empty, boring, and flat."[27] *Mon Oncle* concerns the daily life of the Arpels, a bourgeois couple and their son, Gérard, who live in a modern house in a suburban redevelopment. Hulot is Madame Arpel's brother, and he often looks after his nephew, taking him to the old quarter where he lives. Although once again incident tends to follow incident without much connection, Monsieur Arpel eventually formulates the goal of reforming the carefree Hulot by getting him a job and finding him a wife, and this goal gives the second half of the film a degree of dramatic structure. Roy Armes has suggested that Tati's next film, *Play Time*, takes dedramatization to its limit because it "contains nothing even remotely dramatic in this sense: we simply see people failing to meet, taking photographs, eating, or working."[28] The film is about a group of American tourists arriving at a Paris airport, and it follows them as they wander through a modern redevelopment in the city center, attend a home goods exposition, return to their hotel, and then dine in a newly opened restaurant before leaving on a bus the following day. Monsieur Hulot happens to be visiting a man, Giffard, in a nearby office building, although we never learn why, and he comes across the American tourists as he searches for Giffard before inadvertently ending up at the restaurant where they are dining. There he briefly befriends one of them, Barbara. Although he initially has the goal of meeting Giffard, it is quickly abandoned when he is unable to find Giffard, and the film for the most part once again consists of unconnected events, only some of which are amusing. This is partially true of *Jour de fête* and *Trafic* as well. However, because Tati's characters in these films have jobs that play an important narrative role, unlike in the other films, they have clearly articulated goals. François in *Jour de fête* is a postman, and, inspired by a documentary about the mechanized American postal service, he strives to deliver the mail more efficiently. In *Trafic*, Hulot works for a car company and his goal is to deliver his company's new camper-car, which he designed, to a car show in Amsterdam.

Tati's style has also been called realistic. Kristin Thompson has refined Burch's account of *Les Vacances* by showing that, in fact, Tati often overlaps otherwise discontinuous "small incidents and gags" using long shots, long takes, deep focus, and deep staging so that "one gag may be played out in the foreground, while another minor action is occurring in one part of the background, and the next gag is being set up in another."[29] Bazin argued that the long take and deep focus are inherently realist techniques, leading Jonathan Rosenbaum to contend that *Play Time* "can be regarded as an embodiment of Bazin's most cherished ideas."[30] Instead of the sequential actions of classical narrative, events are interwoven in Tati's films in long, deep focus shots, thereby better approximating the disorganized confusion of perceptual experience in which "several points of interest compete independently for our attention."[31]

What has been less often remarked upon is the way Tati's effort at realism affects the very structure of his gags, something Tati himself was at pains to explicate. In the 1958 interview with Bazin and Truffaut, Tati contrasted his style of comedy with Chaplin's. While Chaplin "is always inventing something," Tati insisted that Monsieur Hulot "didn't invent anything."[32] Tati is referring in Chaplin's films to what Noël Carroll, in his taxonomy of sight gags, calls a mimed metaphor, in which, by way of pantomime, a comic character intentionally equates one thing with another—shoelaces with spaghetti or bread rolls with dancing feet in *The Gold Rush* (1925), for example (fig. 2.1).[33] As Carroll notes,

FIGURE 2.1 The mimed metaphor with bread roles as dancing feet in *The Gold Rush* (Charlie Chaplin, 1925).

even though they recur throughout comedian comedy, mimed metaphors are particularly associated with Chaplin's Tramp character both because of Chaplin's skill as a mime and because the Tramp is highly imaginative and able to see things differently from other people—to see that shoelaces are like spaghetti, for instance. The Tramp is unique, not only because of his unusual physical appearance and alienation from society but because of his inventiveness. This is not the case with Hulot, according to Tati. Even though Tati was a talented mime who, like Chaplin, started his career in the music hall, he stressed Hulot's ordinariness, the fact that "he behaves exactly like any man from Paris or even the provinces."[34]

Carroll believes that mimed metaphors occur in Tati's films, and cites the funeral wreath gag in *Les Vacances* as an example.[35] In fact, as Tati himself explained, it is not a mimed metaphor. Hulot accidentally stops his vintage Amilcar in a cemetery where a funeral is taking place. While rummaging around in the trunk for a hand-crank to restart it, he absent-mindedly throws a spare tire tube onto the ground, where leaves stick to it (fig. 2.2). A uniformed man delivering a wreath to the funeral mistakes the leaf-strewn tube for another wreath and

FIGURE 2.2 Hulot throws a spare tire tube onto the ground where leaves stick to it in *Les Vacances de Monsieur Hulot* (Jacques Tati, 1953).

FIGURE 2.3 The tire tube with leaves is then mistaken for a funeral wreath.

hangs it near the funeral procession, where it loudly deflates as mourners walk past (fig. 2.3). Tati proclaimed that "what happened to Monsieur Hulot [here] could happen to a lot of people. There are many Hulots in life, come to think of it." With Chaplin, on the other hand:

> He would have made the same entrance as Hulot, but, seeing that the situation was turning into a catastrophe . . . he would have ended up with a tire tube in his hand after opening the trunk and would have stuck the leaves on the tube by himself. *For the viewers*, he would have transformed the tube into a funeral wreath.[36]

While Chaplin's character would have intentionally originated the gag, thereby creating what Carroll calls a mimed metaphor, Tati is suggesting that it happens purely *by chance* to Hulot. This gag is instead an example of what Carroll calls an object analog, in which one object is equated with another through visual resemblance rather than the pantomiming of the comedian.[37] This is a crucial distinction, to which I will return in a moment.

Tati sometimes suggested there was a greater affinity between his style of comedy and Buster Keaton's, arguing that Keaton's characters, like Hulot, do not intentionally "construct a system or instigate an action." Instead, they "undergo an experience."[38] Tati is exaggerating the differences between his comic style and Chaplin's, as well as its similarities to Keaton's. Things often happen accidentally to the Tramp. In *Modern Times* (1936), while wandering the streets after being released from hospital, he inadvertently finds himself at the head of a communist march. And although Keaton's characters do not usually resort to mimed metaphors, they routinely construct a system. Carroll calls this the "refunctionalization of an object" gag, wherein an object is used, often ingeniously, for a purpose for which it is not designed.[39] In *The Navigator* (1924), Keaton's character, Rollo Treadway, is attacked by a swordfish while deep-sea diving. He wrestles with it, brings it under control, and uses it like a sword to spear another swordfish that is threatening him. The humor arises from the unexpected and incongruous use to which the swordfish is put as well as the similarity between the fishes' bills and swords.

Furthermore, Hulot is often the source of comedy in Tati's films, especially when he is trying to aid others and slapstick ensues. In *Les Vacances*, while helping the newly arrived aunt of a young woman he has befriended, Martine, carry her suitcases up the front steps into her guesthouse, Hulot mistakes a case left at the top of the stairs for a step and stumbles off it through the house and into the garden. In the restaurant scene in *Play Time*, Hulot attempts to procure a piece of plastic fruit decorating the restaurant's rafters for the American businessman's companion, only to cause part of the ceiling to collapse (figs. 2.4 and 2.5). And in *Trafic*, having driven home a man injured in a car crash, Hulot tries to reposition the vines on the front of the man's house which he had previously disturbed. Hoisting the vines up while perched on the branch of a nearby tree, he slips and hangs upside down. In another object analog, his upside-down position and the flaps of his coat make him look like a bat.

Yet as these examples suggest, Hulot never *intentionally* creates gags, such as mimed metaphors, or refunctionalizes objects in imaginative ways, and this constitutes one of the major differences between Tati's style of comedy and that of his classical predecessors. If Hulot causes humor, he almost always does so "unwittingly."[40] The reason for this unintentional form of comedy is that, in accordance with his democratizing and realist goals, Tati aimed in his Hulot films to demonstrate to his viewers that "everyone is entertaining," that "there is no need to be a comic to perform a gag"—in contrast to Chaplin, Keaton, and other classical comedians, who through their gags emphasize their uniqueness and superior comic skill.[41] "What I've been trying to show is that the whole world is funny," he told Penelope Gilliat in the early 1970s,[42] and he routinely argued in interviews that Hulot was not a "gagman."[43] Unlike the daredevil stunts and other thrills in

FIGURE 2.4 In *Play Time* (Jacques Tati, 1967), Hulot attempts to reach a piece of plastic fruit...

Harold Lloyd's films, or the exotic locations and extraordinary predicaments in which Chaplin and Keaton's characters often find themselves in, Tati's humor is rooted in quotidian objects, places, and actions. It is a comedy of everyday life. By making Hulot an ordinary person in commonplace situations who is almost always the *unwitting* source of humor, Tati was trying to illustrate that the

FIGURE 2.5 ... and accidentally causes part of the ceiling to collapse.

humorous predicaments that befall Hulot could happen to "any absent-minded man who had no comic intention," including the spectator herself.[44] For Tati, no expertise is needed to be funny, meaning that anyone can be funny, that "comedy belongs to everybody."

OBSERVATION OF REALITY AND ALEATORY OBJECT ANALOGS

Rather than from a talented individual who tries to make people laugh, as at the music hall, Tati's style of comedy was instead derived, he claimed, from a more realistic source, namely, the careful observation of reality, the active perception of easily overlooked humorous incidents that occur, often by chance, to everyone, everyday, sometimes unbeknownst to them. Indeed, Tati frequently recounted quotidian occurrences he had witnessed that exemplified the deskilling of comedy he prized:

> One day, I saw a man who wanted an oil change; as he was in a hurry, he stayed in his car. . . . The attendants then raised him, in his automobile, about two meters high. This man was very fat, sitting there in his car reading his paper. The man started changing the oil underneath him, and then I realized one got the impression that the guy was sitting on a toilet.
>
> Now lots of people would have gone by without seeing him; but for me this is the kind of detail that is irresistible. I wanted to stop passers-by and tell them, "Look."[45]

Tati related incidents such as this one in order to show that an ordinary person going about his daily life can be the source of humor without even trying to be funny or being aware that he is. In fact, in this example, humor is not created by anything the man does at all, but rather by his position in the car relative to the oil change going on below him when seen by chance from a particular perspective.

Such occurrences provide the model for a peculiar variant of the object analog—call it the aleatory object analog—that recurs in Tati's films and is one of his most original, brilliant, and modernist comic techniques. As in the funeral wreath gag, it consists of the unplanned, often momentary coincidence of two or more objects (the spare tire and leaves) that together resemble another object (a funeral wreath), thereby creating a comic incongruity. As Lucy Fischer astutely notes, Tati's films "benefit from the legacy of a Surrealist perspective,"[46] and in developing the aleatory object analog, Tati was picking up on the surrealist incongruity strain of comedic modernism we encountered in chapter 1, which celebrated, among other things, Keaton's manipulation of objects in an incongruous manner to achieve his goals. Unlike in Keaton's gags, however, Tati's aleatory object analogs do not issue from Hulot's intentional repurposing of objects, but rather from the "chance meeting," to use Lautréamont's famous phrase beloved by the surrealists, of two or more objects. That these everyday objects are unrelated, and that their combination results in a surprising resemblance to something else, accounts for their marvelous, surreal quality. While Tati was not a surrealist attempting to liberate thought from rationality, as we shall discover in chapter 4, he was deeply disturbed by the uniformity of modern environments, and he doubtless valued aleatory object analogs in part because they disrupted this uniformity, albeit momentarily.

The most well-known and elaborate example of the aleatory object analog in Tati's oeuvre occurs at the end of *Play Time*, when a traffic circle looks like a merry-go-round. A traffic jam causes vehicles to move slowly around a colorful island in the middle of the circle, and some of them bounce up and down as they stop and go. The vehicles begin to resemble seats that go up and down on a carousel, an impression reinforced by cars moving up and down on platforms in a nearby garage as well as colorful balloons and other fairground-like paraphernalia carried by passersby (fig. 2.6 and color figure 3). In this instance, multiple aspects of the mise-en-scène coincide to imply the traffic circle's similarity to a merry-go-round.

FIGURE 2.6 The traffic circle that looks like a merry-go-round in *Play Time*.

FIGURE 2.7 Watering flowery hats in *Play Time.*

Tati's aleatory object analogs, however, typically involve just two or three objects. Also in *Play Time*, a waiter pouring champagne into the glasses of the American tourists at the restaurant appears to be watering the flowers on their hats (fig. 2.7). In *Mon Oncle*, when Monsieur and Madame Arpel look out of the two circular windows on the side of their house at night, their silhouettes make the windows look like eyes with moving pupils (fig. 2.8). During the car crash in *Trafic*, an out-of-control car follows a loose wheel rolling down the road, the car's hood opening and closing as if it is attempting to eat the wheel (fig. 2.9). And again in *Play Time*, when a guard bends down to lock the glass door of the travel agency, the handles of the door resemble horns protruding from his head (fig. 2.10). More standard object analogs, which do not depend on the fortuitous conjunction of two or more objects, can also be found in Tati's films, such as the lampposts that look like the flowers Hulot has given to Barbara at the end of *Play Time* (figs. 2.11 and 2.12). But whether standard or aleatory, in general it is object analogs, rather than mimed metaphors, that occur in Tati's films because they do not need to be intentionally performed by a character.[47]

As Fischer in particular has pointed out, gags such as the ones with the waiter and the guard in *Play Time* are only humorous because they are filmed from a specific angle.[48] It is because the camera is positioned above the traffic circle in certain shots that it looks like a merry-go-round, while it is the slight high angle that makes the door handles look like horns protruding from the guard's head

FIGURE 2.8 Windows as eyes in *Mon Oncle* (Jacques Tati, 1958).

FIGURE 2.9 A car pursues a wheel in *Trafic* (Jacques Tati, 1971).

FIGURE 2.10 Handles as horns in *Play Time.*

when he bends down. And in *Les Vacances*, when the two horses turn their heads to watch Hulot calling on Martine, it appears as though their handler has a horse head because the camera is placed directly in front of him (fig. 2.13). None of these events are intrinsically comic and, like the man in the car witnessed by Tati, the characters in them are not trying to be funny or aware that they are. Rather,

FIGURE 2.11 In *Play Time*, Barbara holds the flowers Hulot has given her . . .

FIGURE 2.12 ...and sees that they look like lampposts.

FIGURE 2.13 Man with horse's head in *Les Vacances*.

they become part of humorous object analogs due to the perspective from which they are seen. Tati employed such gags in order to demonstrate not only that comedy isn't dependent on the skill and intentionality of a clown but that it can arise purely by chance from the coincidence of one's perceptual point of view and a quotidian event.

This is further shown by the observer-figures populating Tati's films, particularly those who are repeatedly shown witnessing and enjoying the comedy happening all around them, such as the old woman in *Jour de fête*; Henry, the Englishwoman, and the German businessman's son in *Les Vacances*; Pichard's wife in *Mon Oncle*; Barbara in *Play Time*; and eventually Maria in *Trafic*.[49] Like Tati observing the man in the car, these characters are active viewers who look out for, and take advantage of, perspectives on comic events that they happen, through happenstance or good fortune, to occupy, and sometimes such events are visible to them alone thanks to their precise spatial locations. In *Les Vacances*, two men outside the Hôtel de la Plage shake hands and are interrupted by water gushing out of the hotel drain pipe, which they dance around to avoid. Only Henry, one of Hulot's fellow guests at the hotel who by chance is strolling nearby on the road overlooking the hotel and the beach, is in a position to see that Hulot is to blame because he has thrown the water from his hand basin out of his attic window and it has run down the drain onto the men (fig. 2.14).[50] While everyone else is preoccupied with the attempt of Arpel's factory manager, Pichard, to fix the fish fountain during the Arpels' garden party in *Mon Oncle*, Pichard's wife alone seems to notice Hulot and his nephew squeezing out Hulot's wet socks and hanging them out to dry from the round bedroom windows, which makes the windows look like eyes crying, and she laughs (fig. 2.15).[51] In the "Ideal Home" exposition in *Play Time*, Hulot shakes hands with the German businessman who sells doors that "slam . . . in golden silence" and accidentally breaks his eyeglasses, which the man is clutching in his hand. When the man puts them on, they resemble the spectacles on display at the exposition with their moveable frames, and he and Hulot stare at each other. Barbara, who by chance is walking in between them, is the only one to notice their stares along with the man's broken glasses and laughs (figs. 2.16 and 2.17). *Trafic* contains another gag involving eyeglasses that foregrounds the role that visual perspective can play in creating humor. Hulot spills a spot of ink on one of the lenses of the glasses worn by the publicity agent, Maria, just as they are about to leave the garage where the camping-car has been repaired. Maria puts them on to inspect the car and mistakes the ink on the lens for a spot on the car's paint job. She orders Marcel, the driver of the truck transporting the camping-car, to clean it off, but as she moves, the spot moves too, and she eventually realizes it is on

FIGURE 2.14 Men dodge water from the hotel drainpipe as seen by Henry in *Les Vacances*.

FIGURE 2.15 Prichard's wife notices Hulot squeezing out his wet socks in *Mon Oncle*.

FIGURE 2.16 The glasses with movable frames at the exposition in *Play Time* . . .

her spectacles, not the car. Laughing, she reenacts the gag by looking at Hulot through her glasses and pointing to the spot she appears to see on his face. Only Maria experiences this gag first-hand (Tati does not provide the viewer with a point-of-view shot through the eyeglasses) because only she wears the spectacles and sees the spot.

FIGURE 2.17 . . . resemble the German businessman's broken glasses, which Barbara laughs at.

Sound, which is central to Tati's comedy and which I will discuss more fully in chapter 3, also plays a crucial role in Tati's object analogs. To some degree, the traffic circle resembles a merry-go-round because of the barrel organ music that accompanies the scene; and the doors, hoods, and trunks of cars in the car exposition in *Trafic* appear to be trying to bite passersby because they sound like jaws snapping shut. Indeed, there are a number of gags in Tati's films that should be described as sound analogs rather than object analogs because they resemble other things aurally, not visually. While the truck transporting the camper in *Trafic* is being repaired in a garage, a damaged car is towed inside. It bounces up and down, and the squeaks it emits approximate cries of pain. The steam expelled from a machine in the plastics factory in *Mon Oncle* sounds like deep, heavy breathing, which is why it lulls Hulot to sleep. Tati is particularly fond of sound analogs that call to mind base bodily functions. The fish fountain in the Arpels' front yard in *Mon Oncle* is absurd in part because it sounds urinary, while the tire that deflates at the funeral in *Les Vacances* is doubly inappropriate because the noise of escaping air evokes flatulence.

There are also occasional gags in Tati's films that should be called aleatory object-sound analogs because they consist of the chance coincidence not of two or more objects, as in aleatory-object analogs, but of an object with a sound from a separate source within the diegesis that together recall something else. When the colonel, another guest at the Hôtel de la Plage, looks out of his hotel window at the fireworks that Hulot accidentally sets off during the last night of his stay in *Les Vacances*, it seems as though he is being fired upon in battle because of both the look *and* the sound of the fireworks exploding all around, an impression reinforced by his binoculars, military hat, and his hasty retreat inside. In *Play Time*, when the air-conditioning is first switched on in the restaurant, a model plane behind the bar that had deflated from the heat reinflates as it cools down, and the loud air-conditioner sounds like the engines of a real jet starting up. In fact, the very first gag in Tati's first feature, *Jour de fête*, is an aleatory object-sound analog along these lines. As the tractor pulling the fairground equipment enters town, a shot of the carousel horses sticking out of the back is accompanied by the neighing of real horses, which are subsequently revealed in the field behind the tractor. Later, when Roger, who runs the fair, flirts with Jeannette, a local villager, in front of the tent where an American Western is being screened, Roger's hat, posture, and the piece of fairground equipment he is holding, along with the dialogue from the off-screen film in which a Westerner is wooing a woman, make him resemble a cowboy with a pistol (fig. 2.18). As with purely visual aleatory object analogs, however, these gags involving sound all happen by chance. No character intentionally devises them, least of all Hulot, and they illustrate the lengths to which Tati went to democratize comedy, to demonstrate that comedy

FIGURE 2.18 Roger looks like a cowboy as he flirts with Jeannette in *Jour de fête* (Jacques Tati, 1949).

is not dependent upon the skill of a talented comedian but can happen, if only accidentally, to everyone and anyone going about his or her daily lives.

OTHER CHARACTERS AND ENVIRONMENTS

While Hulot does not create mimed metaphors or refunctionalize objects, Tati does employ other types of gags found throughout classical comedian comedy. According to Carroll, the most common of these is "the mutual interference or interpenetration" gag.[52] This kind of gag gives rise to humor by way of an incongruity between a character's misinterpretation of an event and the correct interpretation, to which the viewer is simultaneously privy. The spectator of the film perceives both what is really happening in the narrative and that a character, often the comedian, has misunderstood it. The resulting incongruity between the viewer's correct understanding of one or more events and the character's incorrect one creates humor. Mutual interference gags abound in classical comedian comedy. In Max Linder's *Be My Wife* (1921), Max is wooing Mary inside her house while watering a plant nestled in a bust. Her aunt Agatha, who is outside, can see his silhouette along with the bust's against a closed window shade, and it looks to her as though he is pouring water onto her niece's head. In *The Navigator*, in a scene that Tati liked to cite, Rollo and Betsy, the woman he loves, are trying to sleep in separate cabins on the deserted boat on which they are drifting. Betsy, disturbed by a painting of a glaring sailor in her cabin, throws it overboard, and unbeknownst to her, it catches on Rollo's cabin window and swings from side to side as the ship rocks back and forth. Inside the cabin, the sailor's portrait appears and disappears from the window as the boat rocks, and when Rollo sees it, he mistakes it for a real person looking in and jumps out of bed (fig. 2.19). In both mutual interference gags, the incongruity between what is really happening in the narrative, of which the viewer is informed, and a character's misinterpretation of it, creates humor.

Tati often uses mutual interference gags. In *Mon Oncle*, Monsieur Arpel arrives at the plastics factory he manages and walks along its corridors to his

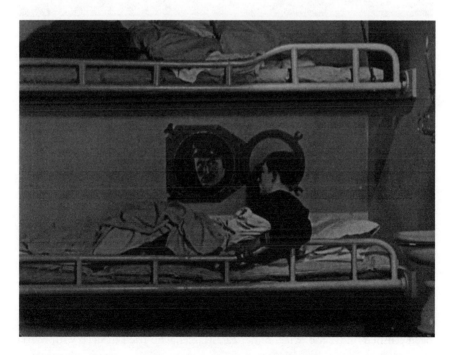

FIGURE 2.19 Rollo mistakes a portrait for a real person in *The Navigator* (Buster Keaton and Donald Crisp, 1924).

FIGURE 2.20 In *Mon Oncle*, Hulot plays with Dacky . . .

office preceded by his dachsund, Dacky. Various workers relaxing on the job see Dacky and, knowing Monsieur Arpel cannot be far behind, get back to work. Hulot, who ironically *is* working, takes time out to lie down on the factory floor to play with the dog (fig. 2.20), and after a few moments, Dacky runs out of sight just as Monsieur Arpel rounds the corner and sees Hulot. To Arpel, it appears that Hulot is lounging on the floor for no reason, and he shrugs his shoulders in exasperation (fig. 2.21). Toward the end of the restaurant scene in *Play Time*, a waiter is carrying the back of a chair that he separated from its seat when his hand became stuck in it. He accidentally knocks it against a woman standing at a table, and she thinks he has brought her a chair to sit on (fig. 2.22). She sits down, but because it has no seat she falls on the floor (fig. 2.23). And in *Trafic*, Hulot is comforting a distraught Maria, who mistakenly believes her beloved dog has been crushed under the wheel of her car. Marcel, who tried to sleep with Maria the night before, sees them from a distance, and they appear to him to be making love (fig. 2.24).

FIGURE 2.21 ... who runs away before Monsieur Arpel rounds the corner.

FIGURE 2.22 A woman at the restaurant in *Play Time* mistakes the back of a seat for a proffered chair ...

FIGURE 2.23 . . . and falls to the ground when she goes to sit down.

FIGURE 2.24 Marcel misinterprets Hulot's attempt to comfort Maria in *Trafic*.

As these examples illustrate, while the structure of such gags is conventional, what is distinctive about Tati's employment of them is that, contrary to David Bellos's assertion, they routinely involve misperceptions on the part of characters other than Hulot.[53] They thereby exemplify Tati's much commented upon tendency to incorporate subsidiary characters into his comedy. For example, Tati delights in having secondary characters inadvertently mimic each other, thereby creating humor by making incongruous people and activities appear similar. In *Play Time*, the waiter taking the order for "turbot à la royale" makes circular hand movements in describing the dish that echo the gestures of the man simultaneously repairing the tile on the restaurant floor behind him, and in *Trafic* a bored policeman yawns and puts his arms behind his head just like a nearby man whose arms are behind his head because he is under arrest (fig 2.25). Later in *Trafic*, after the car crash, all the passengers get out of their cars and stretch their limbs to make sure they are okay, together resembling an exercise class. Indeed, when *Play Time* was released in late 1967, Tati was postulating an evolution in comedian comedy, one that his films recapitulated. Film comedy, he argued, began with individual comedians from the music hall, such as Little Titch, Keaton, Chaplin, and Max Linder. It evolved

FIGURE 2.25 The yawning policeman resembles a prisoner in *Trafic*.

with the emergence of comic duos, particularly Laurel and Hardy, who alternated between the roles of comedian and foil, and took another step forward with the formation of comic groups like the Ritz Brothers and the Marx Brothers, who "passed the cracks and gags around between them like you pass a rugby ball." Now, he claimed, "everyone is in the gag and adds to it."[54] His own films had followed a similar trajectory, he suggested, from *Les Vacances*, in which Hulot is involved in most of the gags, to *Play Time*, in which Hulot is often absent from the screen and many gags are left to others. Although Hulot is once again the unwitting source of much of the comedy in *Trafic*, his final fictional feature, Tati told Jonathan Rosenbaum that "on the basis of my intentions, *Trafic* could have been shot before *Play Time*," which "will always be my last picture" because "there's no star, no one person is important, everybody is; you are as important as I can be."[55]

Tati's theory of the evolution of comedian comedy is hardly plausible, given the role of groups in early film comedies such as those by Mack Sennett. It also downplays the extent to which already in *Jour de fête*, his first feature, Tati de-emphasizes the character he plays, François the postman, who is not seen until approximately ten minutes into the film and whose first gag, in which he is troubled by a bee while cycling, is immediately passed to another person, a farmer scything on a nearby hill. Nevertheless, it is in *Play Time* that Tati's dissolution of the comedian reaches its zenith. By my calculation, before he enters the Royal Garden restaurant at about eighty-three minutes into the approximately two-hour film, Hulot is on screen less than 50 percent of the time, and he is absent for long stretches, including during the film's first ten minutes and the eighteen-minute scene depicting the opening of the Royal Garden. Moreover, even when Hulot appears to be on screen, we cannot always be sure that it is him, as there are at least five Hulot lookalikes who occasion numerous gags: the Englishman with the blue bag at the airport who is mistaken for Hulot by a woman and who drops his umbrella (fig. 2.26); the man with the red scarf who disturbs the German businessman's papers at the exposition, with whom Hulot is confused (fig. 2.27); the man with the red bow-tie and goatee whom Giffard thinks is Hulot (fig. 2.28); the black man on the street whom Giffard also mistakes for Hulot (fig. 2.29); and the young man with a pipe to whom Hulot entrusts the delivery of Barbara's present when she boards her bus at the film's end (fig. 2.30). The absence of the real Hulot from *Play Time* is almost without precedent in classical comedian comedy, and it means that other characters are generating the comedy much of the time in the film.

This depriviling of the comedian is compounded by the lack of information about Hulot's mental states in Tati's films. We saw in chapter 1 how modernists like Léger were drawn to the treatment of the comic as a depsychologized

FIGURE 2.26 Hulot lookalike #1 in *Play Time*; cutouts can be seen in the far background.

object in slapstick because it accorded with their interest in the human body as purely plastic material. Nevertheless, the clown's character typically had goals, desires, and emotions in classical comedian comedy, even if they were rudimentary and functioned purely as a pretext for humor. Keaton's character Rollo in *The Navigator* loves Betsy, is upset when she rejects his marriage proposal, and

FIGURE 2.27 Hulot lookalike #2, rifling through the German salesman's desk.

FIGURE 2.28 Hulot lookalike #3.

wishes to help and protect her once they are trapped together on the ship, while the Tramp in *The Gold Rush* wants to prospect for gold, desires Georgia, and is also distressed when she overlooks him. Tati takes the objectification of the comedian in comedic modernism much further, creating in Hulot a remarkably uncharacterized figure. As Bazin observed, contrary to the commedia dell'arte

FIGURE 2.29 Hulot lookalike #4.

FIGURE 2.30 Hulot lookalike #5.

tradition out of which comedian comedy in cinema arises, Hulot "seems not to dare to exist entirely. He is a wandering whim, a circumspection of being."[56] Excepting what David Bellos astutely calls his "apologetic eagerness to please" others and his readiness to have fun spontaneously with them, for the most part Hulot lacks clearly articulated traits and desires, which is why he seems to wander from one situation to another, becoming inadvertently entangled in them.[57] Even when he does have a goal, as in the first three Hulot films, we are usually not informed of its aim, such as at the beginning of *Play Time* when he visits Giffard at a company called SNC and we never learn why.[58] *Trafic* is an exception because Hulot has the explicitly stated goal of delivering a car to an auto show in Amsterdam. However, as in the other Hulot films, we learn practically nothing about what he feels or thinks about his situation. The range of Hulot's discernible mental states is confined almost entirely to polite reserve, the capacity to enjoy himself on a whim, and embarrassment at the confusions and pratfalls he and others endure. Although his behavior occasionally hints at affection and perhaps more for some female characters such as Martine in *Les Vacances* and Barbara in *Play Time*, unlike his classical predecessors he has no romantic entanglements. Tati's stylistic choices further obscure Hulot's psychology. The use of long shots and lack of close-ups means we rarely see Hulot's facial expressions, which are further hidden by his hat and the pipe he is perpetually smoking. Meanwhile, the already sparse dialogue on the soundtrack, coupled with Hulot's tendency to mumble because of the pipe in his mouth, render him almost mute.

The participation of secondary characters in the humor is a major component of Tati's comic democracy, but Tati's inclusiveness extends beyond other characters to their environments and the objects in them as well as the sounds they make. In chapter 1, we observed that in the 1920s avant-gardists were fascinated by the role of objects in comedian comedy, and René Clair privileged them in his popular modernist films of the late 1920s. Tati developed this variant of comedic modernism by routinely incorporating not just objects but settings into his object and sound analogs, such as the traffic circle-cum-merry-go-round at the end of *Play Time* and the windows that resemble eyes in the Arpels' home. Indeed, in Tati's films, the entire environment often becomes integral to the humor, such as in the switch image at the beginning of *Play Time* in which the airport initially appears to be a hospital. We will see in chapter 4 that the Arpels' house and its furnishings are repeatedly the source of the film's comedy. In *Les Vacances*, Hulot wakes up his fellow hotel guests during the night when he has fun with the hikers at the end of the second day of his stay; when, on the third night, he returns from the funeral in his Amilcar, which has a loud engine that often backfires; and when he sets off the fireworks on the sixth night. Each time the disturbance is conveyed by the same exterior shot of the darkened hotel that shows the guests' bedroom lights turning on one by one as they are awakened by the noise. On the fourth night, it is Hulot's bedroom light we see being turned on when he retreats up to bed after unwittingly disrupting the card game and causing a fight among the hotel guests downstairs in the lobby. In this example, Hulot's comic disruption of the other guests is signaled by way of the lights in the building they inhabit (fig. 2.31).

Another way Tati integrated objects and environments into his comedy was through color. Tati frequently expressed regret at not having shot *Les Vacances* in color in part because of the technique's humorous potential, citing the deepening suntan of the vacationers over their week-long stay and the striped tents on the beach as potential examples. This does not mean color jokes are absent from *Les Vacances*, however, as Tati exploits the contrast between black and white for comic effect on several occasions while incorporating the characters, objects, and settings around Hulot. In the original version of the film, when Hulot is annoying other guests by loudly playing table tennis in the hotel, the waiter walks through the lobby leading one black and one white dog on leashes. The dogs lunge at Hulot's table tennis ball and the waiter becomes caught between them behind a post. The hotel manager, who is dressed in black, begrudgingly rescues him by taking the black dog while the waiter, dressed in white, follows him leading the white one. Later, while en route to the picnic, Hulot tries to position a jack under his car in order to change a flat tire. Lying on a light-colored mat, his legs jut into the road, and by chance he moves them just as a bus passes and leaves a dark tire mark on the

FIGURE 2.31 Lights turning on at the Hôtel de la Plage show that guests have been awoken by Hulot in *Les Vacances*.

road and mat (fig. 2.32). Lowering his legs and pulling the mat out of the way, he sits up and notices the tire mark terminating on the road on one side of his legs and restarting on the other. In a mutual interference gag, to him, it looks as though the bus ran over his legs and he feels them to make sure they are not broken (fig. 2.33).

In his color films, Tati tends to use color to create comic visual analogs in his characters' environments. Disparate objects are made to seem similar in part through their color schemes, and the incongruity between these objects gives rise to humor and, sometimes, mutual interference gags. In *Mon Oncle*, the collar and cuffs of Monsieur Arpel's smoking jacket have the same red and black color pattern as the vest worn by his dog, Dacky (fig. 2.34 and color figure 4); and in *Trafic*, the coat of Maria's dog is identical in color and texture to a duster used at the car exposition to clean cars as well as to a vest worn by a young man. The man and his friends notice the similarity between it and the dog and put the vest under the car's wheel, deceiving Maria into believing her dog has been run over (fig. 2.35 and color figure 5). Toward the end of *Play Time*, when Barbara and Hulot walk past stands selling a variety of merchandise, a yellow sponge falls off of one and Hulot, thinking it is cheese, picks it up and puts it on the adjacent Ideal Cheese stand.

FIGURE 2.32 In *Les Vacances*, Hulot absent-mindedly moves his legs as a bus passes . . .

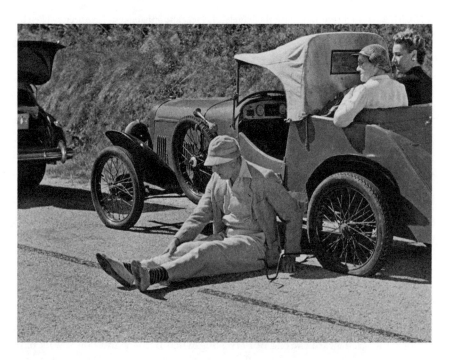

FIGURE 2.33 . . . and checks them when he thinks they have been run over by the bus due to the tire mark.

FIGURE 2.34 The trim of Monsieur Arpel's smoking jacket resembles Dacky's coat as he and his wife gaze at the object floating above their wall in *Mon Oncle*.

FIGURE 2.35 Maria believes her dog has been run over in *Trafic*.

FIGURE 2.36 The blue bag and baby dressed in blue are swapped back in *Play Time*.

A few moments later, when the traffic circle begins to resemble a merry-go-round, two families hail taxis. One has a baby dressed in blue, the other a blue bag, and when they reach their taxis they realize they have confused the two and swap them back (fig. 2.36 and color figure 6). Tati sometimes equates whole buildings and environments using color. In *Mon Oncle*, the plastics factory resembles Gérard's school and his own home in part because of their gray facades (figs. 4.27 and 4.28), while the identical color of the modern buildings depicted on posters advertising disparate tourist destinations in *Play Time* contributes to their uniformity (fig. 4.54). When Barbara is listening to the radio in her hotel room in *Play Time*, the radio is the same shape and color as the modern building visible through her window (fig. 2.37 and color figure 7). This color technique plays a crucial role in Tati's satire of modern life, to which we will return in chapter 4.

In devolving comedy from the comedian to other characters and their environments, Tati is drawing on the variant of comedic modernism, found in Clair's films and discussed in chapter 1, that relies on groups rather an individual comic to create humor. However, in adapting it to the post-World War II context and its democratic concerns, he takes it much further. Tati creates a fictional world in which comedy is diffuse. Rather than being confined to a skilled entertainer, it is anywhere and everywhere, permeating the most mundane aspects of quotidian reality and involving the most ordinary people. It is perhaps no surprise, therefore, that the carnivalesque mode found in *Entr'acte* (1924) and other Clair

FIGURE 2.37 The radio that resembles the facing building in *Play Time*.

films, in which a community joins together in eccentric behavior, re-emerges in some of Tati's. We saw that in *Entr'acte*, Picabia and Clair erase social distinctions and bring the high down low by making the bourgeois mourners look absurd as they chase after the coffin, and I will return to the subject of Tati's depiction of the bourgeoisie in chapter 4. What I wish to emphasize here is how, just as Clair makes it appear that the entire city of Paris is united in the madcap pursuit of the hearse, so Tati sometimes unites a group of people in a carnivalesque moment. The most obvious examples occur in *Mon Oncle* and *Play Time*. In the former, Monsieur Arpel, jealous at the intimate relationship that has developed between his son, Gérard, and his brother-in-law, sends Hulot to work in the provinces. After Arpel and Gérard drive Hulot to the airport, Hulot disappears into the airport terminal with other passengers, and they all appear to be dancing to celebratory extradiegetic jazz music on the soundtrack (fig. 2.38). Arpel and his son then bond for the first time over a comic incident Arpel inadvertently causes in the airport car park (fig. 4.7). Once the jazz band gets going in the restaurant scene in *Play Time* and Hulot causes part of the ceiling to collapse, the haughty, formal behavior of the restaurant's bourgeois patrons, who initially express contempt for the American tourists, gives way to uninhibited revelry enjoyed by all. Their camaraderie seems to spread beyond the confines of the restaurant, infusing the outside world with color and gaiety and thereby altering its very appearance, as will be discussed in chapter 4. Scenes of communal merriment also occur

FIGURE 2.38 The departing passengers who seem to dance at the end of *Mon Oncle*.

in *Jour de fête* on the day of the fete, and while most of the guests at the Hôtel de la Plage in *Les Vacances* never abandon their restrained, regimented behavior, Hulot enjoys a night of carousing with the hikers, which we hear occurring off-screen. In all these examples, the spirit of spontaneous enjoyment associated with Hulot's character spreads though a community, dissolving social differences and uniting people in unrestrained, unselfconscious fun. These are utopian moments in which Tati's vision of comic democracy is realized within the fictional world of his films, and his characters are most aware of the humorous, ludic possibilities in the environments around them.

SWITCH AND ENLIGHTENMENT IMAGES

Tati's comic democracy, however, extends beyond his subsidiary characters and their environments to the spectator. For him, the passivity characteristic of modern life afflicted his audiences too, and he sought to encourage the viewer of his films to take part in the comedy he created on-screen. It was for this reason, he asserted, that he did not use close-ups, thereby encouraging spectators to "see what they see with their own eyes, not what the camera tells them."[59] And in complaining to the editors of *Cahiers du cinéma* about automatic cars, he remarked that he wanted his audiences to "participate more, to let them change the gears for themselves, not to have me do all the work for them."[60] We have examined Tati's use of mutual interference gags, in which the incongruity between a character's incorrect interpretation of a situation and the correct one gives rise to humor. Occasionally in the classical tradition, however, gags are structured around a conflict between the *spectator's*, rather than a character's, initial misinterpretation of an event and the correct interpretation, to which the viewer subsequently gains access. As we observed in the introduction, Carroll calls this a switch image, and while this gag structure does not occur that often in classical comedian comedy, it is more common in Tati's films because it is the spectator who misunderstands what is happening in the film, not a character. Moreover, it is the viewer's error that generates the humor, because we laugh at the discrepancy between what we initially thought was occurring in the film and what is actually happening. We thereby become participants in the comedy.

The best-known example, as discussed in the introduction, is the hospital that turns out to be an airport at the beginning of *Play Time*, although Tati's switch images are usually less elaborate and can occur anywhere. The shot following the woman's pratfall in the restaurant in *Play Time* (fig. 2.23) shows what seems to be her leg sticking up from behind the table as the restaurant manager bends down to help her (fig. 2.39). As she gets up, we infer that during her fall her hand must have slipped into her shoe, as it turns out to be her arm that was sticking up, not her leg (fig. 2.40). In *Les Vacances*, the German businessman seems to be peeping into a beach hut at Martine, who is getting dressed (fig. 2.41). Hulot, thinking he is a voyeur, kicks him in the pants, realizing too late, along with the spectator, that the man is actually behind the hut innocently taking a photograph (fig. 2.42). The daughter of Hulot's concierge in *Mon Oncle* accidentally knocks some tomatoes from a vegetable stand onto the ground and runs away. Hulot, who is standing nearby, is blamed by the stand owner and marches after the girl. A long shot shows him appearing to wag his finger at her in anger (fig. 2.43), but a closer one reveals that he is giving her treats and tapping her on the nose, an affectionate gesture he repeats throughout the film (fig. 2.44). And in *Trafic*, while the mechanic is busy fixing the camping-car, Marcel sees the mechanic's wife, seemingly bare-chested, through the window of their living quarters (fig. 2.45). As he enters, a closer shot discloses that she is holding a baby, and it is the baby's bare bottom that we can see, not her cleavage (fig. 2.46).

FIGURE 2.39 In *Play Time*, it appears to be the leg of the woman who fell that sticks up . . .

FIGURE 2.40 . . . until we see that it is her arm with her shoe on her hand.

FIGURE 2.41 In *Les Vacances*, Hulot thinks the German businessman is a voyeur peering into Martine's beach hut . . .

FIGURE 2.42 . . . and kicks him before realizing the German is taking a photograph behind the hut.

FIGURE 2.43 In *Mon Oncle*, Hulot seems to be berating his neighbor's daughter ...

FIGURE 2.44 ... until it is revealed that he is tapping her affectionately on the nose.

FIGURE 2.45 In *Trafic*, Marcel believes the mechanic's wife is exposing her chest . . .

FIGURE 2.46 . . . until he realizes she is carrying a baby.

Tati sometimes employs a variation on the switch image—also to be found, albeit again infrequently, in classical comedian comedy—in which, at first, the viewer does not understand what is happening in a shot or why, and it is subsequently explained by a change in the mise-en-scène, reframing, or a new shot, which reveals something that was initially hidden. In this variant—call it the enlightenment image—rather than shifting from a misinterpretation to a correct interpretation, as in a switch image, the spectator moves from perplexity to understanding. The source of the humor is thus the *unexpected* explanation for what is occurring in the shot, rather than an incongruity between one interpretation and another. In *You're Darn Tootin'* (1928), Laurel and Hardy—to whom Tati owed a greater debt than to either Chaplin or Keaton—are shown walking down a city street in a medium backward tracking shot (fig. 2.47), and Laurel trips and falls out of the frame while Hardy walks a few more steps unawares (fig. 2.48). Laurel, however, does not reappear, and the viewer wonders what has happened to him until the camera pulls back to disclose that he has fallen head first into a manhole (fig. 2.49). Similarly, in *Jour de fête*, François the postman delivers a letter to a man getting dressed in his Sunday best and inquires if the man is dressing for the village fair (fig. 2.50). The man frowns, and we only understand his reaction when François closes the man's door on his way out and we see a dead body on a bed behind the door—the man, it turns out, is dressing for a funeral rather than the fete (fig. 2.51). In *Mon Oncle*, Monsieur and Madame Arpel are on the steps of their house, while behind them there appears to be an object floating back and forth just above the wall separating their garden from their neighbor's, and a strange clicking sound can be heard (fig. 2.34). When they go upstairs to look into their neighbor's

FIGURE 2.47 Laurel and Hardy walk down the street in *You're Darn Tootin'* (Edgar Kennedy, 1928).

FIGURE 2.48 Laurel suddenly disappears from view and we wonder where he is . . .

FIGURE 2.49 ... until it is revealed he has fallen into a manhole.

garden, a reverse angle shot reveals that the object is their neighbor's hat, and it seemed to be floating above the wall because she is wearing it while seated on a manual lawnmower that she is frantically pedaling back and forth (fig. 2.52). In *Les Vacances*, right before Hulot (and the viewer) mistakes the German businessman for a voyeur, a medium shot of an exercise class, the instructor off-screen, shows

FIGURE 2.50 We wonder why the man frowns when François asks him whether he is dressing for the fair in *Jour de fête* ...

FIGURE 2.51 ...until we discover he is dressing for a funeral.

FIGURE 2.52 The neighbor mows her lawn in *Mon Oncle*.

its members performing calisthenics in time to his whistle. They bend down and the whistle inexplicably stops as they attempt to hold their positions, becoming increasingly uncomfortable. Finally, a reverse angle shot of the instructor discloses that he has been distracted by Hulot, who is asking him a question.

In all of these instances, viewers are denied the omniscience and transparency afforded them by most gags in classical comedian comedy. By hiding a crucial piece of information through framing or mise-en-scène, we are forced to experience, albeit momentarily, the misunderstanding (in switch images) and incomprehension (in enlightenment images) that is typically the lot of characters in the genre. Tati did this quite deliberately, telling Bazin and Truffaut that "the actors are on the same level as the viewers and realize at the same time that some gentleman has, say, forgotten to close the door."[61] Just as Tati devolves gags away from Hulot onto other characters in order to make them take part of the comedy, so he prompts the spectator to participate in the type of humorous mistakes and confusions suffered by characters in comedian comedy films.

THE VIEWER

Tati, however, did not wish to confine his viewers' participation in comedy to their experience of his films. By fashioning gag structures, especially object analogs, in which a range of characters unintentionally play a role, and turning to the furniture of daily life for his comic material, he aimed to show his audiences that they can find humor outside the movie theater because comedy is not reliant on the skill of an expert comedian. Instead, ordinary people like the viewer, often unbeknownst to them, like the man in the car during the oil change, create it every day. He hoped that his films would encourage his spectators to notice and appreciate the comedy in the real world, thereby further countering what he saw as the increasing passivity of modern life. He intended his work to cultivate a more discerning attitude in his viewers by teaching them to be attentive to the comic potential of the quotidian independently of his films. "People are not observant enough," he complained in an interview with the editors of *Cahiers du cinéma* on the release of *Play Time*. "When you observe things, they all look different. Everything should arouse curiosity, a leaf from a tree or a doorknob. *The doorknob at the Royal Garden is there to make you laugh at your own doorknob*."[62] Elsewhere, he maintained that "it is by observation that we see life going on about us and the comedy you can see everywhere you look and that is what I try to do in *Play Time*."[63] In *Cours du soir* (1967), the short film he wrote and starred in while making *Play Time*, Tati is an evening class instructor and the subject of his lesson is observation. In the course of the lesson, he tries to teach his students, who are all men dressed in business suits, mimes and other comic acts by having them carefully observe him performing them before trying them themselves with varying degrees of success. At certain moments, however, he takes them over to the classroom window and has them look at comic events going on *in the outside world.*

Like other modernists, therefore, Tati believed that ordinary perceptual experience in the modern world is deficient in certain respects.[64] According to Tati, we are usually blind to the comedy of everyday life going on around us all the time because we are not observant enough. And he wished to use his art to expand the vision of his audience, which for Tati meant opening their eyes to the comic potential of quotidian reality. Tati thereby shared with much of the avant-garde of the twentieth century the goal of "organiz[ing] a new life praxis from a basis in art," in the well-known words of theorist of the avant-garde Peter Bürger.[65] Like the Dadaists, surrealists, and other avant-garde groups, Tati aimed to transform daily life itself, infusing what Bürger calls the "means-end rationality of the bourgeois everyday,"[66] the emphasis on work and productivity, with the noninstrumental aesthetic. I will return to this at the end of chapter 4. For the moment, I simply want to draw attention to Tati's quintessentially avant-garde ambition to overcome the gulf between art and life, to imbue the world beyond the movie theater with the comedy of everyday life manifest in his films. Moreover, Tati used techniques reminiscent of avant-garde art to accomplish this. In addition to the varieties of comedic modernism he drew on, Tati sought to rid his films of the skilled comedian found in classical comedian comedy. Deskilling, defined as the "persistent effort to eliminate artisanal competence and other forms of manual virtuosity from the horizon of both artistic production and aesthetic evaluation," has been a major strategy in twentieth-century modernism, exemplified, for example, by Marcel Duchamp's usage of ordinary, found objects such as a urinal or bicycle wheel (readymades) as art works, or the Cubists' incorporation of newspaper cuttings into their collages.[67] In addition, Tati employed chance to achieve this goal, as did some avant-garde artists. John Cage devised aleatory procedures to negate his own authorship and intentionality in his sound works, most famously in *4′33″* (1952), in which a pianist or other instrumentalist closes their instrument for four minutes and thirty-three seconds. The piece consists of the sounds that randomly occur in the environment in which the piece is performed. Similarly, as we have seen, Tati based his screen comedy around unintentional comic incidents in order to draw the attention of viewers to the comic potential of the environments around them.

This comparison should not be taken too far, however. While the character played by Tati is never intentionally the source of humor, Tati the director and screenwriter is. It is only within the fictional world that the comedian is deskilled and comedy occurs by chance. In reality, this fictional world and the gags in it have been deliberately and meticulously designed by Tati the filmmaker, who claimed that he never improvised.[68] Tati's films, in other words, do after all foreground the comedian's uniqueness and superior comic skill, but this is the comedian as filmmaker, not just performer. Hence, Tati was quickly embraced in the 1950s by critics at *Cahiers* and elsewhere as an extraordinary artist, one of the few genuine contemporary French auteurs, while Tati himself regularly espoused the *politique des auteurs*, railing against the industrialization of cinema and insisting that films should be made by individuals and express a personal vision.[69] "What troubles me," he told Bazin and Truffaut, "is that young filmmakers today may no longer choose their story, may no longer choose their actors, may no longer do whatever they want. These days, filmmaking has become an industry, on the same level as the car industry."[70] It is not the least paradox of Tati's films that their dissolution of the individual comedian and deskilling of comedy are hallmarks of Tati's singularity and virtuosity as a comic filmmaker.

Nevertheless, like avant-gardists such as Cage, who claimed in a 1943 interview with *Time* magazine that "people may leave my concerts thinking they have heard 'noise,' but will then hear unsuspected beauty in their everyday life," Tati wanted his viewers to exit screenings of his films better able to notice *for themselves* the comedy of everyday life.[71] He purportedly received letters from schoolchildren informing him that, on leaving the movie theater after seeing *Play Time*, it had seemed to them that the film continued in the street outside. "They saw images from the film in the street, and they observed people in the street as they'd done in the theater."[72] How did he design his films to achieve this goal? How did he solve the problem of making his audience more attentive? Tati gives us a clue in the following comment:

> What I like is to observe the people because I do feel that in life, *if you do watch all round*, you begin to see the little everyday things in life that are unique in themselves.... So when you think in *Jour de fête* that the Postman (Tati), is the one who says, "I am the funny fellow in the film. I can fool the bicycle; I can pull a gag; I am the gagman . . ." and that is a little bit of the old time comedy, yes? And what I have been trying with Hulot is to show that the things that happen to Hulot are the things that can happen to everybody. Not just to invent a gag for the audience—to be a good gagman—but to just show that this character, even waiting for an autobus, something unique and funny can happen to him.[73]

The conditional "If you do watch all around" is key to understanding Tati's strategy for fostering an active mode of observation in his viewers when they leave
the movie theater. Once humor is no longer invented for audiences by an expert
comedian, Tati is suggesting that it becomes the responsibility of the spectator
to find it, to discover it in his (Tati's) films and in reality. Unable to passively
receive it from the comic, she must actively look for it in the cinematic and real
worlds. "The viewer must make a little effort," Tati stated when discussing *Les
Vacances* with Bazin and Truffaut, "to enter the comic universe created by Hulot.
If he expects tricks or gags from Hulot, he will undoubtedly be disappointed."[74]
In this respect, the observer-figures populating Tati's films can be understood as
propaedeutic surrogates for the film spectator. Henry, Barbara, and the others
teach us by their example to actively pay close attention not only to Tati's films
but to the world around us in order to see fleeting moments of comedy we might
otherwise overlook, much as Tati himself claimed that he did: "You will not see
anything very funny if you are waiting for someone in London Airport, and they
are twenty minutes late and you are sitting there looking at your watch telling
yourself that they are twenty minutes late. But I would sit there and maybe see
the best show of the week, looking at everyone coming and going."[75]

Tati's approach is to encourage the viewer to actively search for the comedy
when watching his films rather than passively receiving it from the skilled comedian in the hopes that, on leaving screenings of his movies, she will do the same
in the outside world. By being prompted to look for humor in Tati's images and
sounds, he surmises, the spectator will be more inclined to seek out humor in her
daily life. In effect, his films are designed to tutor his audiences in the active mode
of observation required to discern the comedy of everyday life in the real world.
This strategy has no precedent in the prewar avant-garde, and it is perhaps Tati's
most original contribution to comedic modernism. As we shall see in chapter 3,
it deeply informed his comedy, along with his visual and aural filmmaking style
more generally.

CHAPTER 3

THE BEHOLDER'S SHARE

ichel Chion, one of Tati's most astute critics, cites a gag from the
funeral scene in *Les Vacances de Monsieur Hulot* as an example
of Tati's comic democracy. Hulot thanks and shakes hands with
three mourners who have split off from the funeral to help him restart his car.
Mistaking the four for a receiving line, the remaining guests rush over to offer
their condolences. As Chion describes it, Hulot "finds the situation funny and
starts to giggle nervously," followed by the other mourners. "Everybody is able
to laugh and, in turn, be laughed at," concludes Chion.[1] But Chion overlooks
that it is in fact the feather on the hat of a small woman—which, unbeknownst
to her, tickles the faces of Hulot and the other men in the line as she shakes their
hands—that precipitates their laughter (fig. 3.1). As with much of the comedy
in Tati's films, this is easy to miss because of the innovative ways Tati structures
his comic material.[2] Like modernists in general who, in the words of P. Adams
Sitney, stress "vision as a privileged mode of perception, even of revelation, while
at the same time cultivating opacity and questioning the primacy of the visible world,"[3] Tati often designs his comedy so that it is difficult (and sometimes
almost impossible) to perceive. This comic opacity, along with the democratization of gags and the reliance on unintentional forms of humor such as aleatory
object analogs, constitutes the major difference between Tati's comic style and
those of his classical forebears. It is intended to foster precisely the active mode of
observation that, as we noted at the end of chapter 2, Tati hoped his films would
inculcate in his viewers so that they would search for comedy in their daily lives
on exiting the movie theater. The goal of what Jacques Rancière refers to, in the
context of theater, as emancipating spectators by turning them into "active participants as opposed to passive voyeurs" was widely pursued by the avant-garde in

FIGURE 3.1 In *Les Vacances de Monsieur Hulot* (Jacques Tati, 1953), the feather tickles the faces of Hulot and the mourners, making them laugh.

the twentieth century.[4] Tati tried to achieve this goal by obscuring his humor to varying degrees, prodding his audiences to seek it out in his films for themselves rather than passively consuming it, thereby teaching them to be on the lookout for it in reality.

ELISION

Again and again in Tati's films part of a gag occurs offscreen or is hidden by the mise-en-scène so that the viewer, often in tandem with a character, must infer what has occurred during the hidden part of the gag. Rather than being presented with the entire gag, the spectator has to guess at parts of it. Furthermore, Tati sometimes doesn't provide the missing information, and in such cases we never know for certain what has transpired. Tati began using elision in *Jour de fête* (1949), when François the postman is first seen cycling into the village of

FIGURE 3.2 In *Jour de fête* (Jacques Tati, 1949), François rides into Bondu's bar to avoid the falling flagpole.

Sainte-Sévère and, in order to avoid a tottering flagpole, rides into a bar (fig. 3.2). A few seconds later, he reappears on the bar's first-floor balcony while Bondu, the bar's owner, emerges below with François's bike and throws it into the village square in anger (fig. 3.3). This gag is filmed in a single long shot from outside the bar, and we never find out precisely how, somewhat unexpectedly and improbably, Bondu ends up holding François's bike and François gets upstairs. To cite another example, in *Les Vacances*, two women are shown sitting on the beach accompanied by a creaking sound coming from offscreen when the camera suddenly swivels left to reveal the source of the sound—an unmanned winch rapidly unwinding (fig. 3.4). A boat attached to the winch slides down the beach into the sea (fig. 3.5), its occupant falls into the water, and a man who was painting a name onto the side of the boat begins looking for the person who disturbed the winch. Finally, he notices Hulot, who is standing some distance away in front of a pole in his bathing suit. Hulot pretends to dry himself and wring out his towel as if he had been swimming when the winch unwound, but the viewer can see that he is not wet, in part because he is unwittingly toweling dry the pole behind him instead of his back (fig. 3.6). Although Hulot acts suspiciously in this scene,

FIGURE 3.3 François appears on the balcony and Bondu throws his bike into the square.

FIGURE 3.4 In *Les Vacances*, a sudden pan reveals the unattended winch unwinding.

FIGURE 3.5 The boat attached to the winch rolls into the sea.

FIGURE 3.6 Hulot pretends to towel himself dry while the boat painter searches for the person responsible for causing the winch to unwind.

we never learn who unwound the winch, and later in the hotel restaurant the painter can be seen still looking at Hulot inquisitively.

Tati often uses the setting to obscure part of a gag. In *Mon Oncle*, Hulot descends from his penthouse down the rabbit warren of passages and staircases in his old apartment building just as a woman emerges from the shared bathroom dressed only in a slip. The scene is shot from outside the building, and when Hulot encounters her, only his legs are visible through an open window as Hulot turns to face the wall while she passes. Although we cannot see his face, we infer that he does this out of politeness (fig. 3.7). In the "Ideal Home" exposition in *Play Time*, two ladies mistake Hulot for a salesman and give him a broken lamp to repair (fig. 3.34). Continuing an earlier gag, the German businessman and his sales assistant then apologize to Hulot for confusing him with a lookalike who disturbed their papers. Hulot goes to leave their stand, and the cord of the lamp catches on something behind their desk—perhaps the desk itself, or one of their feet—yanking him back (fig. 3.35). He subsequently returns the lamp to the ladies, who ask if it is mended, and on testing it he finds that

FIGURE 3.7 In *Mon Oncle* (Jacques Tati, 1958), Hulot's feet indicate he has turned to face the wall while the woman in the slip passes him.

it now works (fig. 3.36). Not only must we infer that the yanking of the lamp's cord somehow fixed the lamp, but by staging the yanking behind the desk, it is easy to overlook.

Tati sometimes employs elision in ingenious ways to amplify or top gags according to the gag/topper/topper-topper structure found in classical comedian comedy, in which a gag is repeated, varied, and intensified until it climaxes. In *Jour de fête*, a man in a straw hat wheeling his bicycle past the flagpole hears a creaking sound identical to the one the flagpole emitted when it almost toppled onto François, and he looks at it in alarm, assuming, along with the viewer, that it is about to fall over (fig. 3.8). However, in an aural equivalent of the switch image, a reverse-angle shot reveals that the creaking sound is caused by a wooden plank being used nearby by another man to jack up his car (fig. 3.9), and the man with the straw hat, reassured, wheels his bike into Bondu's bar (fig. 3.10). A little later, the gag in which François rides into Bondu's bar to avoid the tottering flagpole and ends up on the second-floor balcony is repeated. Now, however, it is a mutual interference gag (the topper) because, like the man in the straw hat, François is

FIGURE 3.8 In *Jour de fête*, a man in a straw hat hears a creaking sound and turns to see if the flagpole is falling over.

FIGURE 3.9 The creaking sound comes from a man using a wooden plank as a jack, not the flagpole.

FIGURE 3.10 Reassured, the man in the straw hat wheels his bike into Bondu's bar.

FIGURE 3.11 Hearing the creaking sound of the plank, François mistakenly assumes the flagpole is falling and again escapes into Bondu's bar on his bike.

deceived by the creaking sound of the wooden plank into believing that the flagpole is falling over (fig. 3.11). In a further twist (the topper-topper), Bondu the bar owner emerges, as he did before, carrying what he and the spectator assume is once again François's bike and throws it onto the town square in anger, only to discover that the bike belongs to the man in the straw hat who follows Bondu out of the bar, protesting the treatment of his bike (fig. 3.12). Because the part of the repeated gag that is varied (Bondu taking the wrong bike) is elided, the viewer makes an incorrect inference (that it is François's bike).

Mon Oncle contains a gag with a similar structure. Hulot is collecting his nephew, Gérard, from school, and Gérard runs ahead with some other boys to play a prank on drivers in a nearby street. When a car stops at the traffic light, one boy steps on its back bumper while another bangs the lid of a trashcan, thereby deceiving the driver, who cannot see them, into believing his car has been hit by the car behind (the gag) (fig. 3.13). The boys are offscreen the second time they do this, so it is initially unclear to the viewer whether or not the victim, an elderly gentleman, has really been rear-ended (fig. 3.14). He gets out and

FIGURE 3.12 Bondu throws what he thinks is François's bike into the square, only to discover it belongs to the man in the straw hat.

FIGURE 3.13 In *Mon Oncle*, Gérard and his friends deceive a driver into thinking his car has been rear-ended by stepping on its back bumper and simultaneously banging a trashcan lid.

FIGURE 3.14 Offscreen, the boys play their trick on a second driver, an elderly man, who thinks his car has been rear ended.

complains to the woman whom he believes has crashed into him, and a woman in a white hat in the car behind her informs them that they have been tricked by the boys, who run away into an adjacent field (the topper) (fig. 3.15). As the light turns green and the cars inch forward, Hulot walks past, gesturing to Gérard with his umbrella, which distracts the man driving the vehicle behind the woman with the white hat, and he rear-ends her (fig. 3.16). She, however, does not react because she mistakenly believes she has not been hit and is instead the victim of the prank she previously witnessed being played by the boys on others (the topper-topper). To top it off (topper-topper-topper), she berates another boy walking down the street who has nothing to do with the prank (fig. 3.17). Here, it is a character (the woman in the white hat) who makes a false inference about what has occurred beyond her field of vision. However, because of the complexity of the gag, and the fact that part of it occurs offscreen, it is easy for the viewer to misunderstand it or find it confusing.

FIGURE 3.15 A woman in a white hat informs the elderly man that the boys have tricked him, and they escape into an adjoining field.

FIGURE 3.16 Gesturing to Gérard with his umbrella, Hulot distracts a driver who rear-ends the car of the woman in the white hat.

FIGURE 3.17 The woman in the white hat, assuming the boys have tricked her and that her car hasn't been rear-ended, mistakenly berates another boy who has nothing to do with the trick.

Elision can certainly be found in classical comedian comedy, and it usually functions to create humorous surprises. The day after the burglary of the department store in *Modern Times* (1936), a customer selects some fabric from the top of a counter and is startled to discover, along with the viewer, the Tramp asleep underneath it. In Laurel and Hardy's exquisite silent short *Liberty* (1929), the boys, having accidentally dressed in each others' pants, are desperately searching for a place to swap them. They turn off a main street into an alleyway out of view of the camera, and an instant later run back onto the street hotly pursued by a fast-moving truck. In both examples, it is not that the viewer initially misunderstands or is perplexed by what is happening in the shot, as in switch and enlightenment images. Rather, we are amused by the unexpected (re-)appearance of the characters, who are briefly hidden by the framing or mise-en-scène. Tati does something similar in *Jour de fête*, when Bondu cycles into the bar and re-emerges seconds later on the balcony; and in *Les Vacances*, when Hulot chases his out-of-control Amilcar into a country estate and almost instantly reappears pursued by some dogs (figs. 3.18 and 3.19).

FIGURE 3.18 In *Les Vacances*, Hulot pursues his out-of-control Amilcar into a country estate . . .

FIGURE 3.19 . . . and quickly re-emerges pursued by a pack of dogs.

In addition to sometimes failing to provide the missing information and the frequency with which he resorts to elision in his films, however, what is distinctive about Tati's use of this technique is that it tends to last much longer than in the classical tradition. After Hulot is chased by the dogs out of the estate, it is not until some three-and-a-half minutes of screen time later that we see him again *still* being hounded by the dogs. Several events happen in between—the Englishwoman and Martine's aunt are driven back to the hotel by the owners of the estate; the Englishwoman and the German businessman's son look for Hulot at the hotel that night; the boy is mistaken for Hulot when he plays jazz loudly on the record player—and we must infer that Hulot has spent several hours being chased around the French countryside by dogs. In *Play Time*, Hulot leaves the modern apartment of a friend from the army, Schneller, and looks for the button in the vestibule to open the glass door to the street (fig. 3.20). The camera, which is stationed outside, tracks to the right so that Hulot is offscreen, and through the large apartment window we see his friend return to his living room and watch television while taking off his suspenders. Next to it is an identical apartment in which, coincidentally, Giffard lives, and he gets up to walk his dog while his wife sits watching television. Continuing an earlier aleatory object analog, which I analyze in chapter 4, because of the position of the camera and the design of the apartments, it appears as though she and Schneller are gazing

FIGURE 3.20 In *Play Time* (Jacques Tati, 1968), Schneller bids Hulot goodnight in the vestibule of his apartment building.

FIGURE 3.21 Schneller resumes watching TV and, continuing an earlier aleatory object analog, it appears as though he and Giffard's wife in the adjoining apartment are staring at each other.

at each other through the wall between their apartments (fig. 3.21). A cut to a slightly longer shot shows Giffard leaving to walk his dog, and as the camera pans left to keep him in the frame while he passes the friend's apartment, we hear a thud. Schneller, still visible through his window, hears it too, and goes into the vestibule to investigate. A new shot finds him turning on the light to discover Hulot still searching for the button to open the door to the street (fig. 3.22). In this example, Hulot is offscreen for almost two minutes, and it is easy to forget about him due to the comic business in the apartments. Moreover, Tati uses two long takes of approximately ninety and thirty seconds respectively to film the sequence, and not much happens during them. This delay exemplifies one of the most innovative dimensions of Tati's comedy: making the viewer *wait* for a gag's payoff. Occasionally Tati does this using long takes, as when, after Hulot has kicked the German businessman in the pants behind Martine's beach hut (fig. 2.42), he pauses nervously on the other side of the hut to see if the victim will investigate. In a long take, Hulot makes small talk with Martine's aunt for almost twenty seconds before the German businessman emerges (fig. 3.23), and the take continues as, in a mutual interference gag, the man blames an innocent bystander who happens to be dusting sand off his foot while Hulot sprints away (fig. 3.24).

FIGURE 3.22 Almost two minutes after bidding him goodnight, Schnller returns to the vestibule to discover Hulot still searching for the exit button.

FIGURE 3.23 In *Les Vacances*, Hulot nervously makes small talk with Martine's aunt while waiting to see if the German businessman will pursue him for kicking him.

FIGURE 3.24 The German businessman eventually emerges from behind Martine's beach hut to search for the person who kicked him and focuses on a man who is suspiciously brushing sand off his foot.

FRAGMENTED AND RUNNING GAGS

Usually, though, Tati delays the outcome of his gags by fragmenting them, as noted by Noël Burch:

> Tati's genius consists in having extended to his films as a whole the organizational principles which for Sennett and his followers functioned only at the level of the individual gag. For Tati, a gag can be started in one sequence, completed in another, developed in a third, entirely repeated in a fourth, rejected in a fifth, etc. This is just one of the means by which he reaches a formal unity through discontinuity of discourse, an unprecedented achievement in the history of what is called comic cinema.[5]

Burch is pointing to at least two distinct types of gag structure used by Tati—the running gag, in which an already completed gag is subsequently repeated, as in the example of François cycling into Bondu's bar or Hulot being chased by dogs; and the fragmented gag, in which a gag is broken into parts that are dispersed across a sequence or even the entirety of a film. While fragmented gags are more unique to Tati, running gags are found throughout classical comedian comedy and are often combined with the gag/topper/topper-topper structure in which a gag is varied each time it is repeated. Laurel and Hardy in particular were masters of this combination, and as Charles Barr has shown, such gags tend to come in threes in their films: "gag, reversal, new reversal."[6] In *You're Darn Tootin'*, after Hardy has helped Laurel out of the manhole into which he fell head first (gag) (fig. 2.49), Laurel goes to pick up his hat and almost falls in again. Hardy struggles with him to prevent him doing so, and of course falls in himself, but legs rather than head first (reversal) (fig. 3.25). They extricate themselves, and Hardy admonishes Laurel to watch out for manholes as they continue walking down the street, only for Hardy to fall into another one, this time head rather than legs first (new reversal) (fig. 3.26).[7] The running gag involving the boys and the cars in *Mon Oncle* is similar in that the gag is repeated and varied twice in quick succession. Usually, though, Tati's running gags are spread out across a scene if not an entire film. While driving his Amilcar in *Les Vacances*, Hulot nearly knocks down pedestrians on six occasions, the first time some four minutes into the film, the last a little over ten minutes before its end; and in *Mon Oncle*, the street sweeper in the old quarter is shown avoiding work by chatting to passersby about eight

FIGURE 3.25 After Laurel has fallen head first into a manhole in *You're Darn Tootin'* (Edgar Kennedy, 1928), Hardy falls feet first into another manhole.

FIGURE 3.26 Hardy then falls head first into a third manhole.

FIGURE 3.27 An instance of the running gag in *Mon Oncle* in which the street sweeper chats to a passerby instead of working.

minutes after the film has begun, five minutes or so before it finishes, and six other times in between (fig. 3.27).

Hulot's inability to find the button for the door to the street in *Play Time* is not like these examples, however. Rather than a discrete gag that is then repeated and sometimes varied, it is split into two parts by being set up in one shot and then left incomplete in favor of other gags and events, until the camera returns to the vestibule for the payoff two shots and almost two minutes later. Similarly, in *Mon Oncle*, one of Hulot's neighbors is watering some flowers and walking his black-and-white dog outside his apartment building when he is invited into the neighborhood bar for a drink by the street sweeper (set-up) (fig. 3.28). Several other events and gags with different characters follow, including Hulot emerging onto the street accompanied by another man with a black-and-white dog, and it is not until about two-and-a-half minutes later that we briefly see the first man, now inebriated, leave the bar with the dog (fig. 3.29). Tati cuts away again for approximately a minute and a half and returns to him standing on the street rewatering the flowers, where he is again called to the bar by the street sweeper

FIGURE 3.28 In *Mon Oncle*, the street sweeper invites the man with the black-and-white dog into the bar for a drink.

FIGURE 3.29 Two-and-a-half minutes later, the man with the black-and-white dog re-emerges, now inebriated.

FIGURE 3.30 A minute-and-a-half later, the man with the black-and-white dog is enticed back to the bar.

(fig. 3.30). As he stumbles back to the bar, his wife calls him from their apartment window, but he is too drunk to hear, so she calls the dog who pulls the man back toward the apartment (the payoff) (fig. 3.31). In a topper, the dog sees the other black-and-white dog, who is being taken into the bar, and reverses course to follow it, dragging his drunken owner into the bar once more (fig. 3.32). In this example, the payoff and the topper do not occur until almost four minutes after the set-up, and much else takes place in between.

Splitting up gags in this manner allows Tati to interweave and even interpenetrate them. Tati will cut back and forth between fragmented and running gags occurring simultaneously in adjacent locations; and often, the gags will intersect and causally impact each other in unexpected ways. As Jean-André Fieschi and Jean Narboni noted when interviewing Tati for *Cahiers du cinéma* in 1968, the often complex "relations between the gags" that result can be amusing independently of the content of each gag.[8] The fragmented gag with the drunken dogwalker in *Mon Oncle* is intercut with a running sound gag involving a bird, which I will discuss later (figs. 3.83 and 3.84); the elliptical gag of Hulot turning

FIGURE 3.31 The man's wife is unable to attract his attention, so she calls his black-and-white dog, who drags the man back toward his home.

FIGURE 3.32 However, the man's dog is distracted by another black-and-white dog and follows it back into the bar.

away from his scantily clad neighbor in his apartment building (fig. 3.7); the running gag in which Hulot taps his concierge's daughter on the nose (fig. 2.44);
the running gag of the street sweeper avoiding work (fig. 3.27); and a hidden gag
involving Hulot, the street sweeper, and the other man with the black-and-white
dog, which I will also analyze shortly (figs. 3.67, 3.68, and 3.69). Indeed, it is the
"street sweeper avoiding work" gag that initiates the "inebriated dog walker" gag
when the street sweeper invites the dog walker to join him for a drink; and the
latter gag comes to an end when it interacts with the hidden gag and the drunk
man's dog follows the other black-and-white hound back into the bar. Similarly,
the fragmented gag in *Play Time* in which Hulot is mistaken for a sales assistant by the two women with the broken lamp is caused by another fragmented
gag in which Hulot is confused with a lookalike by the German businessman.
Following the setup in which the Hulot lookalike rifles through the contents of
the German businessman's desk (fig. 2.27), Tati cuts away to the third iteration of
a running gag in which Hulot unwillingly takes an elevator, although this time
we see him emerging from the elevator behind a large group of businessmen into
the exposition.[9] As he walks past the display stands still looking for Giffard, the
German, thinking he is the man who disturbed his desk, mockingly invites him to
sit down and "feel at home" while taking off his hat and coat (fig. 3.33). Without
them, Hulot resembles the sales assistants, and he is subsequently mistaken
for one by the two women with the lamp when he finally escapes the German

FIGURE 3.33 In *Play Time*, the German salesman, confusing Hulot with a lookalike who earlier rifled through his desk, sarcastically invites him to take off his hat and coat and "feel at home."

FIGURE 3.34 Without his hat and coat, Hulot is mistaken for a salesman, and two women ask him to fix their broken lamp.

businessman's ire (fig. 3.34). The two gags intersect again moments later when the lamp's cord gets caught behind the German's desk while he apologizes to Hulot (fig. 3.35), which results in the lamp working again (fig. 3.36). Furthermore, while these two gags interweave, several others occur, including a mutual interference

FIGURE 3.35 The lamp's cord gets caught behind the German salesman's desk while he apologizes to Hulot.

FIGURE 3.36 Hulot returns the lamp to the women, and it now works.

gag involving the doors that "slam . . . in golden silence," which the German is selling. Intertwining multiple gags in this fashion is cognitively challenging, as viewers must keep track of several simultaneous lines of action and the ways they interact, thereby forcing them to pay close attention to events.

Tati challenges his viewers further by sometimes combining fragmented gags with elision. Hulot breaks the glass door to the restaurant, and the doorman along with the coat-check woman try to hide the broken glass by sweeping it into a cardboard box (fig. 3.37). The gag is abandoned until, nearly thirteen minutes later, they transport the box of broken glass to the bar, where the restaurant manager asks what is in the box. They tell him that it is ice and pour some of the broken glass into a champagne bucket, which is left on the bar (fig. 3.38). The gag is dropped for others until, almost four minutes later, a waiter delivers a bottle of champagne in a bucket to the table under the broken ceiling and the harried restaurant manager takes out what he thinks is a piece of ice to cool his forehead (fig. 3.39). Perplexed that it doesn't feel cold, he checks his pulse, suspecting he is sick, and walks away in shock. One only comprehends this switch-image if one grasps what has not been shown—that the waiter has delivered the champagne bucket filled with broken glass last seen on the bar, and that it is broken glass the restaurant manager touches to his forehead, not ice. Earlier, the restaurant manager suspects that one of his employees is drinking from a wine bottle in the kitchen, and he puts black grease on the lips of the bottle to catch the offender.

COLOR FIGURE 1 *Play Time* (Jacques Tati, 1967).

COLOR FIGURE 2 *Play Time.*

COLOR FIGURE 3 The traffic circle that looks like a merry-go-round in *Play Time*.

COLOR FIGURE 4 The trim of Monsieur Arpel's smoking jacket resembles Dacky's coat as he and his wife gaze at the object floating above their wall in *Mon Oncle* (Jacques Tati, 1958).

COLOR FIGURE 5 Maria believes her dog has been run over in *Trafic* (Jacques Tati, 1971).

COLOR FIGURE 6 The blue bag and baby dressed in blue are swapped back in *Play Time*.

COLOR FIGURE 7 The radio that resembles the facing building in *Play Time*.

COLOR FIGURE 8 Gérard and his father bond at the end of *Mon Oncle*.

COLOR FIGURE 9 A long shot of Schneller's apartment building in *Play Time* showing Giffard arriving home on the right.

COLOR FIGURE 10 The colorful costumes of audience members in *Parade* (Jacques Tati, 1974).

FIGURE 3.37 In *Play Time*, Hulot breaks the glass door to the Royal Garden restaurant, and the doorman and coat-check woman sweep up the broken glass.

Nearly three minutes later, he sees the head waiter with a black ring on his lips and we must infer that it is the head waiter who has been drinking the wine, even though we never see him do so. In a running gag, additional rings appear on his lips throughout the rest of the scene.

FIGURE 3.38 Almost thirteen minutes later, the doorman and coat-check woman pretend to the restaurant manager that the broken glass is ice and pour it into a champagne bucket.

FIGURE 3.39 Nearly four minutes later, the restaurant manager mistakes the broken glass in the champagne bucket for ice and touches a piece to his forehead.

Tati also refined a more obscure form of the running gag in which, rather than repeating and sometimes varying the same gag, such as cycling into a bar, different gags are built around a recurring motif. One such motif in *Les Vacances* is liquid. Starting with the tea that spills because of the wind from the door to the hotel lobby that Hulot leaves open when he first arrives at the Hôtel de la Plage, Hulot directly or indirectly causes someone to get wet, or he gets wet, on nine occasions. To top it off, when he accidentally sets off the fireworks in the penultimate scene, he desperately tries and fails to collect water from a revolving sprinkler in a watering can in order to douse them. Another motif is disturbing, or failing to disturb, peoples' sleep. Hulot wakes up the hotel guests during the night, as indicated by their bedroom lights being turned on one by one in the darkened hotel, when he has fun with the hikers at the end of the second day of his stay; when, on the third night, he returns from the funeral in his Amilcar, which has a loud engine that often backfires; and when he sets off the fireworks on the sixth.[10] A similar running motif gag in *Play Time* involves glass. This motif is inaugurated by a switch image in which the doorman to Giffard's building initially appears to both the viewer and a passing worker to be standing outside on the street (fig. 3.40). The worker approaches him to ask for a light only to realize that doorman is in fact inside the building and a pane of glass separates them, and he must enter the door of the building to obtain the light for

FIGURE 3.40 In *Play Time*, a man approaches the doorman to the SNC building to ask for a light . . .

his cigarette (I return to the theme of the confusion caused by glass as well as the barrier it erects between people in *Play Time* in chapter 4) (fig. 3.41). In addition to this switch image, Hulot thinks he sees Giffard across the street because of Giffard's reflection in a glass door and leaves the building where Giffard is in

FIGURE 3.41 . . . only to realize (along with the viewer) that a glass wall separates them and he must enter the building to light his cigarette.

FIGURE 3.42 In *Play Time*, Giffard's reflection leads Hulot to believe he is across the road in another building.

fact located (mutual interference gag) (fig. 3.42); Giffard bangs into a glass door and injures his nose when he mistakes a Hulot lookalike for Hulot outside in the street and runs after him (mutual interference gag) (fig. 2.28); it appears as though the families of Giffard and Schneller can see each other through their shared apartment wall when viewed from the street through their large glass windows (aleatory object analog) (fig. 3.21); it seems to a small crowd gathered in the street that workers are dancing while moving a plane of glass on the floor above the restaurant (aleatory object analog) (fig. 3.43); Hulot breaks the glass door to the restaurant (slapstick) (fig. 3.37); the restaurant manager confuses the broken glass with ice (switch image) (fig. 3.39); and during a shot of an ice cream truck in the traffic circle-cum merry-go-round, the camera pulls back to reveal that the truck is being filmed through a window from inside a building (switch image) (figs. 3.44 and 3.45). When the window is open and shut, the reflection of Barbara's departing bus on the window pane (along with the cries of delight of the tourists inside the bus) makes it appear as though the bus is going up and down (aleatory object analog) (fig. 3.46). I describe such running motif gags as an obscure form of the running gag because the relation between their constituent gags is more abstract. Whereas running gags proper tend to repeat the same events using the same characters—Laurel and Hardy falling down manholes;

FIGURE 3.43 Men appear to be dancing as they move a pane of glass during the opening of the Royal Garden restaurant.

FIGURE 3.44 What seems to be an exterior shot of an ice cream truck in the traffic circle . . .

FIGURE 3.45 ... turns out to have been shot through a glass window from inside a building.

Hulot almost running down pedestrians—the actions and people in running motif gags vary considerably, as the glass motif gags in *Play Time* demonstrate. Their component gags are instead connected by an abstract concept—liquid, sleep, glass—and the connection between them can therefore be harder for audiences to divine.

FIGURE 3.46 Barbara's bus, reflected in the window, seems to go up and down as the washer moves the window.

Running and fragmented gags are not always easy to distinguish, as the difference between a whole gag and a part is sometimes not clear. One differentiating characteristic is that, unlike a completed gag that is subsequently repeated, the setups that are separated from their payoffs in fragmented gags— Hulot leaving his friend's apartment in *Play Time*; the man with the dog going into the bar in *Mon Oncle*—are not amusing in themselves but become so retroactively when we reach their payoffs. By fragmenting gags Tati once again renders his comedy opaque to the viewer who, on encountering a setup without an immediate payoff, searches for its comic significance, which remains unclear until the payoff takes place sometime later. Indeed, given the time that elapses between set-up and payoff as well as the distraction of other gags and events that occur during it, the spectator might forget the setup and fail to comprehend the payoff when it arrives.

POTENTIAL GAGS

Tati not only delays payoffs but in certain cases dispenses with them altogether, so that the viewer is tricked by a setup into anticipating a payoff that never arrives. Once again this technique, which Burch calls a truncated gag, is not totally unprecedented in the classical tradition, but Tati uses it more frequently than his predecessors. In Keaton's brilliant first solo short, *The High Sign* (1921), a banana peel is thrown on the street by the leader of the Blinking Buzzard gang (fig. 3.47).[11] Because of its overuse in slapstick to upend clowns, the viewer naturally assumes that one or more of the characters will slip on the peel, but instead they walk over it and the set-up is forgotten. Keaton's character even makes the high sign, a gesture signifying membership in the criminal gang, to the camera after he has avoided the peel, as if to say that viewers should expect something more sophisticated from him than primitive slapstick gags involving banana peels (fig. 3.48). Similarly, in *Jour de fête*, François the postman is handed a boxed-up cake—another archetypal cause of pratfalls in slapstick—to deliver on his rounds. Almost immediately, not looking where he is going, he and his bike become caught between a horse and cart, but he does not drop the cake (fig. 3.49). Nor does he drop it when he arrives at the residence to which he is delivering it, even though he gesticulates wildly while recounting a story to a man with a hose (fig. 3.50). The man gives the hose to François and takes the cake out of harm's way, and we never see it again. Now, however, we suspect François will soak two passing policemen with the hose as he continues telling the story

FIGURE 3.47 In *The High Sign* (Buster Keaton, Edward F. Cline, 1921), the leader of the Blinking Buzzard gang drops a banana peel on the ground.

FIGURE 3.48 Keaton walks past the banana peel and makes the high sign to the camera.

FIGURE 3.49 In *Jour de fête*, François gets caught between a horse and cart while carrying a cake.

FIGURE 3.50 François demonstratively recounts a story while delivering the cake to a man with a hose.

FIGURE 3.51 Relieved of the cake, François continues telling the story to two policemen while holding the hose.

while gesturing frantically (fig. 3.51). But once again our expectations are frustrated when the policemen leave and, unexpectedly, François falls into a hitherto unseen hole (fig. 3.52). In this instance, Tati rewards us for our patience with a gag, although not the one anticipated. In subsequent films this is not always the case. In *Les Vacances*, a little boy buys two ice cream cones and has to climb some stairs and negotiate a door in order to deliver one to another boy, heightening our expectation that he will drop them, but he manages to accomplish his task successfully and we cut to other characters without incident (fig. 3.53). And in the restaurant scene in *Play Time*, a waiter carrying a dessert is distracted by the collapsed ceiling and unknowingly passes the plate over the head of a dancer just as the dancer bends over, barely missing him (fig. 3.54). Again we cut to a new shot without a compensatory gag. The fish-seasoning gag in *Play Time* is a fragmented example of a truncated gag. Thrice over the course of the restaurant scene a fish dish ordered by a couple is seasoned, leading us to expect that, when it is finally served to them, it will be unpalatable. But they are replaced by a new couple who send the dish away, and throughout the rest of the scene, a waiter can be seen

FIGURE 3.52 Finally, François falls into a hidden hole while holding the hose.

FIGURE 3.53 A boy carrying ice cream cones in *Les Vacances*.

FIGURE 3.54 In *Play Time*, a waiter carrying a desert barely misses the head of a dancer.

carrying it as he tries to locate the couple who ordered it, which he fails to do even though he often passes them on the dance floor (fig. 3.55).

In addition to disappointment at the lack of a payoff, one effect of truncated gags is that the viewer searches in vain for the comic potential of the setup to be realized. There are two other kinds of potential gags in Tati's films. Sometimes when watching them we get the impression that we are witnessing a short section of a larger gag, one that we cannot understand or find funny because we are shown too small a part of it. During lunchtime on the second day in *Les Vacances*, a boy goes down some stairs onto a street looking back at a man who can be seen, his back to the boy, through an open window listening to the radio. The boy walks offscreen followed by other children and we cut to something else. This might be part of a gag involving the boy sneaking away from his father to join his friends, but we never find out who the man or the boy are, or their relation to one another, and so the boy's actions are not funny. Nor is it particularly amusing in the airport scene at the beginning of *Play Time* when a uniformed officer berates a subordinate (fig. 3.56); or when, in *Jour de fête*, the music from the merry-go-round in the town square occasions a boy to run out of the establishment adjoining Bondu's bar and a man immediately pulls him back inside (fig. 3.57)—although in all these cases we can imagine gags that would make these events comic. I will return to the role of the viewer's imagination toward the end of this chapter.

FIGURE 3.55 A waiter searches for the couple who ordered a fish dish and unknowingly passes them as they leave the dance floor.

FIGURE 3.56 An army officer loudly berates a subordinate in *Play Time*, while the couple with the baby carriage make their way to the departure gate in the top right corner.

FIGURE 3.57 A boy is prevented from joining the fair in *Jour de fête*.

Incomplete gags such as these overlap with another kind of potential gag first identified by Jean-Luc Godard.

> [Tati] is capable of filming a beach scene simply to show that the children build-
> ing a sandcastle drown the sound of the waves with their cries. He will also shoot
> a scene just because at that moment a window is opening in a house away in the
> background, and a window opening—well, that's funny. This is what interests
> Tati. Everything and nothing. Blades of grass, a kite, children, a little old man,
> anything, everything which is at once real, bizarre and charming. Jacques Tati
> has a feeling for comedy because he has a feeling for strangeness.[12]

Godard, ever the astute critic, is pointing to the fact that Tati often directs our attention to details of setting, costume, or behavior that have the potential to be funny but that, in their current form, are merely strange or bizarre in the sense of being unusual or out of place. In *Jour de fête*, a man driving a horse and cart tries to decide how to steer the cart while keeping a white blouse clean, and he eventually opts for holding the blouse up in the air with one hand and the reins

FIGURE 3.58 In *Jour de fête*, a farmer holds a blouse in one hand while driving his cart with the other.

with the other (fig. 3.58). At the beginning of the second day in *Les Vacances*, Martine opens her bedroom window to look out at the beach, which is empty save for some striped tents and a man doing stretching exercises while jogging (fig. 3.59). And in the airport scene at the start of *Play Time*, a visiting dignitary arrives and is surrounded by reporters while a label on his briefcase flaps loudly (fig. 3.60). None of these are gags in the traditional sense, although they involve incidents—the man holding up the blouse while steering, the jogger's exercises, the label—that are incongruous in that they are (ever so slightly) out of the ordinary. Sometimes their comic potential is exploited later on, as when Hulot follows and mimics the exercising jogger in *Les Vacances* after the winch debacle. Usually, however, they are never returned to, as is the case with the man holding the blouse and the flapping label, and their frequent occurrence in Tati's films points to his dislike of conformity and standardization, a topic to which I will return in chapter 4. For the moment, suffice it to say that such incongruous details, along with incomplete and truncated gags, further obscure the comedy by hinting at its possibility yet failing to realize it, either by dispensing with the

FIGURE 3.59 In *Les Vacances*, Martine looks out at the beach while a man does stretching exercises below.

FIGURE 3.60 The flapping label on the briefcase in *Play Time*.

payoff (truncated gags), presenting only a fragment of a larger gag (incomplete gags), or focusing on incidents that are perhaps interesting but not funny in themselves (incongruous details). They can leave the viewer, who is expecting and searching for the comic significance of an event, frustrated at being unable to locate it and perhaps even bored by the lack of full-blown comedy in a number of shots and sequences. Yet by prodding the spectator to look for their comic meaning, these potential gags and unusual details help realize Tati's goal of fostering the more active mode of vision he desired for his audiences. So do the life-size cutouts of people and cars, which Tati starts placing in the background of shots as the party of American tourists leaves the airport at the beginning of *Play Time* (fig. 2.26). As Kristin Thompson puts it, "we may scan the backgrounds looking for cutouts, rather as we scan for bits of comic action."[13] Indeed, the cutouts are an example of the incongruous details Tati sprinkles throughout his films. They are not particularly funny and are certainly not gags. Instead, to use Godard's words, they are strange and bizarre, and they encourage us to pay attention to the environment around the characters and probe it for significance.

HIDDEN GAGS

Most radical of all in the context of Tati's opaque comedy are the hidden gags populating his films. As we saw in the introduction, critics have long noted that, unlike classical filmmakers, Tati routinely abstains from drawing our attention *to* events, and Tati himself suggested that he avoided close-ups because he wanted his audience to "see with their own eyes, not what the camera tells them."[14] Moreover, Jonathan Rosenbaum, Kristin Thompson, and others have shown how Tati, using long takes, long shots, deep staging, and deep focus often stages several events simultaneously in different parts of the frame, thereby making it difficult if not impossible to watch them all. The fact that the camera tends to be some distance away from them accentuates the difficulty. All of this is true of gags as well. Subtle ones are easily overlooked because they are not indexed and magnified by push-ins and close-ups. Furthermore, they compete for our attention with the events and gags surrounding them, which have not been bracketed out of the shot. The result is a lack of clarity and emphasis relative to traditional comedian comedy, and the viewer is often confused because she misses information crucial to understanding a gag. When the Dutch police are inspecting the camper in *Trafic*, Hulot releases the steam that has built up inside the car from the internal shower through a valve above the car's headlight. Conversing with

FIGURE 3.61 In *Trafic*, Hulot traps steam under his hat . . .

a policeman, he walks in front of the car, and as Maria approaches to discuss some paperwork she is holding, he puts his hat on, inadvertently trapping some steam inside it (fig. 3.61). Because this is filmed in a long shot, the steam trapping incident occupies a small portion of the frame, and Maria's angry gesticulations with the paperwork along with Hulot's conversation with the policeman make it hard to notice. If it is missed, the next shot, in which Hulot raises his hat to greet some other policemen and releases the trapped steam, is difficult to comprehend (fig. 3.62).

A more complex example occurs in *Play Time* when the German businessman introduces Hulot to his dining companions and Hulot, in the center foreground of the shot with his back to the camera, bows at each one in turn. Behind them is the table of American tourists, and another man, who is partly obscured by Hulot, approaches Barbara and asks her to dance. As she gets up, one of the tourists sitting next to her happens to glance at Hulot, mistakes his bow at one of the German businessman's companions for an invitation to dance, and eagerly accepts (fig. 3.63). There are four zones of action in this shot—Hulot bowing in the foreground, the businessman's friends acknowledging his bows in the mid-ground, Barbara getting up to dance just behind them, and her friend

FIGURE 3.62 ... and releases it when raising his hat to some policemen.

FIGURE 3.63 In *Play Time*, while Barbara gets up, Hulot's bow to the German salesman's dinner companions is mistaken for an invitation to dance by one of the American tourists behind them.

misinterpreting Hulot's bow in the background—and it is difficult to keep track of them all. The result is that the viewer is potentially as confused as Hulot when Barbara's friend joins him for a dance (a mutual interference gag) followed by Barbara and her suitor. To top it off, when the two couples walk onto the crowded dance floor in the next shot, another man thinks Barbara's friend is asking him to dance. As she shakes her head, Barbara's suitor begins dancing with her, leaving Barbara to dance with Hulot. Again, this is hard to see as it is filmed in a long shot packed with dancing people, leaving the spectator wondering how Hulot and Barbara end up together.

Tati's tendency not to use mobile framing to manage the viewer's attention has led Rosenbaum and others to characterize *Play Time*'s visual style in Bazinian terms as democratic because it supposedly gives the events on screen equal weight and leaves the viewer free to look at what he or she desires—as is the case, according to Bazin, in the films of William Wyler and others. However, as we noted in the introduction, Tati uses time-honored methods such as movement, color, frontality, the power of the center, the gazes of characters, and sound to direct the viewer's attention. In the *Play Time* example just discussed, Barbara and her friend are wearing bright green and red dresses while Hulot's jacket is brown, ensuring they stand out relative to the other characters dressed in black, white, or gray. Moreover, the three important actions—Hulot bowing, Barbara being asked to dance, her friend mistaking Hulot's bow for an invitation to dance—occur in the center of the frame, and these characters stand above the subsidiary ones, who remain seated and relatively still. One of the German businessman's companions looks up at the man who asks Barbara to dance, cueing us to notice him too, and Barbara's friend glances at Hulot just as he is bowing to the woman sitting directly in front of her, making it more likely that we will see her. Meanwhile, although it is difficult to make out their words, the voices of the German businessman and Barbara's friend are clearly audible above the music and the background din of restaurant conversation. Admittedly, this is a perceptually dense shot, and it is very difficult for the viewer to apprehend everything in it. Nevertheless, Tati is using mise-en-scène and sound to direct our attention to the important information, ensuring we have a chance of noticing it.

In some cases, however, Tati seems to be deploying these techniques for the opposite reason: to distract spectators from a gag or one of its parts. The viewer is prompted to pay attention to one thing while a gag is happening elsewhere, as we saw in the case of the couple with the baby carriage at the beginning of *Play Time*. Tati often uses character movement to hide a gag. In *Play Time*, when the restaurant doorman goes to the bar with the cigars he has purchased for the American businessman, he feigns fumbling for the man's change (fig. 3.64). The impatient American tells him to keep it and Tati cuts to a reverse-angle long

FIGURE 3.64 In *Play Time*, the doorman pretends to search for the American businessman's change.

shot of the bar, the doorman now on the far left of the frame. As he looks down to count the change, which he had in his hand all along, the restaurant architect crosses in front of him and stops at the bar in the center of the shot (figs. 3.65 and 3.66). Here, Tati masks the doorman's deception (he deliberately delayed finding the change so that the American would tell him to keep it) by having him

FIGURE 3.65 As the doorman counts the change he has pocketed, the architect crosses in front of him . . .

FIGURE 3.66 ... and moves to the bar.

lower his head just as the architect, dressed in brown with his head up, captures our attention by moving in front of him. It is therefore easy to miss the doorman counting the change followed by his self-satisfied smirk. Similarly, during the fragmented gag involving the drunk dog-walker in *Mon Oncle*, Hulot emerges from the bar with the street sweeper and the other man with a black-and-white dog. They stand chatting in an unbalanced long shot, the man with the dog in the center of the frame, Hulot and the street sweeper on the right (fig. 3.67). The man with the dog walks to the left, momentarily balancing the shot but distracting the spectator away from a small mutual interference gag in which Hulot taps his pipe on what he thinks is the heel of his shoe only to discover that his shoe has come off and he is tapping the heel of his foot (figs. 3.68 and 3.69). Earlier, when collecting his nephew from school, Hulot walks along the street with Gérard perpendicular to the camera in a long shot. Three of Gérard's friends run ahead and Gérard hands his satchel to his uncle and runs after them (fig. 3.70). Meanwhile, a boy walking with his mother behind Hulot drops a sheaf of papers and runs after the other boys as his mother gestures in anger toward him (fig. 3.71). As the boy passes him, Hulot turns toward the mother, thinking she is berating him because he has caused the papers to fall (another mutual interference gag), and bends down to pick up them up (fig. 3.72). The distance of the camera and the amount of movement in this dense shot make it almost impossible to see this gag. In these examples, far from giving events equal weight and allowing the viewer

FIGURE 3.67 In *Mon Oncle*, Hulot converses with the street sweeper and a man with a black-and-white dog.

FIGURE 3.68 The man with the dog moves to the left of the frame just as Hulot taps his pipe on the heel of his foot rather than his shoe.

FIGURE 3.69 As the man with the dog moves back to the right, Hulot looks down to see what happened.

FIGURE 3.70 In *Mon Oncle*, Gérard runs ahead with his friends, leaving his uncle to hold his satchel.

FIGURE 3.71 The boy behind Hulot drops a sheaf of papers as he runs ahead to join the other boys, angering his mother.

FIGURE 3.72 Thinking he caused the papers to fall, Hulot turns around to pick them up.

to choose which to look at, Tati's style prods us to notice one event and thereby overlook another.

Another method Tati uses to hide gags is to stage them or one of their parts in the far background while employing the mise-en-scène to obscure or distract our attention from them so that they are barely visible. Perhaps the most extreme example occurs when Hulot is buying Barbara a gift at the end of *Play Time*. A shot from inside the store of the street shows a cheese stand in the foreground and a number of colorfully dressed people walking along the road in the mid- and backgrounds. For a split second a young boy being forced by a parent to try on an oversized black plastic coat in the clothes store across the street can be seen through the throng of people and traffic before Tati cuts away (fig. 3.73), and he is briefly visible again a few shots later when Hulot's lookalike searches for Barbara to give her Hulot's present. There is so much to occupy us in the fore- and mid-grounds of these shots that the boy in the distance is hardly noticeable. It is therefore easy to miss this setup for a payoff that occurs a few moments later at the traffic circle, when the boy's father goes to slap the boy's face and misses because the boy ducks down inside his stiff plastic coat (fig. 3.74).

Tati utilizes less perceptually dense versions of this schema in earlier films. In *Les Vacances*, the German businessman is taking a photograph of his family and friends outside the hotel when he is interrupted by a phone call. They maintain their pose while he runs into the hotel (fig. 3.75). In a low-angle shot

FIGURE 3.73 In *Play Time*, a boy is barely visible in the background trying on a coat.

FIGURE 3.74 Later, the boy takes refuge in his coat as his father moves to smack him.

FIGURE 3.75 In *Les Vacances*, the German businessman runs inside the hotel to answer a phone call, leaving his family and friends posed for a photograph.

from behind the group looking up the embankment to the road above, they maintain their poses with one man tipping his hat, and Hulot, partly obscured by the embankment wall, speeds past in his Amilcar in the far background. His wave to the man, whom he thinks is tipping his hat at him, is barely visible (fig. 3.76). The same is true when, a little bit later, a woman crossing the road with her dog is almost knocked down first by Hulot in his Amilcar and then a bus. In another low-angle shot looking up the embankment from the hotel, the bus driver can just be seen berating Hulot behind the embankment wall in the distance while Henry and his wife walk toward the hotel in the foreground (fig. 3.77). As Hulot is leaving the SDRC coal derivatives factory in *Mon Oncle*, a man hanging up his hat is hardly noticeable in a long shot through the factory door (fig. 3.78). Hulot again mistakes the gesture for a salutation, and tips his hat in return (fig. 3.79).

FIGURE 3.76 In a reverse angle, Hulot is barely visible waving from his car in the background of the shot.

FIGURE 3.77 As Henry and his wife walk toward the hotel, Hulot is just visible in the background of the shot being berated by the bus driver.

FIGURE 3.78 In *Mon Oncle*, a man hangs up his hat and coat . . .

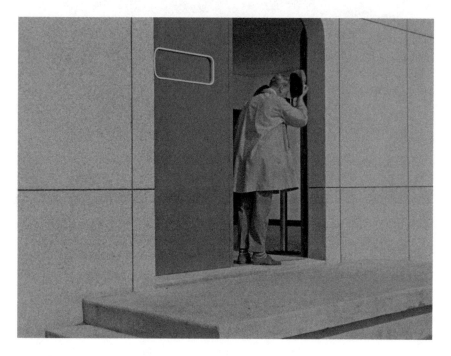

FIGURE 3.79 ... which Hulot misinterprets as a greeting, which he reciprocates.

SOUND

This far, I have focused almost exclusively on Tati's sight gags and the degree to which they are obscured using visual means. They run along a continuum from transparent, easily intelligible gags of the sort employed by classical comedians to barely perceptible hidden gags that are not to be found in the classical tradition. In between are gag structures that occur in classical comedian comedy but are used more frequently by Tati or are in some way radicalized by him in order to render his comedy more opaque: the switch and enlightenment images that initially deceive or confound the viewer; elided gags, parts of which occur offscreen or are masked by the mise-en-scène; running and fragmented gags that are dispersed and intertwined throughout a scene if not an entire film; the class of potential gags whose comic significance is never realized, either because they are truncated, incomplete, or consist merely of incongruous details; and the subtle gags filmed in long shot that compete for the viewer's attention with surrounding events and gags that are staged in the far background. However, as the example of the airport scene at the beginning of *Play Time* suggests, sound is also integral to Tati's comic style. The baby's crying helps deceive the viewer into thinking that the airport is a hospital, and his parents' dialogue persuades us that the man is there because he is sick rather than seeing his wife off on a trip. Indeed, given Tati's reputation as a visual comedian who uses dialogue sparingly, a surprisingly large proportion of his gags are dependent on sound, including the spoken word.

The mere presence of synchronized sound in Tati's films might seem to constitute a departure from classical comedian comedy of the silent era. But diegetic sounds often played a role in silent comedian comedy, whether in the form of dialogue conveyed by intertitles or noises left to the viewer's imagination when not approximated by the live sound effects that typically accompanied comedies by the 1920s.[15] In Laurel and Hardy's *The Finishing Touch* (1928), Laurel takes revenge on a female antagonist who has just punched him by tearing a piece of sandpaper as she bends down. In a mutual interference gag, she misidentifies the tearing sound—which would have been mimicked during many screenings by an accompanying organist or drummer—as the back of her dress ripping and backs away, embarrassed. In *The High Sign*, Keaton's character, who works at a firing range, attaches a dog to a bell and a bone to a piece of string behind the range. In order to deceive his boss into believing he is a sharpshooter, he steps on the string every time he shoots at a target inside the range so that the dog lunges at the bone and rings the bell, signifying the target has been hit (refunctionalization of an object gag). And in *You're Darn Tootin'*, Laurel kicks Hardy's French horn into the street and it is run over. Hardy blows into it to see if it still works, and an intertitle reads "flat," a pun on both the flat sound it makes and the fact that it has been flattened. This latter example points to the crucial role of intertitles in silent comedian comedy, which often commented ironically or sarcastically on the narrative or conveyed amusing dialogue or jokes. In *The High Sign*, an intertitle mocks the Blinking Buzzard gang using alliteration (fig. 3.80). Clearly, the absence of prerecorded synchronized sound did not mean that humor was confined to sight gags in silent comedian comedy.

As the creaking plank in *Jour de fête* and the crying baby in *Play Time* demonstrate, it is sometimes sounds in Tati's films that are misinterpreted by characters and spectators, giving rise to mutual interference gags and switch images. In *Mon Oncle*, Hulot's concierge is sitting outside his apartment building plucking a chicken when a passing cyclist squawks and the concierge jumps, thinking the chicken she is holding is still alive (mutual interference gag); and when Hulot's Amilcar rolls down the hill into the country estate in *Les Vacances* (fig. 3.18), the spare tire, to which a horn is affixed, falls off and rolls along beside it, the horn squeaking each time it passes under the tire (fig. 3.81). In another

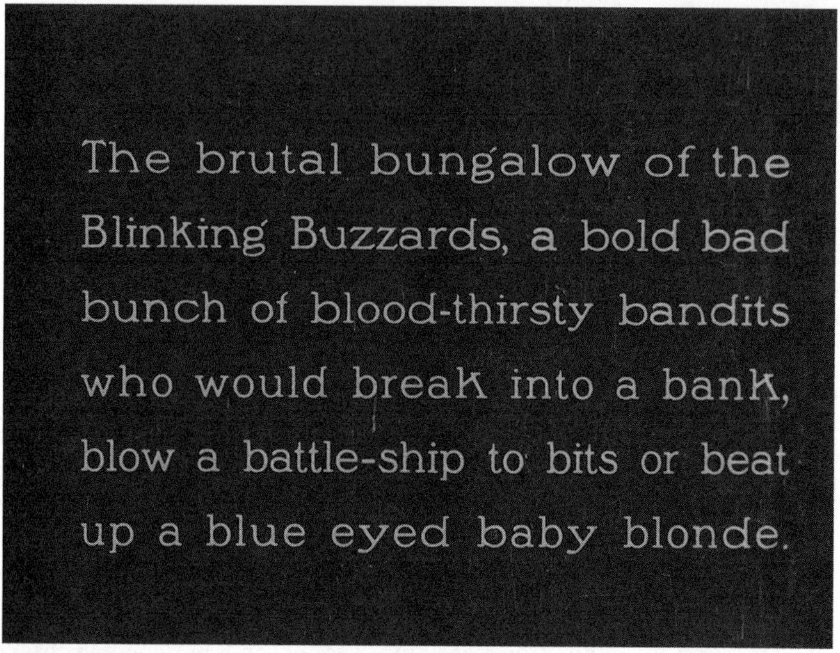

The brutal bungalow of the Blinking Buzzards, a bold bad bunch of blood-thirsty bandits who would break into a bank, blow a battle-ship to bits or beat up a blue eyed baby blonde.

FIGURE 3.80 Alliterative inter-title from *The High Sign*.

FIGURE 3.81 In *Les Vacances*, the horn on Hulot's spare tire squeaks as it rotates . . .

FIGURE 3.82 ... and the squeaks are mistaken by a nearby hunter for the sounds of a bird.

mutual interference gag, a hunter inside the estate mistakes the horn's squeaks for a bird at which he shoots (fig. 3.82). In the switch image involving glass and the ice cream truck at the end of *Play Time* (figs. 3.44 and 3.45), it is partly because we hear someone order from the ice cream vendor in the traffic circle that we assume the camera is outside, when in fact it is inside a building filming Barbara's departing bus through a closed window.

Tati frequently incorporates sound into his other gag structures as well. We wonder what has disrupted the exercise class in *Les Vacances* in part because the offscreen instructor ceases blowing his whistle, and the unusual clicking sound accompanying the floating object in *Mon Oncle* helps provoke our curiosity about what is behind the wall of the neighbor's garden (fig. 2.34). Again in *Mon Oncle*, Hulot adjusts a window in his penthouse and a bird twitters loudly offscreen when the window is in a particular position (fig. 3.83). The connection between the two remains mysterious until a reverse-angle shot reveals that the bird sings when light reflected from Hulot's windowpane falls on it (fig. 3.84). In these enlightenment images, Tati uses sound to make us aware of and inquisitive about something we cannot see because it lies beyond the edge of the frame or is hidden by the mise-en-scène, and the subsequent unanticipated explanation

FIGURE 3.83 In *Mon Oncle*, Hulot adjusts a window . . .

FIGURE 3.84 . . . to reflect sunlight onto a nearby bird, which twitters in delight.

for the sound creates humor. In other cases, the source of the sound is visually elided, and it is the sound itself that gives rise to comedy. When François returns to the post office after a night of drunken revelry in *Jour de fête*, he goes offscreen to shave, and the camera lingers on two postmen stamping letters. The exaggerated sounds of ancient plumbing groaning, creaking, and seemingly exploding as François, offscreen, runs water and bangs on the pipes disturbs them several times, just as the noise of Hulot having fun with the hikers offscreen at the end of the second day of his stay in *Les Vacances* wakes up other guests in the hotel.

A number of Tati's running and fragmented gags are also built around sounds. The guests relaxing during the evenings in the lobby of the hotel in *Les Vacances* are disrupted by loud music when Hulot plays a jazz record on the second night; he turns up the volume of the music at the masked ball on the fifth; the German businessman's son plays Hulot's jazz record on the sixth; and the hotel manager inadvertently turns it on again when awoken by the fireworks later that same night. In *Mon Oncle*, the gag in which Madame Arpel switches on the urinary-sounding fish fountain to impress visitors is repeated and varied eight times.

The gurgling, squirting fountain is also an example of Tati's tendency to exaggerate and distort the sounds made by certain objects and settings. Sometimes the result is equivalent to the incongruous details highlighted in the image. The distinctive bass twang made by the door to the dining room in *Les Vacances* is not particularly funny, nor is the flapping of the ticket on the dignitary's briefcase arriving at the airport in *Play Time*. Rather, Tati underscores such sounds because they are out of the ordinary and therefore counter the uniformity and standardization he feared. Often, however, Tati magnifies sounds in order to render the objects that make them absurd, such as the ancient plumbing in the post office in *Jour de fête*. This is especially true of the noises made by modern technologies, whose volume and intensity are often out of all proportion to their functions. In order to inform Giffard that Hulot has arrived for their meeting, the doorman of the modern office building in *Play Time* must perform an elaborate ritual of button pressing on the intercom, which issues a protracted series of beeps, crackles, and gurgles before the doorman finally gets through to someone who cannot initially understand him due to the poor sound quality (fig. 3.85). In *Mon Oncle*, Madame Arpel shows off her kitchen to the female visitors at the garden party. Offscreen we hear her shrieking "sterilization," "ventilation" above the din made by the gadgets she is demonstrating, which sound like industrial drills and ventilators. The noises made by the gadgets built into the camper in *Trafic* are equally preposterous—the shower, for instance, makes a long, loud burp before emitting water. Such exaggerated sounds are aural equivalents of the use of color to liken incongruous objects and settings. The absurdly

FIGURE 3.85 The intercom in *Play Time*.

loud clicking of Madame Arpel's shoes on the concrete floor of her home in *Mon Oncle* is echoed by the almost identical sound of the shoes of Monsieur Arpel's secretary on the cement floor of the factory, while the polished voice of the woman who makes announcements over the loudspeaker in Barbara's hotel in *Play Time* is similar to the announcer's voice at the airport. As these examples suggest, in many respects Tati's satire of modern life is articulated through his soundtrack, an issue I will take up in chapter 4.

An unusual feature of Tati's soundtracks is the frequent absence of sound perspective.[16] Traditionally in classical narrative cinema, the closer the camera is to something, such as a character speaking, the more the sound of that thing is given prominence on the soundtrack. Background noises are muted and rendered indistinct, while narratively important dialogue tends to be privileged above all else. Tati, however, often refrains from drawing the viewer's attention to significant information in the image, and the same is true on his soundtracks. In some scenes, sounds from sources both near and far are given equal weight, including the overlapping dialogue of multiple characters and noises from offscreen, and we only hear snatches of conversation amidst a cacophony of sounds. Moreover, the dialogue we do catch tends to be insignificant if not banal, and Tati tends to privilege background noises, such as the twang of the dining room door in *Les Vacances*, while minimizing if not eradicating voices and other sounds we would normally expect to hear. The result is that viewers can overlook narrative events

including gags when confronted by long shots depicting multiple actions generating a variety of sounds.

When Hulot leaves the restaurant with Barbara in a long shot in *Play Time*,
several events occur simultaneously. A woman in a white dress and her husband
walk across the shot into the cloakroom on the left to retrieve their coats, Barbara
is on the right in her green dress looking behind her, and another woman in a
blue dress on the far left of the shot waits for her coat. Even though the camera is
positioned outside the restaurant looking into the vestibule, the noise of people
singing, dancing, and talking offscreen is as loud as it was in the previous shot
from inside, and the voices of the people in the vestibule are therefore only
occasionally audible above the din. Thus, it is easy to miss the husband of the
first woman in the white dress mistakenly give a tip to a patron standing in the
middle of the shot (fig. 3.86) followed by the patron's verbal protest to the nearby
doorman that the tip is not for him (fig. 3.87). Similarly, in a high-angle long shot
of the garden party in *Mon Oncle*, most of the guests are congregated around
the table in the center-left of the shot while Pichard, Monsieur Arpel's factory
manager, is up to his shoulders digging in the gravel to repair the fountain on
the right. Behind him, Hulot, embarrassed that his shoes are wet from having
accidentally stepped in the fountain pool, is hiding behind a small hedge. Several
actions then occur simultaneously: Monsieur Arpel calls for Pichard and turns
toward him, the neighbor walks behind Arpel toward Hulot with a plate of food
and, on the way, bends down to Pichard, exclaiming "Honor to the worker,"

FIGURE 3.86 In *Play Time*, a man mistakenly tips a restaurant patron . . .

FIGURE 3.87 ... who angrily gives the tip to the doorman.

Georgette (the Arpels' maid) moves into the foreground to pick up a plate Hulot left on a chair, and Madame Arpel, in the middle of the shot, jokingly reprimands her husband for making Prichard work. In addition to the overlapping lines of dialogue spoken by these characters, we hear the sound of the gravel Pichard is digging, the chatter of the other guests around the table, and the loud laughter of Pichard's wife. Given everything that is going on visually and aurally, it is not hard to overlook Hulot running away, and the neighbor, who has brought a plate of food for him, searching for him in vain from beneath her ridiculous hat, which partly blocks her view (fig. 3.88).

However, on other occasions Tati uses sound to highlight gags that might otherwise be missed. Earlier in the party the guests relocate from one part of the garden to another. As two of them carry a table down some steps in a long shot, the most prominent sound is of liquid, which directs our attention to the contents from a jug on the table pouring perfectly into a nearby cup because of the incline (fig. 3.89). When the camper is being inspected by Dutch police in *Trafic*, a loud scraping sound (in addition to a medium shot) draws our gaze to Hulot accidentally ruffling up the hair of a cop with his arm, and in subsequent shots the man appears with a quiff. And in an action-packed shot in *Play Time* of various people sitting and standing around a table with Barbara playing the piano in the background accompanied by the aging chanteuse, a fizzing sound is clearly audible above the singing and chatter, which alerts us to the restaurant

FIGURE 3.88 During the garden party in *Mon Oncle*, the neighbor searches for Hulot, who can be seen running away in the background.

FIGURE 3.89 In *Mon Oncle*, the contents of a jug on a table pour into a cup as the table is tilted.

FIGURE 3.90 In *Play Time*, the restaurant manager prepares a drink of Alka-Seltzer . . .

manager dissolving some Alka-Seltzer in a glass of water (fig. 3.90). This action turns out to be a set up for a mutual interference gag, as Hulot, mistaking the glass of bubbling liquid for champagne, drinks from it and grimaces at the taste (fig. 3.91).

Nor is it true that dialogue is never privileged, and in fact some of Tati's gags are dependent on it. Earlier in the restaurant scene, the manager overhears a couple talking about an international financier who is dancing in a ridiculous fashion, and he passes on the information to the head waiter who is standing next to him (fig. 4.57). Seconds later, the manager realizes the couple is discussing a different, almost identical man who is dancing equally absurdly, and he again informs the head waiter (fig. 4.58). His words can be heard above the restaurant noise, for if they weren't, the joke about how easy it is to confuse men of finance would be lost. When Maria finishes changing her outfit in her car outside the exposition in *Trafic*, two workers standing nearby make lewd comments about her. However, the language they use—"Look at those accessories," "Well equipped," and "Uh oh, cross traffic" when another woman approaches—could be applied to cars, and the irony is comic. Even in *Les Vacances*, whose dialogue André Bazin famously described as insignificant, words sometimes play a role in the humor. The aleatory object-sound analog involving the colonel being bombarded by fireworks is in part set up by his perpetual prattling throughout the film about military matters as well as the commands he issues during the

FIGURE 3.91 ... which Hulot mistakes for a glass of champagne.

picnic; and the German businessman accidentally swims in the wrong direction when called to the phone for the umpteenth time by the waiter. Nor is dialogue the only means of verbal humor in Tati's films, as he occasionally uses written signs to ironic effect. As we have seen, Ideal Cheese is the name of the stand on which Hulot deposits the yellow sponge in *Play Time*; and in *Trafic*, one of the wrecked cars towed into the police station has a Just Married sign on it. In a switch image in *Mon Oncle*, Gérard's parents watch him adoringly through his bedroom door doing his homework, his back to them and the camera. After they leave, a reverse-angle shot reveals that he is in fact blowing water through a plastic tube attached to the blowhole of a whale pictured on the front cover of his textbook, which is called *Sciences Naturelles*.

The above examples in which dialogue is audible demonstrate that the absence of sound perspective in Tati's films is confined to specific sequences. The noise of something, such as characters talking, will often increase in volume the closer the camera is to it as in classical narrative cinema. During the funeral scene in *Les Vacances*, for instance, the dialogue between Hulot and the mourners helping him restart his car becomes louder when Tati cuts to closer shots of them and quieter when he cuts away. Yet even when employing this convention, Tati will sometimes turn it on its head for comic effect. The convention is designed to ensure, along with mobile framing, that we clearly perceive the most important thing in a shot. Tati, however, often stages the most significant action at some

FIGURE 3.92 In *Les Vacances*, we cannot hear Hulot explaining how he was propelled into the river by the tow rope.

distance from the camera out of earshot, thereby creating an aural ellipsis in which we can see but cannot hear what is happening. Later in *Les Vacances*, on the day of the picnic, Hulot steps on the rope being used to tow his broken-down Amilcar as the rope becomes taut and it propels him into the nearby harbor. When he gets out and explains how he ended up in the water to the tow truck driver and a passerby, Tati films them in a long shot (fig. 3.92). The convention of sound perspective dictates that we cannot hear what he is saying because he is too far away, but we can imagine his words as he mimes the sequence of events to his incredulous interlocutors. In *Mon Oncle*, the switch image in which Hulot appears to berate his concierge's daughter for dropping the tomatoes deceives us in part because it is filmed from a distance and we cannot hear Hulot's words (fig. 2.43); and in *Play Time*, the aleatory object analog involving Schneller and Giffard's families appearing to watch each other through their shared apartment wall works because the camera is filming from the street and we therefore cannot hear the sounds of their television sets (fig. 3.21). In general, for reasons we will explore shortly, Tati uses visual and aural ellipses in order to encourage the viewer to imagine what is happening offscreen or out of earshot.

Tati also deceives or confuses the viewer about the source of the music on his soundtracks. Music we assume to be extradiegetic is suddenly revealed to be emanating from within the narrative world or vice-versa, and sometimes its source is ambiguous. In *Les Vacances*, the extradiegetic jazz theme returns when Martine puts on a record at the beginning of the second day, and we therefore assume it is coming from her phonograph. However, the music continues without alteration over a cut to the beach where we are too far from Martine's room to hear it, suggesting it might be extradiegetic after all. Tati later repeats but reverses this gag when music fades in at the end of the cemetery scene and continues across a cut to the hotel at night where we see Henry and his wife depart for their evening stroll followed by Martine closing her bedroom window. Because it is not interrupted by these temporal and spatial shifts, we suppose the music is extradiegetic until Martine looks down the stairs inside the guest house at an elderly gentleman who appears to be listening to it on a radio. The music subsequently fades out when Tati cuts away from the guesthouse. In *Mon Oncle*, Monsieur Arpel calls Hulot from his boss's office to inform him that he has a job at the plastics factory. The jubilant French accordion music that had previously appeared to be extradiegetic can be heard down the crackling phone line, as if there are street musicians performing it near the public phone from where Hulot is speaking. However, when we cut to Hulot cycling away from the phone booth (having left the phone off the hook so that Arpel's boss can still hear the music on his phone line), no musicians are in sight, and the film never reveals a diegetic source for the music, which we hear numerous times again. After Hulot leaves the apartment of his army-buddy, Schneller, in *Play Time* and looks around in wonder and confusion at the tall, identical modern office and apartment buildings surrounding him, the film's familiar extradiegetic theme fades in although in a new, slower arrangement with an organ. It continues uninterrupted across a cut to a shot of a radio in Barbara's hotel room, and the music now seems to be accompanying a radio advertisement for Quick Cleaner. A variation on this type of gag involves characters who somehow know the extradiegetic theme music. In *Mon Oncle*, when Hulot and Gérard are driven home in a horse-drawn cart by the people they befriended when trying to get rid of the defective plastic tubing, the group sings along to the extradiegetic French accordion theme simultaneously playing on the soundtrack; and at the police station in *Trafic*, a prisoner plays a slow, wistful version of the film's theme tune on his mouth organ accompanied by the whistling and singing of his cell mates.

INDIVIDUALITY

The deception and confusion engendered by such musical gags is, as we have seen throughout this chapter, a central principal of Tati's comic style. Although many of Tati's gags are transparent and afford viewers the omniscience typical of classical comedian comedy, others are, to varying degrees, rendered opaque through ellipsis, fragmentation, dispersal and intertwining, being left unexploited, or being filmed in such a manner that they are barely perceptible. Tati's soundtracks similarly oscillate between highlighting gags, as in the example of the pouring jug on the table in *Mon Oncle*, and obscuring them, as when there is no sound perspective and a cacophony of sounds competes for our attention, or offscreen noises make us aware of what is being visually elided. I have argued that Tati deliberately obscures some aspects of his comedy in order to encourage his viewers to search for it in his images and sounds. By forcing them to look for the humor in his films, he hoped his audiences would become more like himself—that is, observers who deliberately seek out the comedy of everyday life outside of the movie theater. They would become active participants in the comedy happening all around them in their daily lives, thereby counteracting the passivity Tati viewed as characteristic of modernity.

However, there was another, related reason for Tati's comic opacity, which is that Tati believed it fostered individual responses to his films. I have already noted Tati's hostility to standardization, which he associated with modernity, and his love of the unique, such as the incongruous details he frequently highlights in the image and on the soundtrack. This concern extended to his audiences. Whereas television and mainstream films are experienced uniformly thanks to the control they exert over the viewer's attention, his style, he suggested, permitted audiences a degree of choice over what to perceive. "It is partly the picture you make it, what you see, what you choose," he stated.[17] One spectator, for example, might watch the boy trying on the black plastic coat in the background of the shot of the cheese stand in *Play Time* while another tracks the two women in the foreground complaining about Hulot's use of English. Indeed, Tati suggested that *Play Time* empowered the viewer to the degree that he (Tati) was no longer its author. Instead, "it's the way you like it or you don't. . . . It's not a picture that you say, 'I am the Author, I am the Director; I am the Gagman and here, Ah ha ha ha.' Maybe the man you will find funny in the film will not be the same one someone else will find funny. You may find everyone funny or no one funny."[18]

Statements such as these conflict with Tati's frequent espousal of the *politique des auteurs* and his use of mise-en-scène, sound, and occasionally the mobile frame to direct the viewer's attention toward (and sometimes away from) a gag. Earlier in the interview from which the above quotation is extracted, for example, he discusses his use of color "to help the audience look where I think it is important to look," and in general Tati's dissolution of the individual comedian and democratic filmmaking style are, paradoxically, hallmarks of his authorial signature. Nevertheless, that spectators notice gags overlooked by others and vice-versa when watching Tati's films means they can have quite different experiences of them.

Nor is this diversity of responses confined to perception, as for Tati observation was bound up with imagination. He reported that, while watching people in the streets, he often fantasized about what they were saying to each other because they were out of earshot, and in the interview with *Cahiers du cinéma* in 1968 following the release of *Play Time*, he recounted a story of a guest who left a dinner party only to knock on the door half an hour later explaining that he had been unable to locate the exit out of the garden in the dark. This prompted Tati to amuse himself by imagining what had happened to the man in the intervening thirty minutes, and the story he invented reached fantastic proportions.[19] Tati's style, particularly his use of visual and aural ellipsis as well as his potential gags, affords the viewer many opportunities to engage in similar acts of imaginative reconstruction. By leaving events offscreen, spectators can arrive at their own conjectures about what has happened beyond the frame— when, for example, Hulot is unable to find the button to exit the vestibule of Schneller's apartment in *Play Time* or is chased by dogs out of the country estate in *Les Vacances* and reappears hours later still being hounded by them. And by filming the events in Schneller and Giffard's apartments from the street, the conversations between the characters inside are elided and we must infer them for ourselves on the basis of their behavior. Meanwhile, potential gags are imagination pumps, prompting viewers to devise their own scenarios for how they might become fully-fledged gags. Tati's style, in other words, counteracts the standardization that is putatively inherent in modern life and mass culture, and that for many is typified by cinema, both by making it likely that one viewer will miss what another perceives and by allowing spectators to imagine their own scenarios to fill in visual and aural ellipses.

Explicating Tati's rationale for his comic style has required touching on his critique of modernity, which we must now consider in much more depth. But whatever one thinks of this critique, it is worth bearing in mind that it motivated

Tati's comic and stylistic innovations. Tati was by no means a formalist, at least if by this contested term one means an artist who experiments solely for the sake of artistic innovation. Rather, his aesthetic inventions were motivated by his profound beliefs about the modern world, and it is to the precise nature of these beliefs and the ways they play out in his films that we now turn.

CHAPTER 4

SATIRIZING MODERNITY

TATI AND MODERNIZATION

Tati's feature film–making career coincided almost exactly with the thirty-year period of rapid economic growth in postwar France that has come to be known as *les trente glorieuses* (1945–1975).[1] Consumption and incomes rose by a third between 1949, the year that saw the release of Tati's first feature film, *Jour de fête*; and 1958, when his third, *Mon Oncle*, appeared. In these same years, the amount of privately owned cars more than doubled, while the quantity of home appliances such as vacuum cleaners increased by 400 percent.[2] From 1958 until 1974, when Tati's final feature, *Parade*, received its premiere at the Cannes Film Festival, per capita income grew by 80 percent, and the number of households owning a refrigerator and washing machine rose from one in four to nine out of ten and three out of four respectively.[3] As Kristin Ross puts it in her influential account of postwar French modernization, during the three decades in which Tati was making his feature-length films, France was transformed from a "rural, empire-oriented, Catholic country" into an "industrialized, decolonized, and urban one" with "unusual swiftness."[4]

According to Ross, in France, "unlike in the United States, [modernization] is experienced for the most part as highly destructive."[5] For her, Tati is the "greatest analyst of postwar French modernization" in part because his films convey this destructiveness, and she is hardly alone in holding this view.[6] The prevailing opinion of Tati's films is that modernization is their central theme and that they are critical of the changes it wrought in postwar France, particularly suburbanization, the widespread adoption of architectural modernism, and the burgeoning car and consumer cultures. "The foes in all five Tati feature films are modernity, inhuman efficiency, deadening routine," states Gerald Mast.[7] For some, their critique of modernization is one of their defects. Jean-André Fieschi decries their "worn-out," "reactionary" ideology, which he characterizes as the "classic world vision of the *petite bourgeoisie française* (that of the films of René Clair), flattering and catering to the most suspicious sort of individualism, the most maudlin sentimentality, the little *bistro*, the little dog, facile nostalgia, bewilderment when confronted with a modern world fundamentally not understood."[8] For most, it is a virtue. "*Mon Oncle* is to progress what the pacifist film is to war," writes Armand Cauliez, "a defense and illustration of individual liberties, the humble pleasures of existence and simple human happiness. This cry of revolt is the profound song of a humane person, a small crack in the edifice of logic."[9] Lucy Fischer views Tati's work "in its totality" as a "clear, considered, and profound exploration of a select number of themes," chief among them being the "malign effect" of the assembly line on work, leisure, objects, and architecture.[10] James Harding argues that *Play Time*, along with *Mon Oncle* and *Trafic*, "pleaded for a sense of proportion and humanity among the brutal architecture and mechanical nightmares of the consumer society."[11] And Laurent Marie claims that "Tati criticizes the alienating impact of technology" in a manner akin to the avant-garde situationist group.[12]

Tati's stated view of modernization, however, was more nuanced and contradictory than this critical consensus might lead one to expect. To be sure, he often railed against what he saw as the uniformity and authoritarianism of modern environments; the anonymity and lack of communication they fostered; the passivity engendered by the automation of everyday life; and the standardized, even mechanical behavior of modern people. He also frequently expressed nostalgia for the past. In the interview with André Bazin and François Truffaut that appeared in *Cahiers du cinéma* in 1958, he reminisced:

> I miss the old buses with their open-air upper decks. The new buses have lost their personality. In Paris, these platforms were wonderful meeting places. And everyone had his own way of pulling the little chain to request a stop. . . . There were conversations too, lots of them. Today people get on the bus, and, inside, it may be more practical, but I'm not so sure: the driver is in a glass cage, one no longer knows whether one should buy a movie or a bus ticket from him, he deals with you through a small porthole but he does not answer you, for he cannot. People must wait in line, whereas this process used to go much faster; you just stepped onto some stairs, everyone pushed, you climbed, and, in brief, you go to your place.[13]

Yet Tati rejected the charge that his films were unequivocally critical of modernization. "Hulot is not a reactionary," he insisted about the character he played in four of his six features. "He is not against progress."[14] And he acknowledged the benefits of modernization while pointing to its costs: "All over the world, people are now living in surroundings which make everything more comfortable for them—work, home life, holidays. This greater ease makes for more efficiency. The trouble is, though, that the top people seem to have forgotten to leave room for adjustment and for spare time."[15] In the 1968 interview with the editors of *Cahiers du cinéma*, he dismissed the accusation that he was attacking modern architecture. If he were, he demurred, he would have modeled Tativille, his elaborate, expensive set for *Play Time*, on the ugliest modern buildings. Instead, he deliberately designed it "so that no architect could criticize my set," using the "most beautiful" buildings he could find.[16] "My job is not to criticize," he persisted, but instead "to bring a little smile" to peoples' faces.[17] Yet a few years later, when asked by Jonathan Rosenbaum about the buildings in *Play Time*, he did criticize modern architecture while still acknowledging its beauty:

> In New York sometimes, when you're very high up and look out the window, you have a marvelous vista of lights—it's very impressive. But if you go down the elevator at say, six in the morning, what you see isn't so impressive. It looks like you're not allowed to laugh or whistle or be yourself: you have to push the button where it says "push," there's not much way of expressing yourself.[18]

Such shifting statements suggest that Tati's view of modernization was more ambivalent, even conflicted than is usually acknowledged, as do several recurring features of his films.[19] Some have claimed that Monsieur Hulot actively attacks the modern world much like the Tramp in the opening scene of Charlie Chaplin's *Modern Times* (1936) disrupts the factory in which he works (fig. 4.1). Lucy Fischer argues that, just as "the Tramp sabotages the assembly line," so Hulot "openly infiltrates the enemy lines and launches a direct assault" on modern life when he visits his "fireworks blitzkrieg on the sleeping guests" in the hotel at the end of *Les vacances de Monsieur Hulot*, and "encourages the Royal Garden guests to destroy the restaurant's sterile decor" in *Play Time*.[20] But in fact Hulot does neither of these things intentionally.[21] He inadvertently lights the fireworks in *Les vacances* when he seeks refuge from a pack of dogs inside a hut at night and strikes a match to view his surroundings, and he then tries desperately to put them out. In *Play Time*, he mistakenly causes the restaurant's ceiling to collapse when attempting to procure a piece of fruit decorating the rafters for the

FIGURE 4.1 The Tramp squirts oil at the other factory workers in *Modern Times* (Charlie Chaplin, 1936).

American businessman's dancing companion (figs. 2.4 and 2.5). Far from then encouraging other diners to follow his example, he apologizes profusely to the restaurant manager and the architect.

Rather than an outlaw/fugitive who wages war on society, Hulot is instead an example of what film theorist Steve Seidman calls the loner/reject character type recurring throughout comedian comedy, one who is "excluded from the social mainstream" not out of choice but because he is "hopelessly naïve and innocent, unable to function in society, or to contribute to it."[22] Indeed, like many of the characters played by Buster Keaton and Harold Lloyd, and unlike, say, the Marx Brothers, Hulot tries hard to fit in with those around him. As David Bellos puts it, his posture and behavior express an "apologetic eagerness to please" as well as acute embarrassment when he fails to do so.[23] Yet in certain contexts he fails to conform despite his best intentions, and his misunderstandings and pratfalls set him apart from others and are the source of much humor. Without a doubt, it is aspects of the modern world to which Hulot is frequently unable to acclimatize himself, and in this respect, Tati updates the comedian-as-outcast

SATIRIZING MODERNITY ✦ 179

strain of comedic modernism discussed in chapter 1. We saw in that chapter that modernists identified with the comedian's eccentricity and concomitant failure to fit into society not only because they viewed themselves as outsiders. They also perceived in the clown's estrangement a resistance to the social forces that repelled them, such as the philistinism of the bourgeoisie, the utilitarianism of commercial culture, the rationalism of modern life, and so on. Tati seized on the convention of the alienated clown, crafting in Hulot a character who is unintentionally comic because he finds it difficult to conform to the modern environments being erected after the war and the forms of behavior they engendered. But this is not because Hulot is hostile toward them—for he does his best to adjust to them—but because, as we shall soon discover, they *confuse* him. New buildings, technologies, and objects that, for the most part, are navigated with ease by other characters are perplexing and mysterious to Hulot. His bewildered rather than antagonistic reaction to modern environments indicates that Tati's intention was to create in Hulot a character who is alienated from modernity in the sense that he is struggling to adapt to the rapid changes in modern life rather than being necessarily opposed to them. "People like me have not been able to adapt," Tati complained to Bazin and Truffaut. "All this change came too fast. It came so fast that lots of people have been left behind. And what do we do with them now?"[24]

The same can be said of François the village postman, Tati's character in *Jour de fête* who, having seen a documentary about the mechanized postal service in the United States, tries and fails to emulate the speed and efficiency of American postal workers when making his rounds on his bicycle. Although he is different from Hulot in many respects, like Hulot he does not actively resist change. On the contrary, he does his best to embrace it but is ultimately unable to. Moreover, by the time we reach *Trafic* in the early 1970s, Hulot appears to have become acclimated to modern life. Far from being the unemployed castoff from modernity of previous films, he now works for a car company designing a gadget-laden camping vehicle and is no longer confounded by modern technologies and buildings. While his eagerness to please still occasionally lands him in trouble, for the most part the film's comedy derives from its satire of car culture rather than from Hulot's ineptness in the modern world. Meanwhile, modern settings are sometimes sources of play, humor, and even wonder in Tati's films, suggesting that for Tati they could be enchanting as well as alienating. The most famous example is the traffic circle at the end of *Play Time*, which resembles a merry-go-round (fig. 2.6), but there are others such as the camper in *Trafic* with its creative and amusing gadgets, or the bouncing plastic jug in the kitchen of the Arpels' house in *Mon Oncle*, in which Hulot takes obvious delight.

The depiction of Americanization in Tati's work seems equally equivocal. I observed at the beginning of chapter 2 that the influx of American movies, advertisements, books, popular music, and consumer items into France in the postwar era prompted the country's intellectual and artistic elite to start accusing American culture of imperialism, of erasing cultural differences through homogenous, mass produced products that pacify consumers. There are certainly traces of this viewpoint in Tati's films, particularly *Play Time*. Most obviously, the film's title exemplifies the penetration of (American) English into the French language (Franglais) that guardians of French culture were becoming increasingly anxious about, and English words and phrases are sprinkled throughout the conversations of the film's French characters and are visible in their environs. The restaurant in which most the film's second half takes place is called the Royal Garden, and its head waiter sometimes greets even French diners in English. "Drugstore" is emblazoned on a fluorescent sign on the side of a nearby pharmacy-cum-bar (fig. 4.2), and when Barbara decamps there with some of the other diners following their night of revelry at the restaurant, she innocently asks Hulot how to say *drugstore* in French. Outside, Barbara and Hulot pass a stall labeled Ideal Cheese, and there are prominent signs advertising the *Herald Tribune* and Marlboro cigarettes. Hulot pops into a store to find Barbara a gift, telling her in English that he'll be right back, and two passersby loudly complain that they cannot understand him and that he should be

FIGURE 4.2 English signs outside the restaurant in *Play Time* (Jacques Tati, 1967).

FIGURE 4.3 An American serviceman interrupts Barbara taking a photograph of the flower seller in *Play Time*.

speaking French. The previous day, Barbara had been repeatedly interrupted while trying to take a photograph of a flower vendor, including by two teenagers dressed in American-style jeans, sneakers, and bomber jackets who are listening to American popular music on a transistor radio. An American off-duty serviceman then asks Barbara to stand by the flower vendor so that he can take a picture of them both, further impeding her (fig. 4.3). When her party of American tourists enters the nearby home furnishings exposition, one of them announces in delight that it has "American stuff," and while she is getting dressed at her hotel that evening, Barbara listens to a radio advertisement for Quick Cleaner. It is little wonder that, at the beginning of the film on arriving at the airport with its French and English signs and its modern design, another member of Barabra's party proclaims that she "feels at home."

Yet, it is significant that, in other instances, it is Americans and American culture that disrupt the homogeneity of the modern environment, thereby allowing for the carnivalesque, utopian moments of communal enjoyment mentioned in chapter 2 to emerge. As I observed in chapter 1, the European avant-garde of the 1910s and 1920s contrasted what they viewed as "America's wild and primitive modernity" with "Europe's tradition-bound character," and the association of America with a revitalizing primitivism is also present in Tati's films.[25] One of the first arrivals at the restaurant in *Play Time* is a rowdy American businessman, who tells his female companion that they're going to have a "hot time tonight,"

and he is a major catalyst of the merriment that ensues. As the dancing intensi-
fies, it is he who first tries to reach the piece of fruit on the ceiling's rafters before
the taller Hulot grasps it for him, causing part of the ceiling to collapse (figs.
2.4 and 2.5). The American then uses the dangling rafters as a partition to create
his own makeshift nightclub within the restaurant, initially admitting only those
whose backs have been imprinted by the restaurant's chairs, the backs of which
are shaped like crowns (fig. 4.4). He buys champagne for the group inside his
club, who gather around a table laughing, and he begins wearing the glasses of the
German businessman, which Hulot broke earlier in the day (fig. 4.5). When the
ceiling collapses further and scares the jazz band away, the American businessman jumps up on stage and asks for volunteers to replace them, and he is the one
who places a red, white, and blue coaster on the black semicircular shutter above
the chef's head, making it look as though the chef is wearing a bicorne hat with
a cockade (fig. 4.6). Throughout the restaurant scene, he can be seen enjoining
everyone else to sing, dance, and have fun, and it is in part because of his example
that the rigid, supercilious behavior of the restaurant's French patrons gives way
to unconstrained gaiety. Their attitude also changes because of the American jazz
music played by the band of black musicians.[26] Once the band begins performing, the diners dance in a more frenzied, unselfconscious manner, their number
increasing until the dance floor is a mass of bodies.

FIGURE 4.4 The American businessman's makeshift nightclub in *Play Time*.

FIGURE 4.5 The American businessman, wearing the German salesman's broken eyeglasses, directs the festivities in *Play Time*.

American jazz music also plays an important role at the end of *Mon Oncle*, when it appears as though the passengers at the airport from which Hulot is departing are dancing (fig. 2.38). Monsieur Arpel then bonds with his son for the first time and, laughing, they drive out of the airport parking lot the wrong way

FIGURE 4.6 The American businessman creates an object analog in *Play Time*.

FIGURE 4.7 Gérard and his father bond at the end of *Mon Oncle* (Jacques Tati, 1958).

in Arpel's American car, a pink and lime green 1956 Chevrolet Bel Air (figs. 4.7 and 4.15). While this car is an example of the Arpels' conspicuous consumption, it also introduces bright colors and variety into the otherwise uniformly black, gray, and white carscape we have seen throughout the film, just as the green, red, and other vivid colors of the clothes worn by Barbara's party of American tourists punctuates the muted colors of the French bourgeoisie in the Royal Garden (color figure 8). It is also worth noting that modernization is depicted in these films as just as much European as American in origin. It is European architectural modernism that is satirized by the Arpels' house in *Mon Oncle* (a point to which I will return), and its modern gadgets are made in Monsieur Arpel's French factory. In *Play Time*, the company selling the doors that "slam . . . in golden silence" is German, as is the malfunctioning air conditioner in the Royal Garden, which is one reason the restaurant's French architect is unable to operate it.

In the following, I aim to convey some of the complexity and ambivalence of Tati's satire of modernity in *Mon Oncle* and *Play Time*, the two films in which he systematically depicts characters interacting with ultramodern environments. (Although I will briefly mention *Trafic* at the end, the film follows Hulot and his fellow workers as they transport their gadget-laden camping-car in a truck from Paris to an exposition in Amsterdam, and it mostly transpires on the roads in between as well as the garages where their truck and camping-car are taken for repairs and the police station where it is impounded.) While *Play Time* largely takes place within a cluster of new, high-rise commercial and residential buildings in Paris, *Mon Oncle* is set in the old quarter of Saint-Maur, just beyond the Bois de Vincennes southeast of the city, where Hulot lives, and a nearby redevelopment, where Hulot's sister, Madame Arpel, and her family reside in a pseudo-modernist house. Ross, like other critics, argues that the scenes of the Arpels in their suburban home offer a "critique of the kind of life it is possible to live inside hypermodern suburban architecture."[27] But as we have seen, Tati protested that he was not criticizing modern architecture in his films, and he objected that *Mon Oncle* "is not about the house"[28]:

> I am sure if a young couple were married and went to live in that house, they would be happy . . . because they would put down a little ground and they would play football with their children. They would have the big window for the sun to come into their home; they would cook with all the modern facilities and they would be happy. It is not the architecture I am complaining about in *My Uncle*, it is the way the people use it that is the problem.[29]

Is Tati right that it is the *particular use* of the suburban home by the Arpels that he criticizes, or is the house itself, along with modern environments in general, that are his target, as Ross and other critics maintain?

MON ONCLE AND THE BOURGEOISIE

By the mid-1950s, the housing shortage in the Paris region was both acute and well publicized. A 1954 study found that 36 percent of families begun in 1948 remained unhoused by 1952, and 29 percent of married couples under the age of twenty-five lived with their parents. An estimated 80 percent of the housing stock in the city had been built before 1914, and most of it was overcrowded and primitive. Around 65 percent of residences only had one or two rooms, and many lacked utilities such as a toilet (51 percent) and a bathtub or shower (80 percent). The *îlots insalubres*—the seventeen areas designated as slums in the early part of the century because of their high rates of tuberculosis—still existed, and dotted around Paris were impoverished shanty towns.[30]

As the economy expanded after the war, Paris was rapidly redeveloped, and between the mid-1950s and mid-1970s an astonishing 24 percent of the surface of the city was demolished and rebuilt.[31] In some cases, whole neighborhoods were razed and replaced by modern-high rise office and apartment buildings of the sort mimicked by Tativille in *Play Time*, such as the slum area (*îlot* 4) around the Place d'Italie in the Thirteenth Arrondissement and the Front de Seine to the south of the Eiffel Tower in the Fifteenth.[32] Most of the new housing, however, was private and expensive, with government-subsidized accommodation accounting for only about a fifth. This was nowhere near enough stock to meet the increasing demand for affordable homes resulting from population growth, immigration, and the expanding economy, which drove up rents and property values in the city. The result was an exodus of the working-class and young families to the suburbs, and a decline in the residential population of Paris, which increasingly consisted of the affluent.[33]

In order to accommodate the growing suburban population, the state constructed huge housing projects (*les grands ensembles*) outside the city. These collections of high-rise towers and five- or six-story buildings typically housed 30,000 to 40,000 people each and were connected to Paris via new autoroutes and a suburban railway (the Reseau Express Regional). The surrounding region was also redeveloped. New towns were planned and suburban centers reconstructed, including Creteil, adjacent to Saint-Maur, where Tati shot some exteriors for the modern suburb in which the Arpels reside in *Mon Oncle*. Gray, concrete slabs typical of the new accommodations being erected at the time can be seen in the background whenever characters travel between the old and new quarters in the film (fig. 4.8). Redeveloped suburban centers such as Creteil were also intended to reduce congestion in the city by creating employment, and in addition to new housing they included office buildings, factories for the industry that was increasingly migrating out of the city, and shopping malls.[34] Facilities tended to be dispersed, and residents were more dependent on cars to access them. In *Mon Oncle*, Monsieur Arpel drives his son, Gérard, to school before continuing on to his plastics factory, and he and his wife drive to a restaurant (Rington's) to celebrate their anniversary. When he and Gérard drive Hulot to the airport at the end of the film, industrial parks and office buildings are visible along the route.

It is striking, however, that in most other respects, as David Bellos has astutely noted, the Arpels' home is not at all representative of suburbanization as it was occurring in the Paris region in the mid- to late-1950s.[35] Monsieur Arpel is a bourgeois industrialist who lives with his wife and son in a recently built, detached, single-family house with a large, walled garden on a street of

FIGURE 4.8 The wall that separates the new and old quarters in *Mon Oncle*; modern housing is visible in the background.

similar homes, whereas the vast majority of suburban accommodation being constructed during this period consisted of apartments in towers and blocks intended for the less affluent who could not afford to live in the city.[36] While such housing became the object of widespread criticism in the 1960s for being dehumanizing, it is glimpsed only occasionally in *Mon Oncle* and remains very much in the background. Instead, as the architectural historian Dietrich Neumann has pointed out, the design of the Arpels' home alludes to the cubic houses built by Le Corbusier and other modernist architects in the interwar years and is hardly typical of the small number of single-family suburban homes constructed after the war.[37] Why, then, did Tati invoke prewar modernist architecture in a postwar context? Neumann argues that it was in order to lampoon the bourgeois appropriation of once-revolutionary modernist architecture as a status symbol. As he puts it, "With sharp irony, Tati revealed the transformation in meaning of the forms of classical modernism from avant-garde statement to petit-bourgeois fashion item."[38] It is not postwar suburbanization per se that Tati is attacking in the film, therefore, but rather a particular, and atypical, bourgeois form of it. Indeed, a number of Tati's comments from the period show that he was not opposed to the construction of new towns and suburban centers to alleviate the housing shortage in Paris. In the interview with Bazin and Truffaut, for example, he complains: "What bothers me most today is that Paris itself is being destroyed. This really aggravates me. If we need additional housing, and God knows we do, let's build new cities; there is enough room. But we should not demolish nice old buildings in Paris for the sake of new apartment buildings."[39] Moreover, Tati sometimes characterized his comedy as anti-elitist, claiming it was designed to make fun of powerful people and thereby give ordinary folk a feeling of superiority over them. "I'm always . . . trying to defend the simple man," he told Jonathan Rosenbaum in the early 1970s.[40]

> I *can* make Hulot do all the jokes because I come from the music hall and I can do it quite well, but it's not my way. I'd rather show an important man doing something funny, because then people will look around and say, "Why is he speaking so loud? He isn't really that important." I mean, comedy can put a lot of people down.[41]

As noted in chapter 2, Tati's goal of democratizing comedy resulted in the incorporation of a multitude of secondary characters into his gags, and his humor is by no means confined to important people. Nevertheless, his films do tend to ridicule the bourgeoisie, such as the German businessman and other seaside vacationers in *Les vacances*, the Arpels and their friends in *Mon Oncle*, and the diners at the upscale restaurant in *Play Time*. And Tati remarked,

> *Mon Oncle* was a huge success because it's a slap in the face against the bourgeoisie. It was a genuine film of dissent for the time. I'm not saying that I started May '68, but . . . you know, that's another thing they've said against me. Because in *Mon Oncle*, in fact, what I am saying to a family is this: I'm very sorry, but you seem to be very interested in your car, your factory, in the number of meters of piping that your factory puts out, and then you want your son to be first in his class at school, but there is no human warmth, and so on.[42]

Tati's films thereby perpetuate the satirical strain of comedic modernism identified in chapter 1 and exemplified by works such as René Clair and Francis Picabia's *Entr'acte* (1924), which draws on the conventions of comedian comedy to mock the upper classes.

That Tati is targeting the Arpels' use of their home as a bourgeois fashion statement rather than contemporary suburbanization in general is also suggested by the ways in which the design of their house betrays only a superficial understanding of prewar modernist domestic architecture. Le Corbusier's residences of the later 1920s and 1930s, such as the exquisite Villa Savoye (1928–1931) (fig. 4.9), tended to consist of single geometric volumes (usually cubes) resting on slender columns (*pilotis*). Horizontal strip windows were set flush with unadorned, planar white or colored facades, making the facades resemble thin membranes and creating the appearance of weightlessness. Symmetrical exteriors partly concealed free, asymmetrical interiors in which unconventionally situated rooms were ingeniously positioned in order to create a play of space and light along what Le Corbusier called an architectural promenade. The Arpels' home, by contrast, is an asymmetrical pyramid of cubes. Vertical, rectangular windows and doorways punctuate large expanses of thick wall on the ground floor, creating the impression of mass that architects of the International Style attempted

FIGURE 4.9 Le Corbusier, *Villa Savoye*, 1928–31.

FIGURE 4.10 Villa Arpel in *Mon Oncle*.

to dispense with and minimizing natural light in the interior (fig. 4.10). Inside, the plan is relatively open, but none of the rooms is unconventionally situated and there is no play with space or light, let alone an architectural promenade. If anything, the house resembles the irregular, vertical aggregations of cubes first explored by Theo van Doesburg in his effort to translate de Stijl principles into architecture in the late 1910s and subsequently taken up by Robert Mallet-Stevens in his designs for the Villa Noailles (1924–1933) and other houses in the mid-1920s (fig. 4.11). However, whereas rectangular planes of primary color were essential to de Stijl architecture, as evidenced by the exteriors of van Doesburg's plans and the interior of the extraordinary Rietveld Schroder House (1924), the walls of the Arpels' home, both inside and out, are a monochromatic gray, except for what appear to be blue girders on one side of the house. Meanwhile, although the walls are largely unadorned, on the second floor the facade is corrugated, as is part of the ground floor wall to the right of the entrance (fig. 4.12). Both the corrugation and the blue girders seem purely decorative, violating the modernist

FIGURE 4.11 Robert Mallet-Stevens, *Project for a Villa*, 1924.

© 2019 Estate of Robert Mallet-Stevens/Artists Rights Society (ARS), New York/ADAGP, Paris.

FIGURE 4.12 Villa Arpel in *Mon Oncle*.

FIGURE 4.13 Robert Mallet-Stevens, *Villa Noailles*, 1924–1933.

prohibition on ornament as exemplified by the outside of Mallet Stevens's Villa Noailles (fig. 4.13). Finally, on the second floor are two circular windows, which unbalance the building and look incongruous relative to the vertical rectangular windows of the ground floor, and which become the basis of an aleatory object analog that allows Tati to mock the building: when Monsieur and Madame Arpel look out of them at night, their silhouettes make the round windows look like eyes with moving pupils (fig. 2.8). Rather than express a coherent functional or aesthetic rationale, the Arpels' house seems more like a bricolage of improperly understood stylistic elements associated with 1920s domestic modernist architecture that have been chosen because they are fashionable. Indeed Tati's artistic collaborator, Jacques Lagrange, who helped design the set of the house that was built in the Victorines studio in Nice, described the Arpels' home as a "montage," an "architectural pot-pourri" consisting of features he had seen in a variety of magazines and cut and pasted together.[43]

Further evidence for the view that Tati is criticizing a particular bourgeois form of suburbanization can be found in his satire of the Arpels' behavior in and around their house, which he directs at their stereotypically bourgeois attitudes, particularly their concern with status. Most of the scenes at their home take place in their walled garden, in which a large, metallic, urinary sounding fountain in the shape of a fish is prominently on display. The Arpels turn it on whenever they are visited by someone whom they wish to impress, occasioning one of the most prominent running gags in the film, which is repeated and varied seven times before Hulot accidentally breaks the fountain at a garden party the Arpels are hosting. Madame Arpel switches on the fountain erroneously the second, fourth, and fifth times when her husband returns from work, Hulot visits, and a grocer delivers food for the party. On each of these occasions she turns it off once she realizes that the person at the door is not someone she needs to make an impression upon. She also fails to switch on the fountain when she misidentifies her neighbor, whom she does wish to impress, as a salesperson before the garden party, an error she quickly rectifies when she realizes who is at the door.[44] Moreover, the fountain is just one example of the Arpels' conspicuous consumption. Madame Arpel derives great satisfaction from showing off her new house and its latest gadgets to visitors, which she does three times in the course of the film, and for her and Monsieur Arpel's anniversary she has their manual garage door replaced by an automatic one, while he buys her a new American car, the pink and lime green 1956 Chevrolet Bel Air.

Tati also associates the Arpels with other putatively bourgeois attitudes that have long been mocked by the modernist avant-garde. As historian of the bourgeoisie Peter Gay has argued, "an elemental urge . . . toward the rationalization of life, away from . . . unresisted impulse" became a major hallmark of bourgeois culture in the nineteenth century, and it manifested itself, among other ways, in the "rejection of the direct expression and public gratification of bodily needs" and the embrace of "delay, modulation, control."[45] The Arpels are obsessed with control, and one form this takes is their concern with cleanliness. The first time we encounter Madame Arpel we see not her but the wand of her vacuum cleaner as she vacuums her front door, and throughout the film she is constantly cleaning her home, garden, and car. Her kitchen gadgets and rubber gloves enable her to avoid touching food—as if in direct satire of Norbert Elias's famous contention that the civilizing process consisted in part of increasing prohibitions on physical contact with food[46]—and she is distressed when her husband takes Hulot to the airport without his gloves. When her well-dressed son, Gérard, returns with Hulot from playing with his lower-class friends on wasteland in the old quarter, she scrubs the boy from head to toe, and while showing off her house to an acquaintance, she pounces on a stray leaf that has blown onto the winding garden path. The white kitchen, which looks like a sterile dentist's office, is also reminiscent of a factory. Indeed, Madame Arpel informs a visitor that the contents of her sparsely furnished home were designed in her husband's factory, and the loud clicking of her shoes on the concrete floor of her living room is identical to the sound made by the shoes of Monsieur Arpel's secretary on his factory's cement floor. The furniture itself has been chosen for design rather than comfort, as indicated when the neighbor gasps as she sits awkwardly on a tubular couch, and Hulot must turn another couch on its side in order to get a good night's sleep on it.

Conversely, what Gay calls unresisted impulse appears to be absent from the Arpels' lives, as is painfully evident in their relationship with their son. Neither plays with him, and Gérard is usually positioned in shots away from his parents in the background or off to one side, forced to amuse himself (fig. 4.14). Nor do they say much to him except to harangue him about tidying his room and staying clean, and at one point, when Gérard runs into the house to talk to his

FIGURE 4.14 The neighbor visits the Arpels in *Mon Oncle*; Gérard is playing by himself in the background.

mother, he is confronted by a loud, automatic vacuum cleaner in her stead. On the one occasion Monsieur Arpel presents him with a gift, a toy train, he puts it down in front of the boy and immediately walks away. Gérard's nonplussed reaction is in sharp contrast to the howl of laughter he later emits when Hulot gives him a paper mannequin. In general, it is with the spontaneous and carefree Hulot, rather than his parents, that Gérard enjoys a close relationship, and he has fun in and around the old quarter, where Hulot benevolently watches over him as he plays with his friends.

Finally, the first part of the film's ending seems to support, albeit indirectly, Tati's contention that it is the use of their home by the Arpels—a use we have characterized as stereotypically bourgeois—that is the object of his criticism rather than modern suburbia itself. In part out of jealousy at Hulot's close relationship with his son, Monsieur Arpel sends his brother-in-law to work in the provinces, and Hulot's departure occasions the first moment of genuine intimacy and fun between Arpel and Gérard in the film. They drive Hulot to the airport, and as he is swept into the terminal by the throng of passengers, Hulot and several others appear to be dancing in time to the upbeat extradiegetic jazz music on the soundtrack (fig. 2.38). Standing in the car park, Arpel whistles at Hulot and unwittingly distracts a passerby, who walks into a lamppost. Gérard, who often deliberately plays this whistling trick on pedestrians with his friends from the old quarter, hides from the angry victim with his father behind their car, and in a gesture of affection he had previously reserved exclusively for Hulot, takes his father's hand (fig. 4.7). They turn to each other smiling, jump in their pink and green car and, laughing, exit the car park the wrong way (fig. 4.15). Perhaps Gérard and his father can after all enjoy the warm, playful relationship that existed between nephew and uncle, the viewer is left wondering, as the celebratory jazz music continues and a pack of dogs from the old quarter run into the car park.

Here, no abandonment, destruction, or modification of modern suburbia has been required in order for Arpel and his son to become closer. The scene was shot, according to Marc Dondey, at Orly airport, and the gray facade of the airport terminal is consistent with the modern architecture seen throughout the film.[47] Rather, it is Arpel's *attitude* that has, if only momentarily, changed, from one of bourgeois delay, modulation, and control to the antibourgeois enjoyment of unresisted impulse. All that is needed is a transformation of consciousness, Tati seems to be suggesting, in order for people to come together and have fun— "I feel sad because I have the impression that people are having less and less fun" Tati told Bazin and Truffaut[48]—and this can happen anywhere, even in the car park of a busy modern airport. And if this is true of an airport parking lot, surely

FIGURE 4.15 Monsieur Arpel and Gérard exit the airport the wrong way in the pink and lime green 1956 Chevrolet Bel Air at the end of *Mon Oncle*.

it is also true of the Arpels' suburban house, implying that a family with a different, nonbourgeois attitude could indeed be happy in it, as Tati suggested.

MON ONCLE AND MODERN ARCHITECTURE

And yet Tati's claim that he is taking aim only at the Arpels' use of their suburban home, and not the house itself, is ultimately implausible. The bourgeois attitudes he satirizes in the film are *reinforced* by certain features of the modern suburban environment the Arpels inhabit, features to which he consistently draws the viewer's attention. Indeed, some of these features *embody* the Arpels' bourgeois values, thereby making a clear distinction between the Arpels and their suburban surroundings difficult if not impossible to maintain. In attempting to democratize comedy, Tati incorporated not just secondary characters into his humor but also the environments around them, as discussed in chapter 2. In doing so, he frequently targeted modern characteristics of his settings, which are often the focus of his gags, and by exaggerating them, he renders these features ridiculous and laughable.

We have already noted that the Arpels neither play nor converse much with their son, and that he tends to be isolated in the frame away from them. This theme of separation is introduced in the film's first scene, when a pack of small dogs roams through the old quarter of Saint-Maur, exploring and urinating on the trash on the side of the road before running into the sanitized new quarter. A dachshund wearing a black and red jacket breaks away from the other, less well-bred dogs, and squeezes through the railings of a gate to what we soon discover is the Arpels' residence (fig. 4.16). As the others forlornly watch their compatriot depart, Madame Arpel greets the dog, Dacky, with a cry of horror at his dirty state, and picks him up at arm's length, presumably to wash him, much as she will do later with Gérard. Immediately, therefore, the design of the Arpels' modern home with its high gate and wall, which separate Dacky from his pack and clearly demarcate public from private space, is contrasted with the communal lifestyle of the old quarter where the dogs, like the inhabitants, mix freely and spontaneously together.

FIGURE 4.16 Dacky is separated from the other dogs in *Mon Oncle* by the high wall and gate of the Villa Arpel.

This contrast is underscored after Gérard returns home, much as Dacky did, covered in dirt from playing with his friends in the old quarter. Once he is suitably cleansed, Madame Arpel sits him in the kitchen in silence, adjusts his plastic swivel chair, and serves him an egg which has been prepared using several gadgets and that she holds at a distance with metal tongs while wearing rubber gloves. Sullen and uninterested, he slouches over his plate, and his mother asks him if he is ill before she is distracted by her husband. As his parents converse outside, Gérard is left alone in the all-white kitchen with the evening light fading. The high garden wall is visible through the window behind him, and the sound of children playing together beyond it in the distance can be heard. Gérard turns to look longingly in their direction, the somber moment lightened only by his hiccups (fig. 4.17). To further emphasize Gérard's illness—his isolation behind the wall and gate of the house—Tati immediately cuts to the square in the old quarter, which is full of people, warm colors, and noise as the inhabitants shop in the market, Gérard's friends play together, and neighbors pop in and out of the local cafe for a drink (fig. 4.18). Indeed, except for during the credit sequence and the final shot of the film (fig. 4.30), the square is never shown without at least two

FIGURE 4.17 Gérard hears children playing beyond the garden wall in *Mon Oncle*.

FIGURE 4.18 People congregate in the square of the old quarter in *Mon Oncle*.

people together in it, and usually there are many more. Tati, by contrast, often frames Gérard alone in front of or behind the bars outside his bedroom window, making it appear he is in jail (fig. 4.19).

The critique of modern suburbia as alienating is hardly original to Tati, and it was becoming particularly pronounced in France in the late 1950s as old, working- and lower-middle class quarters in and around Paris started being redeveloped. Such neighborhoods, while often dilapidated and containing overcrowded, primitive housing, were seen as fostering a particularly communal way of life. Due to the small size of apartments, with several people if not families sharing one or two cramped rooms as well as facilities such as bathrooms, residents were forced to spend a lot of time outside in public spaces with friends and neighbors. Local cafés, shops, and markets provided them with places to congregate and socialize, and such quarters often enjoyed a high degree of social stability and cohesion, with people staying in them throughout their lives and rarely venturing beyond their boundaries.[49]

FIGURE 4.19 Gérard by the bars of his window in *Mon Oncle*.

Saint-Maur, according to Tati, was in reality just such a place, as he experienced first-hand while shooting *Mon Oncle*:

> In the small neighborhood of Saint-Maur, the three tenants on the ground floor, who were living in only one room (get this!), built us a small makeup area with a partition around it—inside their own room! They even gave us the key. On the same street, there is a lady who buys groceries for her neighbors. I felt that these people knew one another and helped each other out.[50]

In *Mon Oncle*, although Hulot several times enters and leaves his penthouse on the top floor of his ramshackle apartment building in Saint-Maur, we never see him inside it except for when he adjusts his window pane to reflect light onto a caged bird opposite, and even here he is focused on what is outside. Instead, when in Saint-Maur, Hulot is almost always shown in the square and other public spaces fraternizing with neighbors he meets by chance. Even when walking down the maze of corridors and stairs to exit his building he encounters other tenants, including on one occasion a woman dressed only in a slip emerging from the communal bathroom. This is in sharp contrast to his in-laws, who never leave the private spaces of their house, car, and factory except when Monsieur Arpel picks up Hulot to take him to the airport, and who only associate with friends inside their walled home. In Saint-Maur, everyone seems to know and trust each other to the point that Hulot makes no effort to conceal the key to his apartment that he conspicuously leaves on the ledge above his front door; and a local merchant relies on his customers to deposit the correct payment on his stand for the produce they select while he sits some distance away conversing with a friend.

Yet Tati lamented, "I have the impression that this kind of generosity has almost disappeared from our world,"[51] and the sense of the communal lifestyle of Saint-Maur being under threat from the physical destruction of the neighborhood is palpable in *Mon Oncle*. The first part of its opening credit sequence takes place on a construction site where gray, concrete slab buildings of the sort seen later in the background are being built, and instead of extradiegetic music we hear the loud, abrasive sound of pneumatic drills. This same sound is heard again at the film's end when Monsieur Arpel and Gérard drive into Saint-Maur to pick up Hulot and workers are demolishing old buildings on its outskirts (fig. 4.20).

FIGURE 4.20 The old quarter being destroyed in *Mon Oncle*.

Meanwhile, whenever characters travel on foot between Saint-Maur and the Arpels' modern suburb, they do so by crossing a partially destroyed wall bordering the old quarter (fig. 4.8). The physical destruction of Saint-Maur along with Hulot's departure portends the extinction of the communal way of life its architecture fostered among *les petites gens*, the film seems to imply, to be replaced by one in which bourgeois families are literally walled up in their own private spaces, watching television, dining, or driving in cars *alone* instead of mixing with others in public.

The film highlights two other features of the Arpels' modern suburb that bolster their bourgeois attitudes. Like the architecture of their home, the Arpels' garden is a pastiche of prewar modernist design. Modernist gardens of the interwar years typically consisted of flat, abstract, graphic patterns created by the symmetrical arrangement of geometrical, colored planes employing concrete, glass, and other modern materials. Vegetation was sculpted and incorporated into the overall composition, which could only be perceived and appreciated from limited points-of-view at some distance, and fountains, pools, or metallic sculptures were placed at focal points. Such gardens were often conceived of as exterior rooms that extended "outward the domain of the interior ensemble, including its sharply redefined vocabulary" and were therefore under the control of the architect, who coordinated them with the house plan.[52] The Arpels' garden exhibits all of these characteristics with one important exception. Just as their home has no coherent functional or aesthetic rationale, their garden lacks the overall pattern or composition crucial to modernist gardens, such as Gabriel Guevrekian's triangular garden at the Villa Noailles (1926) (fig. 4.21). Instead it is a hodge-podge of geometrical colored planes punctuated by a needlessly winding path and randomly positioned sculpted plants and hedgerows, pointing once again to the role of fashion and status in Arpels' choices (fig. 4.22). Nevertheless, as in prewar modernist gardens, rather than an open setting through which one wanders freely and spontaneously in order to appreciate nature, the walker's route through the Arpels' garden is heavily prescribed by its design, thereby satisfying the Arpels' stereotypically bourgeois desire for control. In fact, the stepping stones that, along with the winding path, dictate where pedestrians can walk become the object of another running gag in which characters—particularly Hulot and Georgette, the Arpels' maid—repeatedly struggle to remain on the stones. This gag climaxes in the garden party when the fountain breaks and the guests attempt to relocate to another part of the garden to avoid getting wet. Filmed through the garden fence, the aperture created by the fence's slats frames the guests' feet, highlighting their difficulty staying on the stepping stones while carrying the garden furniture, and Hulot eventually

FIGURE 4.21 The restored Guevrekian Garden at the Villa Noailles.

FIGURE 4.22 The garden at the Villa Arpel in *Mon Oncle*.

mistakes a lily-pad in the fountain pool for a stone and steps into it, soaking his shoes and socks.

As funny as this gag is, the stepping-stones and winding path are examples of what Tati saw as a sinister aspect of modern environments, namely their authoritarianism. In the earlier quoted interview in which he discusses modern high-rise buildings in New York City, he complains in particular that "you have to push the button [in the elevator] where it says 'push,' there's not much way of expressing yourself,"[53] and in conversation he often returned to the theme of the annihilation of individuality by modern environments that prescribe one's behavior within them. In the Arpels' residence, it is not just the stepping stones and winding path that have this function but also the round mats on the terrace, which indicate where the Arpels should stand and place their chairs when dining and watching television (fig. 4.12). Nor is this control of placement confined to the Arpels' house, as throughout the film, Tati uses high-angle shots to repeatedly draw the viewer's attention to the numerous arrows, lines, and other road markings that constrain the positions and movements of cars and pedestrians in the Arpels' modern suburb (figs. 4.23 and 4.24). Once again, this stands in

FIGURE 4.23 Road markings in *Mon Oncle*.

FIGURE 4.24 Road markings in *Mon Oncle*.

sharp contrast to the disorder of the square and other public spaces in Saint-Maur, which pedestrians traverse freely. And it is, significantly, through Monsieur Arpel's disregard of the arrow pointing to the exit when he drives out of the airport car park the wrong way at the end of the film that Tati conveys the transformation in his attitude from one of bourgeois delay, modulation, control to the antibourgeois enjoyment of unresisted impulse (fig. 4.15).

Finally, and perhaps most obviously, the film emphasizes the uniformity of the Arpels' modern suburban surroundings, which for Tati epitomized the assault on individuality in modernity. "Paris will end up looking like Hamburg," Tati predicted to Bazin and Truffaut when discussing the rebuilding of the city. "And it is uniformity that I dislike. You go to a café on the Champs-Elysees these days and you get the impression that they will soon announce the landing of Flight 412; you don't know anymore if you are in a pharmacy or a grocery store."[54] It is in *Play Time* that Tati takes his satire of modern visual and aural homogeneity to its fullest; for example, in the opening switch image in which an airport initially looks and sounds like a hospital. But already in *Mon Oncle* there are a number of gags that make fun of the regularity of modern suburbia. When Monsieur Arpel drives Gérard to school and continues on to his plastics factory in the opening scene, his gray and white 1951 Oldsmobile Super 88 can barely be differentiated from other similar cars all driving in formation, while the facade of his factory is nearly identical to the outside of his son's school (figs. 4.25 and 4.26). The SDRC coal derivatives factory, where Arpel sends his brother-in-law to interview for a job, is at first sight indistinguishable from Arpel's own plastics factory, and the cubic structures of both, with blue girders running up their sides, echo the design of his house (figs. 4.27 and 4.28). Arpel's suit is the same shade of gray as the walls of his factory and home, and the collar and cuffs of his smoking jacket have the same color and pattern as his dog's jacket (fig. 2.34). I have already noted that the shoes of his wife and secretary make an identical sound on the cement floors of his home and factory, and many of the noises made by Madame Arpel's kitchen gadgets mimic those produced by her husband's factory.

Even though it is wrong to view *Mon Oncle* as a condemnation of modern suburbanization in general in the Paris region of the late 1950s, given the film's exclusive focus on a specific, somewhat atypical bourgeois suburb, it was disingenuous of Tati to deny that the film is critical of the Arpels' home. As we have seen, in interviews he frequently fulminated against what he saw as the alienation, authoritarianism, and homogeneity of modern environments, and his film systematically calls attention to and satirizes these features of modernity as they are manifested in the design of the Arpels' house and its suburban

FIGURE 4.25 In *Mon Oncle*, the exterior of Monsieur Arpel's plastics factory . . .

FIGURE 4.26 . . . resembles the exterior of Gérard's school.

FIGURE 4.27 In *Mon Oncle*, the exterior of Monsieur Arpel's plastics factory . . .

FIGURE 4.28 . . . resembles the exterior of the SDRC coal derivatives factory.

surroundings. It also contrasts them with the freer, more communal lifestyle enabled by the architecture of Saint-Maur, which, the film implies, is under threat of extinction from the rebuilding of Paris and its environs. Indeed, the second half of the film's ending reiterates these themes, thereby tempering the optimism of the first. After Monsieur Arpel and Gérard, laughing, leave the airport parking lot the wrong way to the accompaniment of the upbeat extradiegetic jazz music, the pack of dogs from Saint-Maur reappears in the car park. But suddenly, the mood changes. The music is abruptly replaced by the roaring of a plane's engines, and there is a cut to a long shot of two policemen, their backs to the camera, standing guard nearby. This shot not only alludes to the uniformity of modern suburbia by way of the indeterminate structure the policemen are watching over but also its repressive character when two of the dogs venture forward and then, their paths blocked by the policemen, are forced to retreat (fig. 4.29). The dogs escape back to the old quarter where they are joined by Dacky and are once again free to wander. But the closing shot of the dogs in the town square is filmed through a window across which a sheer

FIGURE 4.29   At the end of *Mon Oncle*, the dogs turn back, their path blocked by policemen . . .

FIGURE 4.30 . . . and congregate in the now empty square of Saint-Maur.

curtain blows shut, and for the first time in the film the square is devoid of people even though it is daytime (fig. 4.30). It is hard to avoid the shot's somewhat heavy-handed implication that the curtain is closing on a communal way of life in favor of modern suburbs like the Arpels'.

Nevertheless, Tati was not being insincere in expressing his belief that another family could enjoy a lifestyle very different from the Arpels' in their home. Tati was no cultural determinist, if by this is meant believing human beings to be mere products of their environments. Quite the contrary, for him, the environment reflects the *attitudes* of its inhabitants, which is why, when his characters embrace what he saw as an authentic, ludic approach to life, even the most austere modern setting becomes a playground. As we will see, this assumes its most elaborate form in Tati's oeuvre at the end of *Play Time*. But already in *Mon Oncle*, as a result of Monsieur Arpel's change of heart, the airport parking lot is transformed into a place where people seem to be dancing, passersby walk into lampposts, and one can exit a car park the wrong way in a pink and lime green car.

PLAY TIME, MODERN ARCHITECTURE,
AND THE COMEDY OF CONFUSION

Play Time targets the same features of the modern setting as *Mon Oncle*, further calling into question Tati's assertion that he refrained from criticizing contemporary architecture in his films. Although the high-rise buildings through which Hulot wanders in search of Giffard in the film's first half consist largely of offices and commercial spaces rather than residences, the aleatory object-analog mentioned in chapter 3, in which it seems as if the families of Giffard and Schneller can see each other through their shared apartment wall, affords Tati the opportunity to once again highlight and mock the putative alienation caused by modern domestic architecture. By chance, Hulot encounters Schneller, an old friend from the army, on the street outside what Schneller calls the ultramodern building in which he has recently purchased an apartment, and reluctantly accepts Schneller's invitation to come inside for a drink. Tati films the scene from outside the apartment building, and we must imagine the conversation as Schneller introduces Hulot to his wife and daughter and shows off his living room and its gadgets, visible through the large pane of glass that constitutes the exterior wall (fig. 4.31). Meanwhile, Giffard, who just happens to live next door,

FIGURE 4.31 In *Play Time*, Schneller shows off his modern apartment to Hulot.

arrives home in a taxi, his nose bandaged from banging into a glass door when pursuing Hulot earlier in the day. Schneller turns on his television, on which there is a boxing match, and Giffard's wife does the same before getting up to welcome her husband. A long shot of their apartment block reveals that the families in the four visible units—Schneller's and Giffard's on the ground floor, and two others located on the first floor directly over their heads—are all watching television, and their TV sets are located in the same position on the adjoining walls between their apartments (fig. 4.32). In the subsequent shot, because the camera is perpendicular to the apartment building, part of the exterior hides the adjoining wall, and it appears as though Schneller and his family are gazing at the Giffards when in reality they are watching the boxing. Tati augments the gag by having the families seem to react to each other when in fact they are responding to the TV. The Schnellers gesticulate wildly while Giffard explains his injury to his wife as if they are in shock at the explanation rather than the fight (fig. 4.33), and later Madame Giffard looks as if she is spying on Schneller as he takes off his jacket and suspenders rather than gazing intently at her television (fig. 3.21). As amusing as this gag is, by making it look as if the apartments are connected and their occupants are communicating with each other, Tati foregrounds their complete separation, and the gag is made doubly ironic by the close proximity of Hulot and Giffard, who have searched for each other in vain throughout much of the day. Even though *Play Time* takes place in urban rather

FIGURE 4.32 A long shot of Schneller's apartment building in *Play Time* showing Giffard arriving home on the right.

FIGURE 4.33 Schneller's family appears to react to Giffard as he explains how he banged his nose.

than suburban Paris and depicts apartments rather than houses, the vision of bourgeois families walled up in their own private spaces watching television is the same as in *Mon Oncle*.

As already mentioned, so is the depiction of modern environments as uniform, which this gag also illustrates. The long shot of the four units reveals them to be almost identical, with the television set, carpeting, and seating in the same position in each. They have similar gray monochrome color schemes and white curtains, and their inhabitants all wear gray, dark blue, or black and white (color figure 9). The gray costumes of Schneller's daughter and wife match the gray walls of their apartment, and their black chairs (reminiscent of the Barcelona chair designed by Mies van der Rohe and Lilly Reich in the late 1920s) are consistent with those in both Giffard's home and his office waiting room (where Hulot marvels at the suction sound the chairs make as they rein-flate after someone has sat on them) (fig. 4.34). Their inhabitants, meanwhile, are all watching the same television program at the same time while repeating other gestures—Giffard and a man in an apartment above take off their jackets in unison, for instance. This is just one example of *Play Time*'s systematic depiction of the modern world as homogeneous. Most famously and obviously, through-out the film we see posters advertising tourist destinations such as Hawaii, Mexico, and Stockholm, and they all picture an identical white and gray high-rise building, thereby fulfilling Tati's prediction that "Paris will end up looking

FIGURE 4.34 The waiting room at SNC in *Play Time*.

like Hamburg" (fig. 4.54). Meanwhile, Barbara and her party glimpse the distinctive landmarks that traditionally individuate Paris—the Eiffel Tower, Sacré-Coeur—only briefly when they happen to be reflected in the windows of the modern buildings. But Tati's vision of a uniform modern world is also evident in small, subtle details, such as the announcer's voice in Barbara's hotel, which is indistinguishable from the flight announcer's voice at the beginning of the film; and the tiny red buttons that adorn the left lapels of *all* the gray-suited company men shown in the portraits hanging on the wall of the room where Hulot waits for Giffard at SNC.

Finally, *Play Time* highlights the authoritarianism of the modern setting, although less systematically than *Mon Oncle*. Several high-angle shots draw attention to the arrows and other directional markings on the road as the bus takes Barbara's party from the airport into Paris, much as they do in the earlier film (fig. 4.35). These arrows are subsequently mimicked by the spiraling fluorescent red arrow on the awning outside the Royal Garden, which seems to command pedestrians to enter, and twice a drunk becomes mesmerized by the arrow and follows it as it lights up, inadvertently ending up inside the restaurant (fig. 4.36). Less noticeable, perhaps, is that Tati instructed his actors to "walk in straight lines" at the beginning of the film so that "everyone follows the lines of modern architecture." "These characters . . . are really prisoners of modern architecture," he claimed, "because it's the architects who have designed things"

FIGURE 4.35 In *Play Time*, the road markings . . .

so that people have to "move in a certain way, always in a straight line."[55] While there are some exceptions to this pattern, it is noticeable in the opening scene at the airport that most of the characters who enter and exit the waiting area walk straight along or at right angles to the line separating the dark gray cubicles

FIGURE 4.36 . . . echo the fluorescent arrow outside the Royal Garden restaurant, which a drunk follows inside.

FIGURE 4.37 In *Play Time*, Giffard walks down the center line of the corridor to meet Hulot.

from the light gray passageway. When the dignitary with the flapping tag on his briefcase enters the arrivals hall behind the party of Americans, he stays on the line separating the gray tiles on the floor (Figure 3.60), as does Giffard when he traverses the long passageway inside SNC to first greet Hulot (fig. 4.37). At the exposition, characters must walk straight down narrow passageways demarcated by the exhibits on either side, and at the nearby travel agent, Hulot marvels at the feet of the agent as he deftly moves from side to side along a straight line on his wheeled stool serving customers, thereby mirroring the lines between destinations on the map above him.

Yet *Play Time* for the most part eschews *Mon Oncle*'s use of stepping stones, mats, and other overtly authoritarian elements of the mise-en-scène to dictate character placement, and I suspect this has to do with another aspect of the modern environment that, while underlined occasionally in the earlier film, takes center stage in *Play Time*. In *Mon Oncle*, Hulot is largely able to avoid modern settings. When caring for his nephew, he takes the boy to the old quarter where he lives and spends most of his time, and he is fired from Monsieur Arpel's plastics factory after only a day. This is perhaps because, when Hulot is forced to visit modern locations, their features routinely confuse him or his eccentric reaction to them confuses others. He thereby disrupts their smooth functioning. While waiting to take Gérard out at his sister's house, Hulot ventures into the Arpels' modern kitchen in search of a drink and discovers a plastic jug that bounces.

After bouncing it up and down on the floor in delight, he spies a drinking glass, which he thinks is made of the same material as the jug, and he drops it on the floor assuming it will bounce too, only for it to shatter. And during his one day on the job at his brother-in-law's factory, the sound of the steam from a nearby plastics machine lulls him to sleep just as the worker overseeing the machine asks him to keep an eye on it while he steps away. Because Hulot's head is nodding as he falls asleep, the worker thinks he is assenting and leaves, and the unattended machine malfunctions, resulting in Hulot's firing.

In *Play Time*, there is no old quarter and Hulot enjoys no respite from the modern world. Nor are there blatant spatial markings such as stepping-stones to guide him. As a result, the confusion he experiences in navigating modern environments, and that he in turn causes others, becomes central to the film's comedy. In particular, Tati systematically uses mutual interference gags to convey Hulot's estrangement from modern settings, thereby coopting the most conventional gag structure in comedian comedy to articulate the modernist theme of alienation from the modern world. Again and again, Hulot mistakes one feature of a modern location for another due to their similarities, just as spectators misidentify the airport as a hospital in the film's opening scene, thereby furthering Tati's depiction of modern environments as uniform. Moreover, Tati sometimes resorts to switch images so that viewers share in this confusion. Even when not in error about his surroundings, Hulot seems perplexed by them, and he investigates the furniture and other objects around him as if seeing them for the first time, as when he marvels at the suction sound made by the chairs in the SNC waiting room. And in performing Hulot, Tati often peers ahead into the distance, as if trying to identify recognizable landmarks and orient himself spatially.

This comedy of confusion begins in earnest once Hulot follows Giffard into the offices of SNC. While politely waiting for Giffard to finish a conversation with somebody in an office cubicle, Hulot wanders into what looks like an alcove with an architectural drawing consisting of red and black lines hanging on its wall (fig. 4.38). However, in a switch image, the alcove turns out to be an elevator car, and before he can get out, its doors close and he is whisked up to a higher floor. When the elevator returns and he gets out, he appears to be in the same location as before (fig. 4.39), but in another switch image we soon realize he is on the floor *above* Giffard and must take an escalator back down to find him (fig. 4.40). Following Giffard into a maze of cubicles, Hulot is confronted by a receptionist sitting at a desk facing him in a corridor between the cubicles (fig. 4.41). He bows, turns a corner, and then enters another, identical corridor perpendicular to the first, searching for Giffard. But unbeknownst to him, in a mutual interference gag the receptionist's desk has rotated ninety degrees so that

FIGURE 4.38 In *Play Time*, Hulot mistakes an elevator for an alcove ...

FIGURE 4.39 ... and ends up on the second floor of the SNC building, which looks identical to the first.

FIGURE 4.40 Hulot must then travel down the escalator to find Giffard within the maze of cubicles.

FIGURE 4.41 Within the maze of cubicles, Hulot greets a receptionist ...

FIGURE 4.42 ... who turns her chair after Hulot has disappeared down a corridor ...

she is still facing him in the second corridor (fig. 4.42), and it looks to him as if he is in the same corridor as before (fig. 4.43). Finally, he locates Giffard and runs after him down another corridor toward a glass door. However, Giffard moves behind a partition, and all Hulot can see is Giffard's reflection in the window of the building opposite. In another mutual interference gag, thinking Giffard is now in that other building, Hulot leaves the first one, and finds himself in the

FIGURE 4.43 ... thereby confusing Hulot when he sees her facing him again in a different corridor.

FIGURE 4.44 At the exposition in *Play Time*, Hulot mistakes a salesman for Giffard.

exposition (fig. 3.42). There, he sees a man with his back to him who, because of his dress, looks like Giffard from behind, and Hulot waits patiently for him, believing he is Giffard (fig. 4.44). When the man turns around, Hulot realizes his mistake (yet another mutual interference gag) but is too polite to stop the man from showing him the chairs he is selling, which are the same as the ones in the SNC waiting room (as well as in Schneller's and Giffard's apartments). Hulot then tries to leave the exposition, but gets caught up in a large group of business-men who sweep him into an elevator. When they get out on a higher floor, their guide realizes he is not part of their group, and Hulot wanders onto a verandah, from which the Eiffel Tower is visible in the distance.

Almost eight minutes of screen time later, during which we see Barbara and her party visiting the exposition and a Hulot lookalike rummaging through the drawers in the German businessman's desk at the stand that sells doors that "slam . . . in golden silence," Hulot reappears from behind another party of businessmen in an elevator and wanders into the exposition. Six mutual interference gags quickly follow. (1) Hulot is mistaken for the Hulot look-alike by the German businessman, who sarcastically invites him to take off his hat and coat and "feel at home" (fig. 3.33) before berating him for opening his desk drawers and then angrily exit-ing through one of his silent doors, which he slams shut (fig. 4.45). (2) Hulot, who turns away from the German for a moment just as he closes the door, turns back, but because the closing was silent, does not realize the German has momentarily departed and thinks he has disappeared (fig. 4.46). (3) Bewildered,

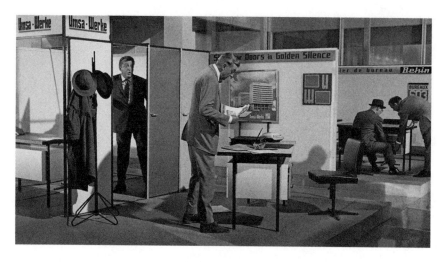

FIGURE 4.45 In *Play Time*, the angry German salesman "slams" one of his silent doors shut as Hulot looks away . . .

Hulot wanders away from the stand and is then confused for a sales assistant by the women with a broken lamp because he is no longer wearing a hat or coat and his jacket and bow tie resemble those of the other sales assistants (fig. 3.34). After the German businessman has apologized to him for his error and he has regained his outerwear, he finally manages to leave the exposition, marveling at the travel

FIGURE 4.46 . . . and Hulot is confused by the German's disappearance when he turns back.

FIGURE 4.47 In *Play Time*, Hulot marvels at the dexterity of the travel agent who rolls back and forth on his stool.

agent on the stool in the process (fig. 4.47). (4) Meanwhile, Giffard, who has been searching for Hulot all the while, sees another Hulot look-alike departing SNC and runs after him, banging into a glass door and hurting his nose (fig. 2.28). (5) The look-alike proceeds on his way and boards a bus, where he grabs a lamppost a man has just purchased, thinking it is one of the bus's stanchions (fig. 4.48).

FIGURE 4.48 In *Play Time*, Hulot lookalike #3 mistakes a lamppost for a stanchion when he boards a bus.

FIGURE 4.49 Hulot also grabs the lamppost when he boards the bus . . .

(6) At the next stop, Hulot boards the bus and repeats the same mistake as his look-alike (fig. 4.49). A few stops further on, the man with the lamppost gets off the bus, and Hulot, still holding it and absorbed in his newspaper, inadvertently does the same (fig. 4.50). It is at this moment that Schneller recognizes him and Hulot reluctantly joins him for a drink. It turns out that, if he hadn't

FIGURE 4.50 . . . and, because he is still holding it, absent-mindedly gets off the bus along with the man carrying the lamppost.

misidentified the lamppost as a metal pole, Hulot probably wouldn't have exited the bus, met Schneller, or ended up at the Royal Garden near Schneller's home.

I have described this series of gags involving Hulot in detail in order to underscore just how many are predicated on some sort of confusion caused by the modern environment's uniformity. Hulot fails to correctly identify the elevator car, the floor he gets off at, the corridor with the receptionist, Giffard's reflection, the door slamming in silence, and the lamppost because, excepting the silent door and Giffard's reflection, they closely resemble other settings and objects. They lack enough distinguishing, individual features for him to tell them apart from the things he mistakes them for, thereby instantiating Tati's complaint to Bazin and Truffaut that "you don't know anymore if you are in a pharmacy or a grocery store."[56] Also noticeable is that this lack of environmental individuality, and the misunderstandings it engenders, extends to people due, primarily, to the similarities in their clothes. It is for this reason that Hulot mistakes the chair salesman in the exposition for Giffard and that Hulot in turn is mixed up with two look-alikes by the German businessman and Giffard, and for a salesman by the women with the lamp. "What I condemn in the 'new' life is precisely the disappearance of any respect for the individual," Tati remarked to Bazin and Truffaut, and in *Play Time*, the assault on individuality Tati saw as endemic in modern settings encompasses people including Hulot, who is mistaken for five similarly dressed men over the course of the film as well as a sales assistant in the exposition.[57] It isn't just uniformity, however, that is responsible for these errors. Some of them, such as the ones involving the silent doors and Giffard's reflection, issue from the way certain materials used in modern construction confound the senses. Because it is transparent, we cannot always see glass and it is therefore inherently befuddling, Tati seems to be implying through the running motif gag of glass (which I discuss in chapter 3), as is a door that closes silently, which we cannot hear. Nor is Hulot alone in making mistakes. While he does so more than other characters, even practiced inhabitants of the modern world occasionally get muddled, as when Giffard runs into the glass door and the German businessman incorrectly identifies Hulot as the man who opened his desk drawers. Indeed, the first gag involving glass is a switch image in which the SNC doorman appears to a passing worker as if he is standing in the street rather than inside a building behind a pane of glass (figs. 3.40 and 3.41). While Hulot, as a result of his naïveté, may be more prone to such errors, we are all ultimately susceptible, Tati seems to be proposing, to the fundamentally confusing nature of the modern environment. As I suggested in the preface, this confusion was perhaps one source of the appeal of Tati's films to viewers, especially those who experienced first-hand the rapid modernization that occurred after World War II (like my father). Anyone who found it difficult to adapt to the new environments being erected after the war might have sympathized or even empathized with the disorientation they engender in Hulot and some of his onscreen compatriots.

PLAY TIME AND THE TRANSFORMATION
OF CONSCIOUSNESS

As with *Mon Oncle*, therefore, it was misleading for Tati to claim that he wasn't criticizing modern architecture in *Play Time*, which is why I argued in the introduction that authors' statements about their intentions are important but fallible guides to the meanings of their films. As we have seen, *Play Time* satirizes the same alienating, authoritarian, and homogeneous characteristics of the contemporary environment that Tati targeted in *Mon Oncle* and that he railed against in interviews, to which he added the effect of confusion; and many of the film's gags take aim directly at its modern locations. That said, the *attitude* of the characters in *Play Time*, and the alteration of the setting to reflect a change in that attitude, assumes an even greater role than in the earlier film.

In his 1968 and 1979 interviews with the editors of *Cahiers du cinéma*, Tati rejected the charge leveled at him by some critics that *Play Time* lacks a structure by pointing to two devices which, he believed, unified the film. Both concern the behavior of the characters.

> When you see the film straight through, you can see much better that everything that looks serious and a bit stiff in the first part becomes funny in the second part. For example, look at the German businessman—the guy with the sound-proofed door—and how he changes his behavior at the Royal Garden; he went along with it, and he is not at all a funny guy himself. This is true of all of the characters. Take the American women who see the same lampposts, the same roads, and the same airport as they did when they arrived, and yet they are freer because the party is still going on (as it often is).[58]

While it is certainly not the case that *all* of the characters seen earlier in the day end up at the restaurant, several do, and they undergo a significant transformation. In addition to the German businessman, who transitions from being an irate seller of silent doors at the home goods exposition to one of the main revelers in the American businessman's makeshift nightclub where he laughingly shares his

FIGURE 4.51 In *Play Time*, the tourist who interrupts Barbara . . .

broken glasses, there is the short, rotund, dour man whom we first see standing and staring gormlessly at Barbara while she tries in vain to take a photograph of the flower seller outside the exposition (fig. 4.51). Later at the restaurant, however, he is to be found dancing, smiling, and clapping as a chanteuse entertains the restaurant patrons once the jazz band has retreated (fig. 4.52). Then there is

FIGURE 4.52 . . . can later be seen dancing at the restaurant.

a second American businessman, Mr. Lacs, whom Hulot first encounters while awaiting Giffard in the waiting room at SNC. Lacs, who clearly has priority over Hulot in Giffard's eyes and, we later learn, is engaged in a business transaction with SNC, brushes off one of the ubiquitous Barcelona chairs and sits down on it, nodding politely at Hulot. Hulot then watches in astonishment as Lacs, sitting erect on the chair in a dark business hat, coat, and suit, performs an elaborate ritual of gestures that includes patting down his trousers, tugging on his shirt sleeves and collar, examining his nails and cracking his fingers, sniffing, checking his watch, smacking his lips, crossing and uncrossing his legs, unzipping his case and pulling out a document which he taps and signs before putting away, clicking his ballpoint pen, sucking on a breath freshener, sniffing a nasal spray, and adjusting his tie (fig. 4.53). He does not stop moving once during the more than sixty seconds he is seated in the waiting room, and his actions take on a rhythmical, almost mechanical quality given the loud sounds they make and the ostentatious, exaggerated manner in which they are executed. Giffard then enters to fetch Lacs, having seemingly forgotten about Hulot, and Hulot must chase after Giffard and try to catch his attention while he engages in the business transaction with Lacs. After Hulot leaves SEC and enters the exposition in the building next door in search of Giffard, Lacs reappears, still fiddling with his shirt and clicking his pen, at the travel agent counter loudly booking a plane ticket to the United States (fig. 4.54). The impression he gives is of a driven, self-important businessman

FIGURE 4.53 In *Play Time*, Hulot watches Lacs tugging on his collar while they wait for Giffard.

FIGURE 4.54 In *Play Time*, Lacs tugs on his collar as he goes to the travel agent counter; posters of different tourist destinations featuring what appears to be the same building can be seen in the background.

who is obsessed with his hygiene and personal appearance to the point that he cannot stop adjusting his clothes and engaging in business activities.

Once at the Royal Garden, he changes. We first see him still pulling on his cuffs and collar as he walks self-consciously among the restaurant tables with a female companion. After the ceiling collapses, the American businessman turns Lacs and his companion away from his makeshift nightclub because they don't have the shape of a crown from the Royal Garden chairs imprinted on their backs, and they start dancing, Lacs continuing to adjust his collar, cuffs, and tie. They go to sit down, and his companion, deceived into thinking that Lacs has brought her a seat by a waiter who is carrying the back of a chair that has come apart from its base, falls on the floor, her hand ending up in her shoe (figs. 2.22 and 2.23). The American businessman then comforts her and admits her and Lacs to his nightclub, where they begin partaking in the festivities. Lacs starts drinking and relaxes to the point that he allows another woman to feed him from a tray of food she is carrying (fig. 4.55). He also listens appreciatively to the music and when the American businessman places the red, white, and blue coaster on the black semi-circular shutter above the chef's head (fig. 4.6), he steps backward in laughter, causing Hulot to fall over. Although he never completely stops adjusting his clothes, and is later berated by the American businessman for worrying about the check, he now seems capable of the spontaneous fun the other characters are enjoying, in sharp contrast to his rigid behavior earlier in the day.

FIGURE 4.55 A woman feeds Lacs during the restaurant scene in *Play Time*.

The second unifying device mentioned by Tati concerns the straight lines along which the characters walk.

> The fact that there's a new nightclub and the club is not really ready, the building is not finished, well, all of a sudden, you see people's individual personalities coming out. You see? Do you have a piece of paper? I'm going to show the structure I came up with myself. Do you have a second? Here, at the start of the film, I tell the actors to walk in straight lines, no curves or bends, so everyone follows the lines of modern architecture. It's all built like that, the maze of offices, the cubicles, it's the architect who decided that, and people go straight and then turn sharply, and turn again sharply. It's the same with the display rooms; no one can do any swerves or bends. Then we get to the nightclub, and already there is something there because the neon sign doesn't work properly and the direction isn't so clear. So, you get a sense that things are a little off, and then you can see from the architect's mistakes that the building is not finished. So people have to go around things, and then the neon sign starts working, but then you have a second swerve because people start dancing, a third swerve, and people are moving around and around, and, well, I'm not a painter, but you can see how it's like a modern painting. We end up with this merry-go-round, and you can see that it's the people in the film who have taken on their own identity against this background, they are living the way they want to. Do you see?[59]

Although there are some exceptions to this pattern, those inside the restaurant, like the characters earlier in the film, initially tend to walk along a straight line as they move from the door through the lobby and between the tables that are arranged symmetrically, as do Lacs and his companion. However, as Tati notes, this begins to change as they are forced to avoid the various things that break. The head waiter, for example, has to stride around a missing tile on the dance floor (which becomes attached to his shoe) (fig. 4.56), while he and others must circumnavigate the ill-placed column containing the air conditioning controls that blocks the passageway from the foyer to the dining area and that Hulot collides with. Once the jazz music begins in earnest, the tempo increases, and the dancers become more uninhibited, they start *circling around* the dance floor instead of moving back-and-forth, as they had before (figs. 4.57 and 4.58).

For Tati, as the above quotations make clear, this adjustment of outlook on the part of the characters, this shift from what Peter Bürger, as I noted in chapter 2, calls the "means-end rationality of the bourgeois everyday"[60] consisting of work and productivity to noninstrumental pleasure in dancing and socializing—from walking in straight lines, with its connotation of moving purposively from point A to point B, to going in circles, which takes you non-purposively back to the same place—gives *Play Time* unity. We watch as the attitude of the characters, much like Monsieur Arpel's at the end of *Mon Oncle*, changes from one of bourgeois delay, modulation, control to the antibour-geois enjoyment of unresisted impulse as they move from the daytime world

FIGURE 4.56 In *Play Time*, the head waiter circles around the dance floor.

FIGURE 4.57 The restaurant manager makes comments about a dancing financier as he circles around the dance floor...

of labor and consumption to the nighttime world of fun and conviviality in the restaurant, and this transition gives *Play Time* a structure. For Tati, this alteration is also an expression of liberation, of taking on your own identity. Rather than conforming to the straight lines along which one is putatively

FIGURE 4.58 ... only to realize that he has mistaken him for another man.

enjoined to walk by modern architecture, the patrons of the Royal Garden begin to chart *their own* circular path around the dance floor and restaurant much as they do in the town square in *Mon Oncle*.

As I argued earlier in relation to *Mon Oncle*, the environment for Tati reflects the attitude of the characters. It is therefore no accident that this change in their behavior is bookended by two alterations to the architecture of the restaurant, both of which are caused unwittingly by Monsieur Hulot. First, he accidentally shatters the glass door to the street (fig. 3.37), thereby breaking the barrier between the restaurant and the outside world and permitting passersby who aren't among the restaurant's bourgeois clientele to wander inside and participate freely in the party. Glass, which has functioned throughout the film to confuse and separate characters, is thereby removed, allowing people to come together in the restaurant, a motif that is reiterated by the glass window that spontaneously opens when the jazz band starts playing, enabling the sound of their music to spill out onto the street. Then, once the dancers have started moving in a circular fashion, Hulot mistakenly causes the ceiling to collapse (figs. 2.4 and 2.5). This encourages the characters to take even greater control of their surroundings, to manipulate them according to their needs and desires, as the American businessman creates his makeshift nightclub, the patrons rearrange the tables and chairs, and they begin serving themselves food and drink and performing music once the jazz band departs (fig. 4.55). Instead of passive inhabitants of modernity regulated by their environs, they have become active participants who alter their environment for their own purposes and are alive to its ludic possibilities, as evinced by the American businessman who puts the red, white, and blue coaster on the black semicircular shutter above the chef's head, thereby creating *his own* object analog by making the chef look as though he is wearing a bicorne hat with a cockade (fig. 4.6).

Crucially, this transformation in the setting cannot be confined to the restaurant now that its door is broken, but it continues the next morning outside in the daytime world of work as the circular motif introduced by the Royal Garden's neon arrow invades the surrounding streets and buildings, which also erupt in color (a third unifying device). In the nearby bar, to which Hulot, Barbara, and their party repair after they leave the restaurant in the early hours, the fluorescent drugstore sign is being fixed, and a priest stands under the letter *O*. In an aleatory object analog, the men working on the sign light up the letter, and its round shape makes it look like a luminous halo hovering above the priest's head (fig. 4.59). Meanwhile, two workers repairing pipes in the bar use them to siphon off some alcoholic drinks, thereby altering the environment for their pleasure, as did the restaurant patrons (fig. 4.60). When Hulot and Barbara leave the bar and

FIGURE 4.59 The letter *O* in the fluorescent sign looks like a halo above the priest in this aleatory object analog from *Play Time*.

walk past the Ideal Cheese stand, the wheels of cheese echo the circular decorations that have now appeared on the facades of the nearby buildings, and while Hulot is purchasing a gift for Barbara, a woman asks a sales assistant to cut out a sample of fabric with a circle on it. In trying to exit the store, Hulot mistakes a round pot with a long red handle for a turnstile, and once Barbara boards her

FIGURE 4.60 Workers repurpose pipes to obtain drinks from the bar in *Play Time*.

FIGURE 4.61 The spinning globe in *Play Time*.

bus, a spinning globe is visible behind her (fig. 4.61). The bus enters the traffic circle, which looks and sounds like a merry-go-round, as colorful flags and other decorations are hung on the surrounding buildings and children carry colored balloons (fig. 2.6 and color figure 3). A revolving red and white cement mixer can be seen driving around the circle, and a cherry picker rotating around a lamppost is visible as Barbara's bus leaves town.

Because the consciousness of the characters has been transformed, the daytime world of labor no longer appears the same as it did in the film's first half. Noninstrumental play and pleasure—the merry-go-round—has permeated it, and families purchase ice cream from a vendor in the traffic circle. Instead of traveling along straight lines as before, the characters and vehicles now journey around a traffic circle, thereby returning nonpurposively to the same place— like the dancers in the restaurant—rather than moving purposively forward. Meanwhile, bright reds, blues, yellows, and greens punctuate the almost exclusively black, white, and gray mise-en-scène of the previous day. It is essential to note that this utopian vision doesn't consist of the *replacement* of work with play but rather their *synthesis*. The aleatory object analog involving the halo and the priest occurs because men are repairing the neon sign, and the workers siphon off drinks from the bar as they are fixing its pipes. The circular motif overtakes the signs and products of businesses selling their wares outside the bar, such as the Ideal Cheese stand, as well as utilitarian vehicles performing

their functions, like the cement mixer and cherry picker. Just as modern suburbia does not need to be destroyed in *Mon Oncle* for Arpel and his son to
become closer, so a revolt against bourgeois capitalism is not required for the
modern city to be transformed into a playground in *Play Time*. Rather, worka-
day, quotidian *time* is infused with *play*. In this respect, although *Trafic* is often
viewed as a lesser film than *Play Time*, *thematically* it can be seen as the logical
culmination of Tati's comedy of everyday life given that, for the first time that
we know of in a Hulot film, Hulot has a steady job, and the film's gags and
other comic devices are completely integrated into his work.

Returning to *Play Time*, one might almost describe it as an expressionist film
seeing as the mental (or rather spiritual) state of the characters is given perceptible form in their surroundings, much like the Arpels' bourgeois mindset. But
even if one doesn't want to go that far, it *is* the case that the setting reflects the
characters' outlook in that its appearance changes when their outlook shifts.
They are now able to see it as a playground where they can enjoy themselves,
which is why it looks different. This change in outlook suggests that, for Tati, the
primary target of his critique was not so much the modern environment itself
but the *attitude* of its inhabitants. What most troubled him about modernity,
I conjecture, was the stereotypically bourgeois ethos of work, productivity, and
consumption that seemed to be overtaking society as it modernized and that
increasingly left no room for noninstrumental pleasures such as play. His goal
was therefore to demonstrate how one can have fun *within* the modern world
rather than to oppose modernization. In devising aleatory object analogs and
other innovative gag structures, his aim was to show how humor may be derived
from the most banal and boring modern locations such as a traffic circle rather
than to resist their construction. While he targets features of modern settings
that he disliked, *Play Time* seems to imply that these features will dissolve once
the correct, playful mentality is adopted. One could stay that, for Tati, the environment is an epiphenomenon that supervenes on the behavior of the characters.
All that is needed is the mode of active observation I discussed in chapter 3, in
which one is on the lookout for the ludic possibilities in one's surroundings, and
they will no longer appear austere and alienating. As she leaves town on the bus,
Barbara notices that the flower Hulot has given her, in an object analog, resembles the lampposts they are passing (figs. 2.11 and 2.12). Like the American businessman in the restaurant, Barbara is now able to enjoy *her own* object analog by
perceiving the similarity between the flower and the lamppost, which, for Tati,
means that "the party is still going on."

It is of course this transformation of consciousness that Tati also desired to
effect in his viewers, as I showed in chapters 2 and 3. By deemphasizing his comic

character and placing the responsibility for finding humor in his films partly on his audiences' shoulders, he encouraged us to actively attend to the comedy of everyday life putatively happening outside the movie theater. In effect, he wished to wean his audiences from their dependence on both Hulot *and* his films for a comic experience so that they could discover it for themselves all around them. His was the quintessentially avant-garde goal of closing the gulf between art and life and "organiz[ing] a new life praxis from a basis in art."[61] Such an ambition might strike us today as hopelessly naïve and utopian, as do so many modernist projects. But whether or not this is the case, we can continue to appreciate the considerable ingenuity with which Tati went about trying to realize his democratic and participatory aims. We can still marvel at his extraordinary comic innovations, particularly his use of elliptical, fragmented, dispersed, intertwined, unexploited, and barely perceptible gags, even if we might be skeptical of the transformative impact he hoped they would have. Tati once said that comedy is a "big garden to which everyone contributes his own pebble. Some bring large stones, some small pebbles."[62] Tati's comic opacity, along with his dissolution of the comedian, democratization of gags, and aleatory object analogs, constitute a large stone of the first order, and like modernists in general, it is in no small measure due to his beliefs about the modern world that he arrived at these brilliant inventions.

AFTERWORD

Parade, Tati, and Participatory Culture

I have postponed a consideration of *Parade* (1974), Tati's sixth and final feature, until this afterword because, at least on the surface, it appears very different from its predecessors. Most obviously in the context of this book, it does not belong to the genre of comedian comedy. It lacks a fictional narrative centered on an eccentric character who generates humor through his inability or unwillingness to conform to social and other norms. There is no François the postman, Monsieur Hulot, or equivalent protagonist to make us laugh, and most of the gags and other comic structures I previously analyzed are absent. Instead, the film purports to document a live circus performance before an audience in which Tati, assuming the role of master of ceremonies, reprises some of the sporting impressions that made him famous on the music hall stage in the 1930s. Interspersed with his impersonations of a soccer goalkeeper, boxer, fisherman, tennis player, circus horse rider, and traffic cop are acts by an assortment of jugglers, acrobats, magicians, artists, musicians, singers, and dancers as well as a routine in which audience members are invited to ride an obstinate mule. Stylistically, the film also stands apart. It was shot on video, 16 mm, and 35 mm over a three-year period, and its shots therefore differ in texture and image quality. More importantly, the film employs the variable framing that is largely absent from Tati's previous features in order to direct the viewer's attention to relevant details. It even includes close-ups (fig. 5.1), which Tati derisively associated with television, and indeed it was filmed for Swedish TV in Stockholm. These technical, stylistic, and formal divergences perhaps explain why critics usually regard *Parade* as a minor film, the work of an old man wallowing in his past—his early career in the music hall—rather than innovatively forging ahead. Far from "the clowning glory of [Tati's] career," it is a "public exercise in personal

FIGURE 5.1 A close-up of the feet of the orchestra members and their belongings in *Parade* (Jacques Tati, 1974).

nostalgia," declares David Bellos, one that asks to be viewed "at least in part as a sentimental self-depiction."[1] Bellos echoes the opinions of many who reviewed the film on its release. *Positif*, for instance, labeled it a "parenthesis...in the series of Tati's films,"[2] while John Pym in the *Monthly Film Bulletin* called it "an image of unadulterated sentimentality."[3]

Yet as Kristin Thompson and Jonathan Rosenbaum argue in what remain the two best analyses of the film, *Parade* is in many respects continuous with Tati's earlier work and, in its own way, is just as innovative and audacious.[4] In fact, I think it is the film in which Tati most clearly expresses his artistic intentions. As we have seen throughout this book, Tati sought above all else to create a democratic, participatory form of comedian comedy, and his goal of involving viewers in his humor, while training them to perceive it for themselves in the world outside the movie theater, motivated many of his comic inventions. For the first time in *Parade*, Tati makes this ambition explicit *within* one of his films by employing the quintessentially modernist device—used by avant-garde filmmakers at least since Dziga Vertov and exemplified by films such as Max Ophuls's masterpiece *Lola Montès* (1955)—of depicting an audience in the work as a metaphor for the cinema audience. The spectators are as important as the performers in *Parade*, and the variable framing that is largely eschewed in Tati's previous films is consistently used to draw our attention to them. This allows Tati, in Thompson's words, to represent "literally, his ideal circus audience, and figuratively his ideal cinema audience; sitting in a film theater, we are encouraged to see ourselves as being potentially as active, imaginative, and uninhibited as the people we see watching the circus."[5]

When Tati first enters the circus ring, he announces, while gesturing toward the audience: "We're pleased to present a show in which everyone's invited to participate. The artists and clowns are you and me." *Parade* then systematically breaks down the distinction between viewer and actor, thereby demonstrating, much as his fiction films aimed to, that "everyone is entertaining," that "there is no need to be a comic to perform a gag."[6] A circus, after all, consists of a ring— a circle—and as we saw at the end of *Play Time*, the circular motif represents for Tati the triumph of the noninstrumental value of play and the freedom of the individual to chart her own path rather than conforming to the straight lines of modern architecture. The saturation of the modern environment by circles and bright colors shows that a transformation of consciousness has occurred, that the characters now see this environment as a playground in which they can enjoy themselves, a place to actively play rather than passively consume. In *Parade*, passive consumption is replaced by active participation on the part of the circus audience to the point that it is often not clear who is a performer and who is a viewer. To accentuate this situation, the spectators are dressed in brightly colored costumes that are largely indistinguishable from those of the acrobats and other circus entertainers (fig. 5.2 and color figure 10). In this way, Tati models his ideal cinema audience, and he enjoins us once again to take part in the comedy of everyday life he depicts in his films, thereby attempting to close the gap between art and life. As he put it in a 1979 interview with *Cahiers du cinéma*, "what I wanted was to eliminate the coldness between the screen and the viewers. If you see *Parade* with a full house, that's what happens. You're not waiting for some guy to show up and make you laugh; it's a direct connection between the audience and the screen."[7]

The very first comic moment in the film is an object analog noticed by an audience member. As patrons enter the door to the circus, a young man and his companion laughingly pick up traffic cones and put them on their heads as if they are pointed hats (fig. 5.3). Later in the show, some of the musicians begin arguing. Tati sends them back to their seats and starts conducting the orchestra, but a trombone player approaches him to air his grievances and the music comes to a halt. A woman from the audience grabs and plays his trombone, and the

FIGURE 5.2 The colorful costumes of audience members.

FIGURE 5.3 The first comic moment of *Parade* is an object analog discovered by audience members.

FIGURE 5.4 A woman from the audience grabs a trombone from an orchestra member.

orchestra accompanies her (fig. 5.4). Once the show is over, two small children from the audience remain as everyone else leaves. They enter the ring and play with the props left behind by the performers before they rejoin their parents and the film ends (fig. 5.5). In these and other instances, viewers actively make use of objects in the environment around them to amuse themselves rather than passively consuming entertainment, just as the restaurant diners eventually do in *Play Time*.[8] These sequences also suggest that the spectators, rather than being filmed spontaneously, cinema-verité style, are at times being directed to perform certain actions that have been planned in advance and may even be actors. In fact, half the audience was reportedly made up of extras from Swedish TV, while the two children were hired to play their parts. The fictionality of the audience is further implied by the life-size, black-and-white cutouts of photographs of viewers, reminiscent of the cutouts in *Play Time*, which have been adorned with clothes and other props and placed in some of the seats in the auditorium (fig. 5.6).

Many of the sequences involving the audience seem at least partly staged. During the show, spectators are invited to try and mount a mule that is circling the ring, and, after others fail to stay on the creature, a man in a gray suit enthusiastically volunteers despite his wife's protestations. The mule kicks and brays

FIGURE 5.5 Two children playing on the stage with props at the end of *Parade*.

FIGURE 5.6 Cutouts of audience members behind real ones.

FIGURE 5.7 The mule mounts an audience member.

at him before chasing him out of the ring. He tries again with a second mule, and is able to mount it before being thrown off. The mule then mounts *him* (fig. 5.7) before he runs away and trips over the ring, and by this point his pratfalls suggest that, despite his businessman's appearance, he may be a trained performer. The small boy who plays on the stage at the end of the film then walks up and has no trouble sitting on the mule, indicating that he might be in on the act too. Later, Tati introduces Pia Colombo, a well-known French singer, and she emerges from the audience rather than backstage. It isn't just members of the audience who are performers, however, but also workers in the theater. During the intermission, one bartender is uncorking a champagne bottle behind another with a patently false bald head who is opening a can (fig. 5.8). When the cork pops it looks as if the champagne is spurting out of the bald man's head, and the customers at the bar laugh (fig. 5.9). This is an aleatory object analog gag of the sort I analyzed in chapter 2 and, because it depends on the position of the camera for its effect, is obviously preplanned. Earlier, a magician performing tricks is interrupted by one of the scene decorators who are busy painting scenery beside the stage. The worker begins to compete with the magician, one-upping him each time he does a trick until he

FIGURE 5.8 A bartender uncorks a champagne bottle behind his bald colleague . . .

FIGURE 5.9 . . . and it looks as though liquid is squirting from the man's bald head.

FIGURE 5.10 A magician is one-upped by a set decorator . . .

turns the magician's red handkerchief into a walking stick (fig. 5.10). He is then himself interrupted and one-upped by an audience member, who borrows a walking stick and a red handkerchief from people in nearby seats and proceeds to turn the stick red before transforming it into a second red handkerchief (fig. 5.11). The scene decorators participate in other acts as well, including one in which they juggle with their paintbrushes, and as with the spectators, we cannot always be sure who is a real set decorator and who an entertainer. Just as Tati devolves the comedy away from his major protagonists onto secondary characters in his fiction films, so everyone is potentially a performer in *Parade* even if they are not ostensibly part of the circus troupe.

In this way, as Thompson and Rosenbaum have stressed, Tati creates a hybrid of fiction and documentary in the film, making it unclear where reality ends and performance begins. Our ontological uncertainty about who is a spectator and who is an actor, about what is spontaneous and what is staged, drives home Tati's belief that there shouldn't be a distinction between them, that viewers should be performers too, actively finding and creating comedy in the world around them as many of the audience members and workers in the film do. This ideal is further reinforced by the use of off-stage space. While many of the acts occur inside the

FIGURE 5.11 . . . who is himself one-upped by an audience member.

circus ring, some comic moments happen in other parts of the theater, such as the aleatory object analog with the bartenders. When Tati begins the show by announcing that everyone is invited to participate in it, there is an immediate cut to two of the scene decorators who are painting clown pictures on the side of the ring as if to suggest that they are just as much a part of the performance as the official acts (fig. 5.12). We then see a woman in the lobby struggling to get her small child to enter the auditorium and a cloakroom attendant who is unsure where to place a patron's checked motorcycle helmet, because there are already so many on the shelves of the cloakroom (fig. 5.13). Incidents such as these are not particularly funny and are not full-blown gags. Rather, they are akin to the slightly incongruous or unusual details of the sort Tati peppered his fiction films with. These shots of offstage space involve audience members and workers at the theater, but others include official performers who have strayed away from the ring. A man dressed in a hockey uniform opens and shuts doors in the lobby as if trying to find the auditorium (fig. 5.14), while a violinist in evening dress comes out of the theater to meet a woman in a motorcycle helmet who gives him a bow, which he has obviously forgotten to bring with him. Both appear in the subsequent acrobatic act. Later, during the intermission, shots of backstage show

FIGURE 5.12 The set decorators by the side of the stage.

FIGURE 5.13 A cloakroom attendant has nowhere to put a checked helmet.

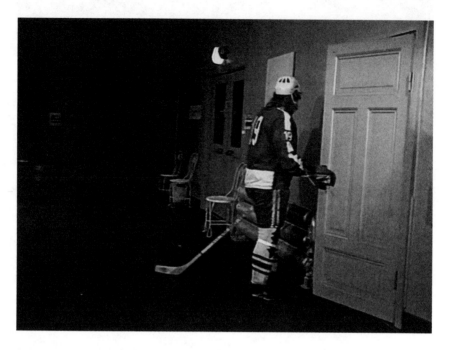

FIGURE 5.14 A man dressed in a hockey costume searches for the stage.

a worker using a ladder as a pair of stilts, and Tati himself wanders backstage, where he performs his impression of traffic cops in different countries for the stage hands and a policeman who happens to be there (fig. 5.15). Not only, in other words, is the distinction between spectator and actor blurred, so is the one between on- and offstage. In Jonathan Rosenbaum's words:

> *Parade* creates a privileged zone of its own in which the free play between fiction and nonfiction becomes an open space to breathe in. It is a utopian space where equality reigns between spectators and performers, children and adults, foreground and background, entertainment and everyday life, reality and imagination—an evening's light diversion that, if taken seriously, as it was meant to be, could profitably crumble the very ground beneath our feet.[9]

I cannot improve on Rosenbaum's description except to say that Tati's other feature films also depict versions of this utopian space, which Tati so desired to make a reality. For Tati, comedy, as we have seen repeatedly, can happen anywhere to everyone if they have the right attitude. In *Parade*, when he

FIGURE 5.15 Tati performs his impersonation of a traffic cop backstage.

first speaks to the audience, Tati uses the same word he does in many other contexts—*participate*—to describe his ambition for his viewers, and all of his features attempt to open our eyes to the comic possibilities of the quotidian world once it is seen as a playground.

ENVOI

It is a convention of studies of great film auteurs of the past to argue for their contemporary relevance. I have largely resisted the temptation to do this in Tati's case because I think his work should be appreciated and valued regardless of whether it remains pertinent today. His comic inventions are alone enough to guarantee his place in the pantheon of major filmmakers of the twentieth century, as I hope this book has demonstrated. However, in closing, it is worth noting that Tati's abiding artistic goal throughout his career—getting his viewers to participate—remains a major concern in contemporary culture and its theorization. In fact, some have claimed that we are living in an especially participatory moment as a result of technological and cultural shifts. Media scholar Henry Jenkins, for instance, contends that the putative media convergence of recent years, in which content increasingly circulates across "different media systems, competing media economies, and national borders," has helped give rise to what he calls a participatory culture.[10]

> The term *participatory culture* contrasts with older notions of passive media spectatorship. Rather than talking about media producers and consumers as occupying separate roles, we might now see them as participants who interact with each other according to a new set of rules that none of us fully understands.[11]

For Jenkins, a participatory culture is one with "relatively low barriers to artistic expression and civic engagement, strong support for creating and sharing creations, and some type of informal mentorship where experienced participants pass along knowledge to novices."[12] He gives as examples fan videos and the many other forms of creative expression that now circulate across the internet and beyond, as well as membership in online communities and shaping the flow of media through blogging. Although Jenkins sees the emergence of participatory culture as more of a cultural than a technological shift, these examples indicate that he ties this culture to the adoption of digital media since the 1980s, as do many commentators.[13]

There is much that could, and indeed has, been said about Jenkins's notion of a participatory culture. All I want to point out here is that, as Tati's example suggests—along with the efforts of many other avant-gardists after World War II that I discussed briefly at the beginning of chapter 2—practitioners have been finding ways to render the experience of media more participatory since long before the digital age. While some digital media might make content creation and other forms of media participation easier and cheaper than their analogue predecessors, this does not mean that participatory forms of engagement with media begin with them. Rather, as the editors of a recent volume about the history of participatory media put it, "active and politically engaged uses of media are not exclusive to our times. As a matter of fact, it is fair to ask the question: Has there ever really been such a thing as a passive audience?"[14] Prior to the digital age, filmmakers working outside the film industry made movies with 16 mm, 8 mm, and analogue video, and they repurposed footage filmed by others, as did Bruce Conner and Guy Debord. Photographers shot photographs or cut and pasted the photographs of others into montages, while write-in campaigns and other forms of audience pressure influenced media content.

Predigital communities formed through involvement in film societies, book clubs, and fan groups, and amateurs launched their own radio and TV stations. Meanwhile, plenty of people today consume digital content without blogging about it or writing fan fiction in response to it. It seems implausible, therefore, to characterize contemporary culture as participatory in contrast to a more passive, predigital past, just as it is wrong to label one medium as inherently more participatory than another, as did Marshall McLuhan in his distinction between hot and cold media. McLuhan believed that film is a hot medium allowing of less participation than a cool one, because it provides audiences with so much information, leaving them little to fill in themselves.[15] Tati's films, however, demonstrate that there is nothing inherently hot about film, given that Tati withheld information about his comedy precisely in order to elicit greater audience participation. Instead, they show that what matters in determining whether a medium allows for participation is how it is *used* in particular circumstances. As Régis Debray put it, McLuhan confuses "technology itself with its usage," thereby "making media an abstract, undifferentiated force," and the same can be said for Jenkins.[16] While one can perhaps talk about degrees and kinds of participation in specific cases, gross generalizations about media and culture of the sort offered by McLuhan and Jenkins are vulnerable to myriad counterexamples.

I have no idea whether Tati's ingenious devices actually elicit the degree and kind of participation their author hoped for from his audiences. This book has been focused on explaining the design of his films, not their outcome. Nevertheless, it is significant that Tati's comic style was shaped by the widespread, enduring wish for more active participation in media. This desire is so pervasive and longstanding because it is born of a fear foundational to what Charles Taylor calls modern identity: the fear that modernity has created "a world dominated by technology, standardization, the decay of community, mass society, and vulgarization" that leaves little room for the individual.[17] This fear and desire were felt acutely by members of the post-World War II avant-garde, as evident in works such as Debord's *Society of the Spectacle* and the democratic surrounds built by artists like Stan VanDerBeek. Tati's singular and enduring achievement was to translate the participatory ambitions of the avant-garde into the mainstream form of comedian comedy and thereby craft a genuinely popular comedic modernism.

NOTES

PREFACE AND ACKNOWLEDGMENTS

1. David Kynaston, *Modernity Britain: 1957–1962* (New York: Bloomsbury, 2015). The phrase "You've never had it so good" was used often in the UK in the 1950s as a political slogan; it comes from a famous speech by British prime minister Harold Macmillan.

2. André Bazin, "Fifteen Years of French Cinema," trans. Bert Cardullo, *Canadian Journal of Film Studies* 18, no. 2 (Fall 2009): 114.

3. Roy Armes, *The Ambiguous Image* (Bloomington: Indiana University Press, 1976), 71.

4. Kristin Thompson, "*Play Time*: Comedy on the Edge of Perception," in *Breaking the Glass Armor: Neoformalist Film Analysis* (Princeton, NJ: Princeton University Press, 1988), 262.

5. Due to the length of its shoot (365 shooting days); the cost of constructing (and reconstructing after it was damaged by a storm) Tativille, a set with real buildings, roads, an escalator, and a power plant; the limited distribution available to films in 70 mm, the format in which it was shot; poor reviews in the French press on its release; and lack of distribution in the United States—Tati was unable to recoup the costs of making the film and his production company, Specta, went into bankruptcy. Among other things, he lost the rights to his films and his home in Saint-Germain.

6. Armes, *The Ambiguous Image*, 71.

7. Alvin Toffler, *Future Shock* (New York: Bantam, 1971), 2.

INTRODUCTION

1. I follow Tati scholar Kristin Thompson in spelling *Play Time* using two words rather than one. See her "*Play Time*: Comedy on the Edge of Perception," in *Breaking the Glass Armor: Neoformalist Film Analysis* (Princeton, NJ: Princeton University Press, 1988), 250n7; and her "Where in the World is M. Hulot?," *Observations on Film Art*, July 22, 2009, http://www.davidbordwell.net /blog/2009/07/22/where-in-the-world-is-m-hulot/. Jonathan Rosenbaum recently argued that the title should be spelled as one word, *PlayTime*, because Tati himself wrote the title as one word in correspondence, and because Macha Makeieff, the rights holder to the Tati estate, has decided to use this version of the title. Rosenbaum also notes: "But what arguably makes '*PlayTime*' better than

either '*Playtime*' or '*Play Time*' is its emphasizing the fact that it isn't either a French *or* an English title. It's a non-word belonging to no existing language except for 'franglais'—the perception of English through a French sensibility, which also produced such relatively new terms in France during the same period as 'parking,' 'weekend,' and 'drugstore.'" (Jonathan Rosenbaum, "*PlayTime*," *Jonathan Rosenbaum* (blog), July 10, 2018, https://www.jonathanrosenbaum.net/2018/07 /playtime-2/). However, evidence can also be found that Tati wrote the title as two separate, capitalized words, as did his art director, Jacques Lagrange (see the photographs in Marc Dondey, *Tati* [Paris: Ramsay, 2009], 195 and 207). Moreover, unlike franglais words such as *drugstore*, *parking*, and *weekend*, there is no such word as *PlayTime* in English. It therefore reads strangely in an English-language context. Finally, and most importantly, in the credits of the film as well as posters for it, the title seems to be spelled as two, capitalized words, and they are colored differently (blue and red), emphasizing that they are distinct.

2. Noël Carroll, "Notes on the Sight Gag," in *Theorizing the Moving Image* (Cambridge: Cambridge University Press, 1996), 151.

3. I use the word *incongruity* here and elsewhere because Carroll's theory of the sight gag, which I am drawing on, is predicated on the so-called incongruity theory of humor (see Carroll, "Notes on the Sight Gag," 147). I briefly address this theory, along with two other prominent theories of humor— the superiority and release theories—in chapter 1. For a lively overview of these and other theories of humor, and a defense of the incongruity theory, see Carroll's *On Humor: A Very Short Introduction* (Oxford: Oxford University Press, 2014).

4. Rudolf Arnheim, *Film as Art* (Berkeley: University of California Press, 1957), 36.

5. Jonathan Rosenbaum, "Tati's Democracy," *Film Comment* 9, no. 3 (May–June 1973): 36.

6. Lucy Fischer, " 'Beyond Freedom and Dignity': An Analysis of Jacques Tati's *Playtime*," *Sight and Sound* 45, no. 4 (Autumn 1976): 234–39.

7. Harold G. Woodside, "Tati Speaks," *Take One* 2, no. 6 (July–August 1969): 8.

8. David Bordwell has explored many of these devices in his *Figures Traced in Light: On Cinematic Staging* (Berkeley: University of California Press, 2005).

9. David Bellos makes no mention of it, for example, in his description of the scene. See Bellos, *Jacques Tati: His Life and Art* (London: Harvill Press, 1999), 261.

10. See Bellos, *Jacques Tati*. Bellos's book is largely a biography, although it contains some insightful analysis of Tati's films.

11. See Penelope Gilliatt, *Jacques Tati* (London: Woburn, 1976); Brent Maddock, *The Films of Jacques Tati* (Metchuen, NJ: Scarecrow, 1977); Lucy Fischer, *Jacques Tati: A Guide to References and Resources* (Boston: G. K. Hall, 1983); and James Harding, *Jacques Tati Frame by Frame* (London: Secker & Warburg, 1984).

12. Some of this is covered in Bellos, *Jacques Tati*.

13. András Bálint Kovács, *Screening Modernism: European Art Cinema, 1950–1980* (Chicago: University of Chicago Press, 2007), 16.

14. P. Adams Sitney, *Modernist Montage: The Obscurity of Vision in Cinema and Literature* (New York: Columbia University Press, 1990), 1.

15. Kovács, *Screening Modernism*, 56.

16. Steve Seidman, *Comedian Comedy: A Tradition in Hollywood Film* (Ann Arbor, MI: UMI Research Press, 1981), 64.

17. Seidman, *Comedian Comedy*, 64.

18. Notable exceptions include Hugh Kenner, *Flaubert, Joyce and Beckett: The Stoic Comedians* (Boston: Beacon Press, 1962); Roger Shattuck, *The Banquet Years: The Origins of the Avant-Garde in France, 1885 to World War I* (New York: Vintage, 1968); Phillip Dennis Cate and Mary Shaw, eds., *The Spirit of Montmartre: Cabarets, Humor, and the Avant-Garde, 1875–1905* (New Brunswick, NJ: Jane Voorhees Zimmerli Art Museum/Rutgers, 1996); Pamela Kort, ed., *Comic Grotesque: Wit and Mockery in*

German Art, 1870–1940 (New York: Neue Galerie/Prestel Verlag, 2004); John C. Welchman, ed., *Black Sphinx: On the Comedic in Modern Art* (Zurich: JRP Ringier, 2010); Michael North, *Machine-Age Comedy* (New York: Oxford University Press, 2008); and William Solomon, *Slapstick Modernism: Chaplin to Kerouac to Iggy Pop* (Urbana: University of Illinois Press, 2016).

19. Recently, William Solomon has coined the term *slapstick modernism* to refer to what he describes as "the coalescence in cultural practice of the artistic experimentation associated with high modernism and the socially disruptive lunacy linked to the comic film genre" (*Slapstick Modernism*, 2). Solomon's account is full of insights into the convergence between modernism and slapstick comedy. However, I continue to prefer the term *comedic modernism* because, as I argue in chapter one, modernists were influenced by a variety of conventions from the genre of comedian comedy, not just slapstick. Furthermore, Solomon argues that modernism and slapstick "for the most part had remained separate throughout the 1920s . . . and then came together in explosive fashion in the United States in the post-World War II era" (*Slapstick Modernism*, 2), when in fact this convergence started occurring long before the 1920s.

20. See, most recently, Owen Hatherley, *The Chaplin Machine: Slapstick, Fordism, and the International Communist Avant-Garde* (London: Pluto Press, 2016).

21. Miriam Hansen, "The Mass Production of the Senses: Classical Cinema as Vernacular Modernism," in *Reinventing Film Studies*, ed. Christine Gledhill and Linda Williams (London: Arnold, 2000), 333.

22. Hansen, "Mass Production of the Senses," 333.

23. Hansen, "Mass Production of the Senses," 341–42.

24. Hansen, "Mass Production of the Senses," 342.

25. Hansen, "Mass Production of the Senses," 343.

26. David Bordwell, Janet Staiger, and Kristin Thompson, *The Classical Hollywood Cinema: Film Style & Mode of Production to 1960* (New York: Routledge, 1988).

27. Hansen, "The Mass Production of the Senses," 340–41. As David Bordwell notes, he and the other authors of *The Classical Hollywood Cinema* nowhere claim that the "transnational and translatable and resonance" of classical Hollywood cinema is due to "its optimal mobilization of biologically hardwired structures and universal [classical] narrative templates." Rather, Bordwell argues that "many aspects of film style are transformations of a variety of cross-cultural skills and practices, *both biological and cultural*," an example being the streamlining and amplification of face-to-face conversation, a cross-cultural universal, in shot/reverse shot (Bordwell, afterword to "Convention, Construction, and Cinematic Vision," in *Poetics of Cinema* [New York: Routledge, 2008], 76).

28. Miriam Hansen, "Fallen Women, Rising Stars, New Horizons: Shanghai Silent Film As Vernacular Modernism," *Film Quarterly* 54, no. 1 (Autumn, 2000): 10–22.

29. Hansen, "Mass Production of the Senses," 342 (my emphasis).

30. Hansen, "Mass Production of the Senses," 337.

31. Hansen, "Mass Production of the Senses," 339.

32. Charlie Keil, "'To Here from Modernity': Style, Historiography, and Transitional Cinema," in *American Cinema's Transitional Era: Audiences, Institutions, Practices*, ed. Charlie Keil and Shelley Stamp (Berkeley: University of California Press, 2004), 62.

33. David Bordwell, *Narration in the Fiction Film* (Madison: University of Wisconsin Press, 1985), 281.

34. Bordwell, *Narration in the Fiction Film*, 285.

35. Bordwell, *Narration in the Fiction Film*, 275.

36. Bordwell, *Narration in the Fiction Film*, 275.

37. Bordwell, *Narration in the Fiction Film*, 283.

38. Bordwell, *Narration in the Fiction Film*, 280.

39. Bordwell, *Narration in the Fiction Film*, 282.

40. Bordwell, *Narration in the Fiction Film*, 36.

41. Thompson, "*Play Time*," 248.
42. Bordwell, *Narration in the Fiction Film*, 282.
43. Bordwell, *Narration in the Fiction Film*, 283.
44. Bordwell, *Narration in the Fiction Film*, 285.
45. Thompson, "*Play Time*," 251.
46. Thompson, "*Play Time*," 252.
47. Thompson, "*Play Time*," 255.
48. Thompson, "*Play Time*," 252.
49. Kevin Thomas, "Jacques Tati: Silent Comedy's Heir," *Los Angeles Times*, November 24, 1972, 33.
50. Thompson, "*Play Time*," 252.
51. Thompson, "*Play Time*," 248.
52. Bordwell, *Narration in the Fiction Film*, 36.
53. Bordwell, *Narration in the Fiction Film*, 293.
54. Monroe C. Beardsley and William K. Wimsatt, "The Intentional Fallacy," in Wimsatt, *The Verbal Icon: Studies in the Meaning of Poetry* (Lexington: University of Kentucky Press, 1954), 3.
55. Berys Gaut, *A Philosophy of Cinematic Art* (Cambridge: Cambridge University Press, 2010), 106.
56. Gaut, *A Philosophy of Cinematic Art*, 112.
57. Gaut, *A Philosophy of Cinematic Art*, 113.
58. Gaut, *A Philosophy of Cinematic Art*, 103.
59. Joanna Robinson, "Did *Twin Peaks* Star Naomi Watts Just Hint That We'll Never See Agent Cooper Again?," *Vanity Fair Hollywood*, July 21, 2017, https://www.vanityfair.com/hollywood/2017/07/twin-peaks-comic-con-naomi-watts-agent-cooper-never-waking-up.
60. Bordwell, Staiger, and Thompson, *The Classical Hollywood Cinema*, 117.
61. Gaut, *A Philosophy of Cinematic Art*, 122.
62. Paisley Livingston, *Cinema, Philosophy, Bergman: On Film as Philosophy* (Oxford: Oxford University Press, 2009), 67–68.
63. Livingston, *Cinema, Philosophy, Bergman*, 69. See Victor Perkins, *Film as Film: Understanding and Judging Movies* (New York: Penguin, 1972), 184.
64. Ted Nannicelli emphasizes the role of the author's responsibility for a work in the agential approach to the appreciation of television he develops in chapter 1 of his *Appreciating the Art of Television: A Philosophical Perspective* (New York: Routledge, 2017).
65. Livingston, *Cinema, Philosophy, Bergman*, 72–73.
66. Livingston, *Cinema, Philosophy, Bergman*, 67–68.
67. A useful survey of some of these theories can be found in Stephen Davies, "Authors' Intentions, Literary Interpretation, and Literary Value," *British Journal of Aesthetics* 46, no. 3 (July 2006): 223–47.
68. See David Davies, *Art as Performance* (Malden, MA: Blackwell, 2004), 89–96.
69. Livingston, *Cinema, Philosophy, Bergman*, 65.
70. Livingston, *Cinema, Philosophy, Bergman*, 99.

1. COMEDIC MODERNISM

1. For an overview of the image of the entertainer including the clown in modern art, see Naomi Ritter, *Art as Spectacle: Images of the Entertainer Since Romanticism* (Columbia: University of Missouri Press, 1989).
2. Louisa E. Jones, *Sad Clowns and Pale Pierrots: Literature and the Popular Comic Arts in Nineteenth-Century France* (Lexington, KY: French Forum, 1984), 12–14.

3. Jones, *Sad Clowns and Pale Pierrots*, 23–24.

4. Robert Storey, *Pierrots on the Stage of Desire: Nineteenth-Century French Literary Artists and the Comic Pantomime* (Princeton, NJ: Princeton University Press, 1985), 18–25. As Storey puts it, "Like the circus (another enthusiasm of [Romantic writers such as] Gautier, Banville, Baudelaire), the *pantomime-féerie* offered frankly infantile fantasy to the habitués of the Funambules" (25).

5. Storey, *Pierrots on the Stage of Desire*, 159–60.

6. Philip Dennis Cate, "The Spirit of Montmartre," in *The Spirit of Montmartre: Cabarets, Humor, and the Avant-Garde, 1875–1905*, ed. Phillip Dennis Cate and Mary Shaw (New Brunswick, NJ: Jane Voorhees Zimmerli Art Museum/Rutgers, 1996), 37.

7. Roger Shattuck, *The Banquet Years: The Origins of the Avant-Garde in France, 1885 to World War I* (New York: Vintage, 1968), 206.

8. See Robert L. Herbert, *Impressionism: Art, Leisure, and Parisian Society* (New Haven, CT: Yale University Press, 1988), chapters 3 and 4.

9. See the first-hand account in Fernande Olivier, *Picasso and His Friends*, trans. J. Miller (New York: Appleton-Century, 1965), 127.

10. Theodore Reff, "Harlequins, Saltimbanques, Clowns, and Fools," *Artforum* 10, no. 2 (October 1971): 38.

11. On the influence of music-hall on Picasso and Marinetti, see Jeffrey Weiss, "'Le Journal Joué': Picasso, Collage and Music-Hall Modernism," chap. 1 in *The Popular Culture of Modern Art: Picasso, Duchamp, and Avant-Gardism* (New Haven, CT: Yale University Press, 1994).

12. See Richard Abel, "American Film and the French Literary Avant-Garde (1914–1924)," *Contemporary Literature* 17, no. 1 (Winter 1976): 90–92.

13. For an overview of the avant-garde's embrace of Chaplin, see Peter Conrad, "The Chapliniad," chap. 18 in *Modern Times Modern Places: Life & Art in the Twentieth Century* (London: Thames & Hudson, 1998).

14. Richard Pells, *Modernist America: Art, Music, Movies, & the Globalization of American Culture* (New Haven, CT: Yale University Press, 2011), 24; 27.

15. András Bálint Kovács, *Screening Modernism: European Art Cinema, 1950–1980* (Chicago: University of Chicago Press, 2007), 16–17.

16. Wanda M. Corn, *The Great American Thing: Modern Art and National Identity, 1915–1935* (Berkeley: University of California Press, 1999), 53–54.

17. Kovács, *Screening Modernism*, 17.

18. Elie Faure, "The Art of Cineplastics," in *French Film Theory and Criticism*, ed. Richard Abel, vol. 1, *1907–1929* (Princeton, NJ: Princeton University Press, 1988), 263.

19. René Clair, *Cinema Yesterday and Today*, ed. R. C. Dale, trans. Stanley Appelbaum (New York: Dover, 1972), 104.

20. Yuri Tsivian, "Charlie Chaplin and His Shadows: On Laws of Fortuity in Art," *Critical Inquiry* 40, no. 3 (Spring 2014): 73.

21. Lucy Fischer briefly considers Tati's relation to Clair, as well as Jean Vigo and surrealism, in *Jacques Tati: A Guide to References and Resources* (Boston: G.K. Hall, 1983), 46–53.

22. Carolyn Lanchner "Fernand Léger: American Connections," in *Fernand Léger*, exhibition catalogue (New York: Museum of Modern Art, 1998), 45.

23. Fernand Léger, "A Critical Essay on the Plastic Quality of Abel Gance's Film *The Wheel*," in *Functions of Painting* (New York: Viking Press, 1973), 21.

24. Léger, "A Critical Essay," 21.

25. Léger, "Painting and Cinema," in Abel, *French Film Theory and Criticism*, vol. 1, 373.

26. Léger, "Painting and Cinema," 373.

27. Fernand Léger, "On Charlie Chaplin," in *Léger: Modern Art and the Metropolis*, exhibition catalogue, ed. Anna Vallye (Philadelphia: Philadelphia Museum of Art, 2013), 153.

28. Alan Dale, *Comedy Is a Man in Trouble: Slapstick in American Movies* (Minneapolis: University of Minnesota Press, 2000), 1; 3.

29. Walter Kerr, *The Silent Clowns* (New York: A. A. Knopf, 1980), 82.

30. Léger, "On Charlie Chaplin," in Vallye, *Léger*, 153.

31. Dale, *Comedy Is a Man in Trouble*, 38; Kerr, *Silent Clowns*, 85.

32. Jennifer Wild, "What Léger Saw: The Cinematic Spectacle and the Meteor of the Machine Age," in Vallye, *Léger*, 147.

33. This impression of a gap between Chaplin the actor and his characters is undoubtedly one reason why Bertolt Brecht argued that Chaplin's acting style "would in many ways come closer to the epic than to the dramatic theater's requirements" (*Brecht on Theater: The Development of an Aesthetic*, ed. and trans. John Willett [New York: Hill and Wang, 1964], 56).

34. See Sherwin Simmons, "Chaplin Smiles on the Wall: Berlin Dada and Wish-Images of Popular Culture," *New German Critique* 84 (Autumn 2001): 3–34; and Jennifer Wild, "The Automatic Chance of the Modern Tramp: Chaplin and the Parisian Avant-Garde," *Early Popular Visual Culture* 8, no. 3 (August 2010): 263–83.

35. Yvan Goll, "The Chaplinade: A Film Poem," trans. Clinton J. Atkinson and Arthur S. Wensinger, *Massachusetts Review* 6, no. 3 (Spring–Summer 1965): 503.

36. Goll, "The Chaplinade," 503.

37. Kerr, *Silent Clowns*, 85.

38. Christopher Green, *Léger and the Avant-Garde* (New Haven, CT: Yale University Press, 1976), 233.

39. Tsivian, "Charlie Chaplin and His Shadows," 82.

40. Viktor Shklovsky, "Literature and Cinema" (extract), in *The Film Factory: Russian and Soviet Cinema in Documents 1896–1939*, ed. Richard Taylor and Ian Christie (London: Routledge, 1988), 99.

41. Shklovsky, "Literature and Cinema," 98.

42. Quoted in Tsivian, "Charlie Chaplin and His Shadows," 82.

43. Luis Buñuel, "Buster Keaton's *College*," in *An Unspeakable Betrayal: Selected Writings of Luis Buñuel*, trans. Garrett White (Berkeley: University of California Press, 2000), 110.

44. Salvador Dalí, "Saint Sebastian," in *Oui: The Paranoid-Critical Revolution, Writings 1927–1933*, ed. Robert Descharnes, trans. Yvonne Shafir (Boston: Exact Change, 1998), 7.

45. Salvador Dalí, "Poetry of Standardized Utility," in Descharnes, *Oui*, 43.

46. Buñuel, "Buster Keaton's *College*," 110.

47. See Robert Knopf, *The Theater and Cinema of Buster Keaton* (Princeton, NJ: Princeton University Press, 1999), 114.

48. Buñuel, "Buster Keaton's *College*," 111.

49. See, for example, Matthew Gale, "*Un Chien Andalou*," in *Dalí and Film*, ed. Matthew Gale (London: Tate, 2007), 82–93.

50. Jean Starobinski, "The Grimacing Double," in *The Great Parade: Portrait of the Artist as Clown*, ed. Gerard Regnier (Jean Clair) (New Haven, CT: Yale University Press, 2004), 17.

51. See Sabine Hake, "Chaplin Reception in Weimar Germany," *New German Critique* 51 (Autumn 1990): 96–97.

52. Sergei Eisenstein, "Charlie the Kid," in *Selected Works*, ed. Richard Taylor, trans. William Powell, vol. 3, *Writings, 1934–47*, (London: BFI, 1996), 245.

53. Eisenstein, "Charlie the Kid," in Taylor, *Selected Works*, 251.

54. The Surrealist Group, "Hands Off Love," in *The Shadow and Its Shadow: Surrealist Writings on the Cinema*, 3rd ed., trans. and ed. Paul Hammond (San Francisco: City Lights, 2000), 179.

55. Goll, "The Chaplinade," 510.

56. Goll, "The Chaplinade," 513.

57. Goll, "The Chaplinade," 514.

58. Rod A. Martin, *The Psychology of Humor: An Integrative Approach* (Burlington, MA: Elsevier Academic Press, 2007), 63.

59. Knopf, *Theater and Cinema*, 121–33.

60. John Lippitt, "Humor," in *A Companion to Aesthetics*, ed. Stephen Davies (Malden, MA: Wiley-Blackwell, 2009), 336–37.

61. Eisenstein, "Charlie the Kid," in Taylor, *Selected Works*, 261.

62. Eisenstein, "Charlie the Kid," 262.

63. Antonin Artaud, *Selected Writings*, ed. Susan Sontag (Berkeley: University of California Press, 1988), 240.

64. Artaud, *Selected Writings*, 241.

65. Artaud, *Selected Writings*, 241.

66. Artaud, "Cinema and Reality," in Abel, *French Film Theory and Criticism*, vol. 1, 412.

67. Clair, *Cinema Yesterday and Today*, 101.

68. Clair, *Cinema Yesterday and Today*, 35.

69. Clair, *Cinema Yesterday and Today*, 100.

70. Clair, "Rhythm," in Abel, *French Film Theory and Criticism*, vol. 1, 368; Francis Picabia,"Instantanism," in *I Am a Beautiful Monster: Poetry, Prose, and Provocation*, trans. Marc Lowenthal (Cambridge, MA: MIT Press, 2007), 318.

71. Clair, "Rhythm," 370.

72. Clair, *Cinema Yesterday and Today*, 69.

73. Clair, *Cinema Yesterday and Today*, 69.

74. Clair, *Cinema Yesterday and Today*, 18.

75. Clair, "Rhythm," 370.

76. Clair, *Cinema Yesterday and Today*, 103, 106.

77. Clair, *Cinema Yesterday and Today*, 83.

78. Steven Kovacs, *From Enchantment to Rage: The Story of Surrealist Cinema* (Rutherford, NJ: Fairleigh Dickinson University Press, 1980), 94.

79. Charlie Chaplin, "What People Laugh At," *American Magazine* 86 (November 1918), 34, 134.

80. Martin, *The Psychology of Humor*, 44.

81. Jones, *Sad Clowns and Pale Pierrots*, 235.

82. Fernand Léger, "*Ballet Mécanique*," in *Functions of Painting*, 49.

83. Léger, "Painting and Cinema," 373.

84. Clair, *Cinema Yesterday and Today*, 81.

85. Léger, "On Charlie Chaplin," in Vallye, *Léger*, 153.

86. Clair's 1928 documentary *La Tour* is about the Eiffel Tower, the setting for his earlier *Paris qui dort* (1923).

87. See, for example, Celia McGerr, *René Clair* (Boston: Twayne Publishers, 1980), 47ff.

88. Dale, *Comedy Is a Man in Trouble*, 10.

89. Clair, *Cinema Yesterday and Today*, 83.

90. Louis Aragon, "On Decor," in Abel, *French Film Theory and Criticism*, vol. 1, 167.

2. COMEDY OF EVERYDAY LIFE

1. Michel Chion, *The Films of Jacques Tati*, trans. Monique Viñas, Patrick Williamson, and Antonio D'Alfonso (Toronto: Guernica, 1997), 24, 25.

2. Stéphane Goudet, *Jacques Tati de François le facteur à Monsieur Hulot* (Paris: Cahiers du cinéma, 2002), 24–25.

3. Jonathan Rosenbaum, "Tati's Democracy," *Film Comment* 9, no. 3 (May–June 1973): 39.

4. André Bazin and François Truffaut, "An Interview with Jacques Tati," trans. Bert Cardullo, *Quarterly Review of Film and Video* 19, no. 4 (October 2002): 288–89. This interview originally appeared in *Cahiers du cinéma* 83 (May 1958): 2–18.

5. Richard Kuisel, *Seducing the French: The Dilemma of Americanization* (Berkeley: University of California Press, 1993), 12.

6. Richard Pells, *Not Like Us: How Europeans Have Loved, Hated, and Transformed American Culture Since World War II* (New York: Basic Books, 1987), 196.

7. Pells, *Not Like Us*, 238.

8. Pells, *Not Like Us*, 239.

9. Guy Debord, *Society of the Spectacle* (Detroit, MI: Black & Red), para. 4, 1.

10. Debord, *Society of the Spectacle*, para. 30.

11. Theodor Adorno and Max Horkheimer, *Dialectic of Enlightenment*, trans. John Cumming (London: Verso, 1989), xiv.

12. Adorno and Horkheimer, *Dialectic of Enlightenment*, 137.

13. Adorno and Horkheimer, *Dialectic of Enlightenment*, 167. For a trenchant critique of these and other views of mass culture, see Noël Carroll, "Philosophical Resistance to Mass Art: The Majority Tradition," chap. 1 in *A Philosophy of Mass Art* (Oxford: Oxford University Press, 1998).

14. Bazin and Truffaut, "An Interview with Jacques Tati," 294.

15. Bazin and Truffaut, "An Interview with Jacques Tati," 296.

16. Rosenbaum, "Tati's Democracy," 40.

17. Kevin Thomas, "Jacques Tati: Silent Comedy's Heir," *Los Angeles Times*, November 24, 1972, 33. Jonathan Rosenbaum reports that when he worked on the unrealized script for *Confusion* with Tati in the early 1970s, it was about television ("The Death of Hulot," *Sight and Sound* 52, no. 2 [Spring 1983]: 95).

18. Harold G. Woodside, "Tati Speaks," *Take One* 2, no. 6 (July–August 1969): 8.

19. Kaira M. Cabañas, *Off-Screen Cinema: Isidore Isou and the Lettrist Avant-Garde* (Chicago: University of Chicago Press, 2014), 3.

20. Tom McDonough, *"The Beautiful Language of My Century": Reinventing the Language of Contestation in Postwar France, 1945–1968* (Cambridge, MA: MIT Press, 2007), 5.

21. Fred Turner, *The Democratic Surround: Multimedia and American Liberalism from World War II to the Psychedelic Sixties* (Chicago: University of Chicago Press, 2013), 3.

22. Turner, *The Democratic Surround*, 126–27.

23. Pells, *Not Like Us*, 282.

24. Bazin and Truffaut, "An Interview with Jacques Tati," 289.

25. Kristin Thompson, "*Parade*: A Review of an Unreleased Film," *The Velvet Light Trap* 22 (January 1986): 77–78.

26. André Bazin, "Monsieur Hulot and Time," in *What is Cinema?*, trans. Timothy Barnard (Montreal, Canada: Caboose, 2009), 41.

27. Noël Burch, *Theory of Film Practice*, trans. Helen R. Lane (Princeton, NJ: Princeton University Press, 1969), 64.

28. Roy Armes, *The Ambiguous Image: Narrative Style in Modern European Cinema* (Bloomington: Indiana University Press, 1976), 71.

29. Kristin Thompson, "Boredom on the Beach," in *Breaking the Glass Armor: Neoformalist Film Analysis* (Princeton, NJ: Princeton University Press, 1988), 97.

30. Rosenbaum, "Tati's Democracy," 36.

31. Rosenbaum, "Tati's Democracy," 37.

32. Bazin and Truffaut, "An Interview with Jacques Tati," 289.

33. Noël Carroll, "Notes on the Sight Gag," in *Theorizing the Moving Image* (Cambridge: Cambridge University Press, 1996), 150.

34. Bazin and Truffaut, "An Interview with Jacques Tati," 291.

35. Carroll, "Notes on the Sight Gag," 150.

36. Bazin and Truffaut, "An Interview with Jacques Tati," 289.

37. Carroll, "Notes on the Sight Gag," 153.

38. Bazin and Truffaut, "An Interview with Jacques Tati," 291. Tati vacillated on this point. Eight years later he claimed in an interview that he was "the opposite of a Chaplin or a Keaton" (Gilles Jacob and Claire Clouzot, "Letter from Paris," *Sight and Sound* 34, no. 4 [Autumn 1965]: 163).

39. Carroll, "Notes on the Sight Gag," 153.

40. Bazin and Truffaut, "An Interview with Jacques Tati," 290. There are one or two exceptions. For example, in *Mon Oncle*, Hulot gives his nephew, Gerard, a paper mannequin of a Tramp-like figure that makes Gerard laugh.

41. Bazin and Truffaut, "An Interview with Jacques Tati," 288.

42. Penelope Gilliatt, *Jacques Tati* (London: Woburn Press, 1976), 69.

43. Harold G. Woodside, "Tati Speaks," *Take One* 2, no. 6 (July–August 1969): 7.

44. Woodside, "Tati Speaks," 7.

45. Bazin and Truffaut, "An Interview with Jacques Tati," 290.

46. Lucy Fischer, *Jacques Tati: A Guide to References and Resources* (Boston: G. K. Hall, 1983), 50.

47. Very occasionally Tati's characters intentionally create object analogs, as when, during the restaurant scene in *Play Time*, the American businessman affixes a red, white, and blue coaster to the black semicircular shutter above the chef's head, making it look as though he is wearing a bicorne hat with a cockade of the sort associated with Napoleon (fig. 4.6). I will return to this example in chapter 4.

48. Lucy Fischer, "*Homo Ludens:* An Analysis of Four Films by Jacques Tati" (PhD diss., New York University, 1978), 97.

49. Nor are these figures always major characters. The fisherman who observes Hulot treading on and breaking his boat in *Les Vacances* is shown only once, as is the businessman conducting a meeting who sees Hulot in the street below gesticulating at Giffard's reflection in *Play Time*. However, such minor characters do not typically appear to enjoy the humor they witness.

50. Fischer is wrong to argue that the observer-figures never appreciate the comedy happening all around them ("*Homo Ludens,*" 86). Clearly, Henry, the Englishwoman, and the German businessman's son do, which is why they say goodbye to Hulot at the end of the vacation while everybody else snubs him.

51. I thank Kristin Thompson for pointing out to me that the water from the dripping socks looks like tears from the round, eye-like windows.

52. Carroll, "Notes on the Sight Gag," 148.

53. David Bellos, *Jacques Tati: His Life and Art* (London: Harvill Press, 1999), 176.

54. "A Conversation with Jacques Tati," *October* 160 (Spring 2017): 111. This interview originally appeared in *Cahiers du cinéma* 199 (March 1968): 6–23.

55. Rosenbaum, "Tati's Democracy," 39.

56. Bazin, "Monsieur Hulot and Time," 40.

57. Bellos, *Jacques Tati*, 168.

58. The resolution of this goal, which is postponed while Hulot gets caught up in various misadventures, occurs off-screen (if it happens at all) when Hulot by chance meets Giffard on the street outside the Royal Garden restaurant and they walk away together.

59. Thomas, "Jacques Tati," 33.

60. "A Conversation with Jacques Tati," 120.

61. Bazin and Truffaut, "An Interview with Jacques Tati," 292.

62. "A Conversation with Jacques Tati," 125 (my emphasis).

63. Woodside, "Tati Speaks," 8.

64. See my *Doubting Vision: Film and the Revelationist Tradition* (Oxford: Oxford University Press, 2008), 100–110, for an account of this fundamental and enduring modernist myth.

65. Peter Bürger, *Theory of the Avant-Garde*, trans. Michael Shaw (Minneapolis: University of Minnesota Press, 1984), 49.

66. Bürger, *Theory of the Avant-Garde*, 49.

67. Hal Foster, Rosalind Krauss, Yve-Alain Bois, and Benjamin H. D. Buchloh, *Art Since 1900: Modernism, Antimodernism, Postmodernism* (New York: Thames & Hudson, 2004), 531.

68. Bazin and Truffaut, "An Interview with Jacques Tati," 293.

69. In "A Certain Tendency of the French Cinema," his notorious broadside against the French film industry, Truffaut listed Tati alongside Jean Renoir, Robert Bresson, Jean Cocteau, Jacques Becker, Abel Gance, Max Ophuls, and Roger Leenhardt as one of the few examples of a genuine French auteur. See François Truffaut, "A Certain Tendency of the French Film Industry," in *Movies and Methods*, ed. Bill Nichols, vol. 1 (Berkeley: University of California Press, 1976), 229. This essay originally appeared in *Cahiers du cinéma* 31 (January 1954).

70. Bazin and Truffaut, "An Interview with Jacques Tati," 298.

71. Quoted in "Percussionist," *Time* 41, no. 8 (February 22, 1943): 68.

72. *In the Footsteps of Monsieur Hulot*, directed by Sophie Tatischeff. CEPEC/La Sept/Antenne 2/INA, 1989.

73. Woodside, "Tati Speaks," 7–8.

74. Bazin and Truffaut, "Interview with Jacques Tati," 291.

75. Woodside, "Tati Speaks," 8.

3. THE BEHOLDER'S SHARE

1. Michel Chion, *The Films of Jacques Tati*, trans. Monique Viñas, Patrick Williamson, and Antonio D'Alfonso (Toronto: Guernica, 1997), 24.

2. I have no doubt that I, too, have missed some of Tati's gags, or parts of them, due to his comic opacity.

3. P. Adams Sitney, *Modernist Montage: The Obscurity of Vision in Cinema and Literature* (New York: Columbia University Press, 1990), 2.

4. Jacques Rancière, *The Emancipated Spectator*, trans. Gregory Elliott (London: Verso, 2009), 4.

5. Noël Burch, "Notes sur la forme chez Tati," *Cahiers du cinéma* 199 (March 1968): 26 (my translation).

6. Charles Barr, *Laurel and Hardy* (Berkeley: University of California Press, 1968), 23.

7. Walter Kerr is therefore wrong to complain that Laurel and Hardy repeat this gag exactly, and in general he fails to see the subtlety and brilliance of their variation of gags. Kerr, *The Silent Clowns* (New York: Da Capo, 1980), 330.

8. "A Conversation with Jacques Tati," *October* 160 (Spring 2017): 113. This interview originally appeared in *Cahiers du cinéma* 199 (March 1968): 6–23.

9. In the previous iteration, he was swept into an elevator by another large group of businessmen, and in the one before that—the first—he mistakenly stepped into an elevator while waiting for Giffard.

10. Tati reverses this gag in two ways: on the fourth night, it is Hulot's bedroom light we see being turned on in the darkened hotel when he retreats up to bed after unwittingly disrupting the card game and causing a fight among the hotel guests downstairs in the lobby; and on three occasions— Hulot's arrival at the hotel; while he is waiting to go riding with Martine in the parlor of the guest-house; and during the fireworks—someone unexpectedly sleeps through the havoc Hulot is causing.

11. *The High Sign* was the first two-reeler Keaton starred in and directed in 1920, although it was not released until a year later.

12. Jean-Luc Godard, *Godard on Godard: Critical Writings by Jean-Luc Godard*, ed. and trans. Tom Milne (New York: Da Capo, 1972), 48.

13. Kristin Thompson, "*Play Time*: Comedy on the Edge of Perception," in *Breaking the Glass Armor: Neoformalist Film Analysis* (Princeton, NJ: Princeton University Press, 1988), 257.

14. Kevin Thomas, "Jacques Tati: Silent Comedy's Heir," *Los Angeles Times*, November 24, 1972, 33.

15. See Rick Altman, *Silent Film Sound* (New York: Columbia University Press, 2004), 385.

16. See Donald Kirihara, "Sound in *Les Vacances de Monsieur Hulot*," in *Close Viewings: An Anthology of New Film Criticism*, ed. Peter Lehman (Tallahassee: Florida State University Press, 1990), 161–62.

17. McCandlish Phillips, "Mr. Hulot Stalks into Town for *Trafic*," *New York Times*, December 15, 1972, 56.

18. Harold G. Woodside, "Tati Speaks," *Take One* 2, no. 6 (July–August 1969): 8.

19. "A Conversation with Jacques Tati," 118–19.

4. SATIRIZING MODERNITY

1. The French economy expanded at an average rate of 4.5 percent per year from 1949 to 1959, and 5.8 percent per year from 1959 until 1971. The growth figures for the United States in the same years are 3.3 percent and 3.9 percent respectively. Robert Gildea, *France Since 1945* (New York: Oxford University Press, 2002), 101.

2. Richard Kuisel, *Seducing the French: The Dilemma of Americanization* (Berkeley: University of California Press, 1993), 104–5.

3. Kuisel, *Seducing the French*, 149–50.

4. Kristin Ross, *Fast Cars, Clean Bodies: Decolonization and the Reordering of French Culture* (Cambridge, MA: MIT Press, 1995), 4. Ross continues: "In the space of just ten years a rural woman might live the acquisition of electricity, running water, a stove, a refrigerator, a washing machine, a sense of interior space as distinct from exterior space, a car, a television, and the various liberations and oppressions associated with each" (5).

5. Ross, *Fast Cars, Clean Bodies*, 21–22.

6. Ross, *Fast Cars, Clean Bodies*, 30.

7. Gerald Mast, *The Comic Mind: Comedy and the Movies* (Chicago: University of Chicago Press, 1979), 294.

8. Jean-André Fieschi, "Jacques Tati," in *Cinema, A Critical Dictionary, The Major Filmmakers*, vol. 2, *Kinugasa to Zanussi*, ed. Richard Roud (New York: Viking Press, 1980), 1001.

9. Armand J. Cauliez, *Jacques Tati* (Paris: Éditions Seghers, 1968), 17.

10. Lucy Fischer, *Jacques Tati: A Guide to References and Resources* (Boston: G. K. Hall & Co., 1983), 15, 18.

11. James Harding, *Jacques Tati: Frame by Frame* (London: Secker and Warburg, 1984), xviii.

12. Laurent Marie, "Jacques Tati's *Play Time* as New Babylon," in *Cinema and the City: Film and Urban Societies in a Global Context*, ed. Mark Shiel and Tony Fitzmaurice (Malden, MA: Blackwell, 2001), 259.

13. André Bazin and François Truffaut, "An Interview with Jacques Tati," trans. Bert Cardullo, *Quarterly Review of Film and Video* 19, no. 4 (October 2002): 295. This interview originally appeared in *Cahiers du cinéma* 83 (May 1958): 2–18.

14. Quoted in Penelope Gilliat, *Jacques Tati* (London: Woburn Press, 1976), 23.

15. Quoted in Gilles Jacob and Claire Clouzot, "Letter from Paris," *Sight and Sound* 34, no. 4 (Autumn 1965): 163.

16. "A Conversation with Jacques Tati," *October* 160 (Spring 2017): 114. This interview originally appeared in *Cahiers du cinéma* 199 (March 1968): 6–23.

17. "A Conversation with Jacques Tati," 114.

18. Jonathan Rosenbaum, "Tati's Democracy: An Interview and Introduction," *Film Comment* 9, no. 3 (May–June 1973): 40.

19. In *The Filming of Modern Life: European Avant-Garde Film of the 1920s* (Cambridge, MA: MIT Press, 2011), I argue that European avant-garde artists of the interwar years were rarely either anti- or promodernization, but typically criticized one or more features of modernity while embracing others, or embraced and criticized the same features simultaneously. The same is true of post-World War II modernists such as Tati.

20. Fischer, *Jacques Tati*, 18, 26. Chaplin's character, it should be noted, only sabotages the assembly line because he has been driven temporarily insane by the pace of work in the factory.

21. As was noted in chapter 2, Tati insisted that Hulot only ever causes humor "unwittingly" (Bazin and Truffaut, "An Interview with Jacques Tati," 290).

22. Steve Seidman, *Comedian Comedy: A Tradition in Hollywood Film* (Ann Arbor, MI: UMI Research Press, 1981), 70.

23. David Bellos, *Jacques Tati: His Life and Art* (London: Harvill Press, 1999), 168.

24. Bazin and Truffaut, "An Interview with Jacques Tati," 297. As I noted in the preface, this attitude approximates what Alvin Toffler termed future shock, "the shattering stress and disorientation that we induce in individuals by subjecting them to too much change in too short a time." Toffler, *Future Shock* (New York: Bantam Books, 1971), 2.

25. Wanda M. Corn, *The Great American Thing: Modern Art and National Identity, 1915–1935* (Berkeley: University of California Press, 1999), 53–54.

26. In this respect, there is perhaps a trace of the primitivism—defined as "an expressed affinity for people or peoples believed to be living simpler, more natural lives than those of people in the modern West"—that Daniel J. Sherman sees as a "pervasive cultural tendency" in France of this period. See Sherman, *French Primitivism and the Ends of Empire, 1945–1975* (Chicago: University of Chicago Press, 2011), 3.

27. Ross, *Fast Cars, Clean Bodies*, 192.

28. Quoted in Harold Woodside, "Tati Speaks," *Take One* 2, no. 6 (July-August 1969), 8.

29. Woodside, "Tati Speaks," 8.

30. Norma Evenson, *Paris: A Century of Change, 1878–1978* (New Haven, CT: Yale University Press, 1979), 232–36.

31. Evenson, *Paris*, 310.

32. It should be noted, however, that high-rise towers, such as the Tour Montparnasse, did not begin appearing in Paris until after the completion of *Play Time*. See Anthony Sutcliffe, *Paris: An Architectural History* (New Haven, CT: Yale University Press, 1993), 169–71.

33. Evenson, *Paris*, 236–38.

34. Evenson, *Paris*, 339.

35. Bellos, *Jacques Tati*, 207.

36. In the Paris region, single-family homes accounted for only about 20 percent of the housing built between 1949 and 1968 (Evenson, *Paris*, 252).

37. Dietrich Neumann, "*Mon Oncle*," in *Film Architecture: Set Designs from* Metropolis *to* Blade Runner (Munich: Prestel-Verlag, 1996), 136.

38. Neumann, "*Mon Oncle*," 136.

39. Bazin and Truffaut, "An Interview with Jacques Tati," 296.

40. Rosenbaum, "Tati's Democracy," 40.

41. Rosenbaum, "Tati's Democracy," 40.

42. "Entretiens avec Jacques Tati," *Cahiers du cinéma* 303 (September 1979): 22.

43. Jacques Lagrange quoted in Marie-Anne Sichère, "Jacques Tati: Où est l'architecte?," *Monuments Historiques* 137 (1985): 88.

44. On the eighth and final occasion the Arpels, who are trapped in their garage, call out to Georgette, their maid, to help them and she thinks they are asking her to turn on the fountain, which she does.

45. Peter Gay, *The Bourgeois Experience: Victoria to Freud*, vol. 1, *Education of the Senses* (Oxford: Oxford University Press, 1984), 58.

46. Norbert Elias, *The Civilizing Process: The History of Manners*, trans. Edmund Jephcott (Oxford: Blackwell, 1994), part 2.

47. Marc Dondey, *Tati* (Paris: Éditions Ramsay, 2009), 139.

48. Bazin and Truffaut, "An Interview with Jacques Tati," 295.

49. Evenson, *Paris*, 255–64.

50. Bazin and Truffaut, "An Interview with Jacques Tati," 295.

51. Bazin and Truffaut, "An Interview with Jacques Tati," 295.

52. Dorothée Imbert, *The Modernist Garden in France* (New Haven, CT: Yale University Press, 1993), 54.

53. Rosenbaum, "Tati's Democracy," 40.

54. Bazin and Truffaut, "An Interview with Jacques Tati," 296.

55. "Entretiens avec Jacques Tati," 15.

56. Bazin and Truffaut, "An Interview with Jacques Tati," 296.

57. Bazin and Truffaut, "An Interview with Jacques Tati," 294.

58. "A Conversation with Jacques Tati," 110.

59. "Entretiens avec Jacques Tati," 15.

60. Peter Bürger, *Theory of the Avant-Garde*, trans. Michael Shaw (Minneapolis: University of Minnesota Press, 1984), 49.

61. Bürger, *Theory of the Avant-Garde*, 49.

62. *In the Footsteps of Monsieur Hulot*, directed by Sophie Tatischeff. CEPEC/La Sept/Antenne 2/INA, 1989.

AFTERWORD: *PARADE*, TATI, AND PARTICIPATORY CULTURE

1. David Bellos, *Jacques Tati: His Life and Art* (London: Harvill, 1999), 319–20. Bellos, to be fair, acknowledges that there is more to the film than this.

2. Paul-Louis Thiraud, "*Parade*," *Positif* 166 (February 1975): 70.

3. John Pym, "*Parade*," *Monthly Film Bulletin* 51, no. 600 (January 1984): 20.

4. Kristin Thompson, "*Parade*: A Review of an Unreleased Film," *The Velvet Light Trap* 22 (January 1986): 75–83; Jonathan Rosenbaum, "The World as a Circus: Tati's *Parade*," in *Goodbye Cinema, Hello Cinephilia: Film Culture in Transition* (Chicago: University of Chicago Press, 2010), 152–59. Rosenbaum's article was originally published in the December 1, 1989 issue of the *Chicago Reader*.

5. Thompson, "*Parade*," 77.

6. André Bazin and François Truffaut, "An Interview with Jacques Tati," trans. Bert Cardullo, *Quarterly Review of Film and Video* 19, no. 4 (October 2002): 288.

7. "Entretiens avec Jacques Tati," *Cahiers du cinéma* 303 (September 1979): 24.

8. Rosenbaum refers to this as "*bricolage* . . . the appropriation of impersonal objects for personal use that enables people to reshape and reclaim their environment" (Rosenbaum, "World as a Circus," 156).

9. Rosenbaum, "World as a Circus," 159.

10. Henry Jenkins, *Convergence Culture: Where Old and New Media Collide* (New York: New York University Press, 2006), 3.

11. Jenkins, *Convergence Culture*, 3.

12. Henry Jenkins, with Ravi Purushotma, Margaret Weigel, Katie Clinton, and Alice J. Robison, *Confronting the Challenges of Participatory Culture: Media Education for the 21st Century* (Cambridge, MA: MIT Press, 2009), xi.

13. See, for example, Aaron Delwiche and Jennifer Jacobs Henderson, *The Participatory Cultures Handbook* (New York: Routledge, 2013), 4.

14. Anders Ekström, Solveig Jülich, Frans Lundgren, and Per Wisselgren, "Participatory Media in Historical Perspective: An Introduction," in *History of Participatory Media: Politics and Publics, 1750–2000* (New York: Routledge, 2011), 1.

15. Marshall McLuhan, *Understanding Media* (New York: McGraw-Hill, 1964), 22–23.

16. Régis Debray, *Media Manifestos* (London: Verso, 1996), 71

17. Charles Taylor, *Sources of the Self: The Making of the Modern Identity* (Cambridge, MA: Harvard University Press, 1989), 456.

BIBLIOGRAPHY

Abel, Richard. "American Film and the French Literary Avant-Garde (1914–1924)." *Contemporary Literature* 17, no. 1 (Winter 1976): 84–109.

Abel, Richard, ed. *1907–1929*. Vol. 1 of *French Film Theory and Criticism*. Princeton, NJ: Princeton University Press, 1988.

Adorno, Theodor, and Max Horkheimer. *Dialectic of Enlightenment*. London: Verso, 1989.

Altman, Rick. *Silent Film Sound*. New York: Columbia University Press, 2004.

Aragon, Louis. "On Decor." In *1907–1929*, ed. Richard Abel, 165–69. Vol. 1 of *French Film Theory and Criticism*. Princeton, NJ: Princeton University Press, 1988.

Armes, Roy. *The Ambiguous Image*. Bloomington: Indiana University Press, 1976.

Arnheim, Rudolf. *Film as Art*. Berkeley: University of California Press, 1957.

Artaud, Antonin. "Cinema and Reality." In *1907–1929*, ed. Richard Abel, 410–12. Vol. 1 of *French Film Theory and Criticism*. Princeton, NJ: Princeton University Press, 1988.

Artaud, Antonin. *Selected Writings*. Ed. Susan Sontag. Berkeley: University of California Press, 1988.

Barr, Charles. *Laurel and Hardy*. Berkeley: University of California Press, 1968.

Bazin, André. "Fifteen Years of French Cinema." Trans. Bert Cardullo. *Canadian Journal of Film Studies* 18, no. 2 (Fall 2009): 104–16.

Bazin, André. "Monsieur Hulot and Time." In *What is Cinema?*, trans. Timothy Barnard, 37–44. Montreal, Canada: Caboose, 2009.

Bazin, André, and François Truffaut. "An Interview with Jacques Tati," trans. Bert Cardullo. *Quarterly Review of Film and Video* 19, no. 4 (October 2002): 285–98.

Beardsley, Monroe C., and William K. Wimsatt. "The Intentional Fallacy." In *The Verbal Icon: Studies in the Meaning of Poetry*, ed. William K. Wimsatt, 3–18. Lexington: University of Kentucky Press, 1954.

Bellos, David. *Jacques Tati: His Life and Art*. London: Harvill, 1999.

Bordwell, David. "Convention, Construction, and Cinematic Vision." In *Poetics of Cinema*, 57–82. New York: Routledge, 2008.

Bordwell, David. *Figures Traced in Light: On Cinematic Staging*. Berkeley: University of California Press, 2005.

Bordwell, David. *Narration in the Fiction Film*. Madison: University of Wisconsin Press, 1985.

Bordwell, David, Janet Staiger, and Kristin Thompson. *The Classical Hollywood Cinema: Film Style and Mode of Production to 1960*. New York: Routledge, 1988.

Brecht, Bertolt. *Brecht on Theater: The Development of an Aesthetic.* Ed. and trans. John Willett. New York: Hill and Wang, 1964.

Buñuel, Luis. "Buster Keaton's *College.*" In *An Unspeakable Betrayal: Selected Writings of Luis Buñuel*, trans. Garrett White, 110–11. Berkeley: University of California Press, 2000.

Burch, Noël. "Notes sur la forme chez Tati." *Cahiers du cinéma* 199 (March 1968): 26–27.

Burch, Noël. *Theory of Film Practice.* Trans. Helen R. Lane. Princeton, NJ: Princeton University Press, 1969.

Bürger, Peter. *Theory of the Avant-Garde.* Trans. Michael Shaw. Minneapolis: University of Minnesota Press, 1984.

Cabañas, Kaira M. *Off-Screen Cinema: Isidore Isou and the Lettrist Avant-Garde.* Chicago: University of Chicago Press, 2014.

Carroll, Noël. "Notes on the Sight Gag." In *Theorizing the Moving Image*, 146–57. Cambridge: Cambridge University Press, 1996.

Carroll, Noël. *On Humor: A Very Short Introduction.* Oxford: Oxford University Press, 2014.

Carroll, Noël. *A Philosophy of Mass Art.* Oxford: Oxford University Press, 1998.

Cate, Philip Dennis. "The Spirit of Montmartre." In *The Spirit of Montmartre: Cabarets, Humor, and the Avant-Garde, 1875–1905*, ed. Phillip Dennis Cate and Mary Shaw, 1–94. New Brunswick, NJ: Jane Voorhees Zimmerli Art Museum/Rutgers, 1996.

Cate, Philip Dennis, and Mary Shaw, eds. *The Spirit of Montmartre: Cabarets, Humor, and the Avant-Garde, 1875–1905.* New Brunswick, NJ: Jane Voorhees Zimmerli Art Museum/Rutgers, 1996.

Cauliez, Armand J. *Jacques Tati.* Paris: Éditions Seghers, 1968.

Chaplin, Charlie. "What People Laugh At." *American Magazine* 86 (November 1918): 34, 134–37.

Chion, Michel. *The Films of Jacques Tati*, trans. Monique Viñas, Patrick Williamson, and Antonio D'Alfonso. Toronto: Guernica, 1997.

Clair, René. *Cinema Yesterday and Today*, ed. R. C. Dale, trans. Stanley Appelbaum. New York: Dover, 1972.

Clair, René. "Rhythm." In *1907–1929*, ed. Richard Abel, 368–70. Vol. 1 of *French Film Theory and Criticism.* Princeton, NJ: Princeton University Press, 1988.

Conrad, Peter. *Modern Times Modern Places: Life and Art in the Twentieth Century.* London: Thames and Hudson, 1998.

"A Conversation with Jacques Tati." *October* 160 (Spring 2017): 109–26.

Corn, Wanda M. *The Great American Thing: Modern Art and National Identity, 1915–1935.* Berkeley: University of California Press, 1999.

Dale, Alan. *Comedy Is a Man in Trouble: Slapstick in American Movies.* Minneapolis: University of Minnesota Press, 2000.

Dalí, Salvador. "Poetry of Standardized Utility." In *Oui: The Paranoid-Critical Revolution, Writings 1927–1933*, ed. Robert Descharnes, trans. Yvonne Shafir, 43–45. Boston: Exact Change, 1998.

Dalí, Salvador. "Saint Sebastian." In *Oui: The Paranoid-Critical Revolution, Writings 1927–1933*, ed. Robert Descharnes, trans. Yvonne Shafir, 3–8. Boston: Exact Change, 1998.

Davies, David. *Art as Performance.* Malden, MA: Blackwell, 2004.

Davies, Stephen. "Authors' Intentions, Literary Interpretation, and Literary Value." *British Journal of Aesthetics* 46, no. 3 (July 2006): 223–47.

Debord, Guy. *Society of the Spectacle.* Detroit, MI: Black and Red.

Debray, Régis. *Media Manifestos.* London: Verso, 1996.

Delwiche, Aaron, and Jennifer Jacobs Henderson. *The Participatory Cultures Handbook.* New York: Routledge, 2013.

Dondey, Marc. *Tati.* Paris: Ramsay, 2009.

Eisenstein, Sergei. "Charlie the Kid." In *Writings, 1934–47*, ed. Richard Taylor, trans. William Powell, 243–69. Volume 3 of *Selected Works.* London: BFI, 1996.

Ekström, Anders, Solveig Jülich, Frans Lundgren, and Per Wisselgren. "Participatory Media in Historical Perspective: An Introduction." In *History of Participatory Media: Politics and Publics, 1750–2000*, 1–9. New York: Routledge, 2011.

Elias, Norbert. *The Civilizing Process: The History of Manners*. Trans. Edmund Jephcott. Oxford: Blackwell, 1994.

"Entretiens avec Jacques Tati." *Cahiers du cinéma* 303 (September 1979): 8–24.

Evenson, Norma. *Paris: A Century of Change, 1878–1978*. New Haven, CT: Yale University Press, 1979.

Faure, Elie. "The Art of Cineplastics." In *1907–1929*, ed. Richard Abel, 258–68. Vol. 1 of *French Film Theory and Criticism*. Princeton, NJ: Princeton University Press, 1988.

Fieschi, Jean-André. "Jacques Tati." In *Kinugasa to Zanussi*, ed. Richard Roud, 1000–1005. Vol. 2 of *Cinema, A Critical Dictionary, The Major Filmmakers*. New York: Viking, 1980.

Fischer, Lucy. " 'Beyond Freedom and Dignity': An Analysis of Jacques Tati's *Playtime*." *Sight and Sound* 45, no. 4 (Autumn 1976): 234–39.

Fischer, Lucy. "*Homo Ludens*: An Analysis of Four Films by Jacques Tati." PhD diss., New York University, 1978.

Fischer, Lucy. *Jacques Tati: A Guide to References and Resources*. Boston: G.K. Hall, 1983.

Foster, Hal, Rosalind Krauss, Yve-Alain Bois, and Benjamin H. D. Buchloh. *Art Since 1900: Modernism, Antimodernism, Postmodernism*. New York: Thames and Hudson, 2004.

Gale, Matthew. "*Un Chien Andalou*." In *Dalí and Film*, ed. Matthew Gale, 82–93. London: Tate, 2007.

Gaut, Berys. *A Philosophy of Cinematic Art*. Cambridge: Cambridge University Press, 2010.

Gay, Peter. *Education of the Senses*. Vol. 1 of *The Bourgeois Experience: Victoria to Freud*. Oxford: Oxford University Press, 1984.

Gildea, Robert. *France Since 1945*. New York: Oxford University Press, 2002.

Gilliatt, Penelope. *Jacques Tati*. London: Woburn, 1976.

Godard, Jean-Luc Godard. *Godard on Godard: Critical Writings by Jean-Luc Godard*. Edited and trans. Tom Milne. New York: Da Capo, 1972.

Goll, Yvan. "The Chaplinade: A Film Poem." Trans. Clinton J. Atkinson and Arthur S. Wensinger. *Massachusetts Review* 6, no. 3 (Spring–Summer 1965): 497–514.

Goudet, Stéphane. *Jacques Tati de François le facteur à Monsieur Hulot*. Paris: Cahiers du cinéma, 2002.

Green, Christopher. *Léger and the Avant-Garde*. New Haven, CT: Yale University Press, 1976.

Hake, Sabine. "Chaplin Reception in Weimar Germany." *New German Critique* 51 (Autumn 1990): 87–111.

Hansen, Miriam. "Fallen Women, Rising Stars, New Horizons: Shanghai Silent Film as Vernacular Modernism." *Film Quarterly* 54, no. 1 (Autumn, 2000): 10–22.

Hansen, Miriam. "The Mass Production of the Senses: Classical Cinema as Vernacular Modernism." In *Reinventing Film Studies*, ed. Christine Gledhill and Linda Williams, 332–50. London: Arnold, 2000.

Harding, James. *Jacques Tati Frame by Frame*. London: Secker and Warburg, 1984.

Hatherley, Owen. *The Chaplin Machine: Slapstick, Fordism, and the International Communist Avant-Garde*. London: Pluto, 2016.

Herbert, Robert L. *Impressionism: Art, Leisure, and Parisian Society*. New Haven, CT: Yale University Press, 1988.

Imbert, Dorothée. *The Modernist Garden in France*. New Haven, CT: Yale University Press, 1993.

Jacob, Gilles, and Claire Clouzot. "Letter from Paris." *Sight and Sound* 34, no. 4 (Autumn 1965): 160–63.

Jenkins, Henry. *Convergence Culture: Where Old and New Media Collide*. New York: New York University Press, 2006.

Jenkins, Henry, with Ravi Purushotma, Margaret Weigel, Katie Clinton and Alice J. Robison. *Confronting the Challenges of Participatory Culture: Media Education for the 21st Century*. Cambridge, MA: MIT Press, 2009.

Jones, Louisa E. *Sad Clowns and Pale Pierrots: Literature and the Popular Comic Arts in nineteenth-Century France*. Lexington, KY: French Forum, 1984.

Keil, Charlie. " 'To Here from Modernity': Style, Historiography, and Transitional Cinema." In *American Cinema's Transitional Era: Audiences, Institutions, Practices*, ed. Charlie Keil and Shelley Stamp, 51–65. Berkeley: University of California Press, 2004.

Kenner, Hugh. *Flaubert, Joyce and Beckett: The Stoic Comedians*. Boston: Beacon, 1962.

Kerr, Walter. *The Silent Clowns*. New York: A. A. Knopf, 1980.

Kirihara, Donald. "Sound in *Les Vacances de Monsieur Hulot*." In *Close Viewings: An Anthology of New Film Criticism*, ed. Peter Lehman, 150–70. Tallahassee: Florida State University Press, 1990.

Knopf, Robert. *The Theater and Cinema of Buster Keaton*. Princeton, NJ: Princeton University Press, 1999.

Kort, Pamela, ed. *Comic Grotesque: Wit and Mockery in German Art, 1870–1940*. New York: Neue Galerie/Prestel Verlag, 2004.

Kovács, András Bálint. *Screening Modernism: European Art Cinema, 1950–1980*. Chicago: University of Chicago Press, 2007.

Kovacs, Steven. *From Enchantment to Rage: The Story of Surrealist Cinema*. Rutherford, NJ: Fairleigh Dickinson University Press, 1980.

Kuisel, Richard. *Seducing the French: The Dilemma of Americanization*. Berkeley: University of California Press, 1993.

Kynaston, David. *Modernity Britain: 1957–1962*. New York: Bloomsbury, 2015.

Lanchner, Carolyn. "Fernand Léger: American Connections." In *Fernand Léger*, 15–70. New York: Museum of Modern Art, 1998.

Léger, Fernand. *Functions of Painting*. Ed. Edward F. Fry. Trans. Alexandra Anderson. New York: Viking, 1973.

Léger, Fernand. "On Charlie Chaplin." In *Léger: Modern Art and the Metropolis*, ed. Anna Vallye, 152–53. Philadelphia: Philadelphia Museum of Art, 2013.

Léger, Fernand. "Painting and Cinema." In *1907–1929*, ed. Richard Abel, 372–73. Vol. 1 of *French Film Theory and Criticism*. Princeton, NJ: Princeton University Press, 1988.

Lippitt, John. "Humor." In *A Companion to Aesthetics*, ed. Stephen Davies, 334–37. Malden, MA: Wiley-Blackwell, 2009.

Livingston, Paisley. *Cinema, Philosophy, Bergman: On Film as Philosophy*. Oxford: Oxford University Press, 2009.

Maddock, Brent. *The Films of Jacques Tati*. Metchuen, NJ: Scarecrow, 1977.

Marie, Laurent. "Jacques Tati's *Play Time* as New Babylon." In *Cinema and the City: Film and Urban Societies in a Global Context*, ed. Mark Shiel and Tony Fitzmaurice, 257–69. Malden, MA: Blackwell, 2001.

Martin, Rod A. *The Psychology of Humor: An Integrative Approach*. Burlington, MA: Elsevier, 2000.

Mast, Gerald. *The Comic Mind: Comedy and the Movies*. Chicago: University of Chicago Press, 1979.

McDonough, Tom. *"The Beautiful Language of My Century": Reinventing the Language of Contestation in Postwar France, 1945–1968*. Cambridge, MA: MIT Press, 2007.

McGerr, Celia. *René Clair*. Boston: Twayne, 1980.

McLuhan, Marshall. *Understanding Media*. New York: McGraw-Hill, 1964.

Nannicelli, Ted. *Appreciating the Art of Television: A Philosophical Perspective*. New York: Routledge, 2017.

Neumann, Dietrich. "Mon Oncle." In *Film Architecture: Set Designs from Metropolis to Blade Runner*, ed. Dietrich Neumann, 134–39. Munich: Prestel-Verlag, 1996.

North, Michael. *Machine-Age Comedy*. New York: Oxford University Press, 2008.

Olivier, Fernande. *Picasso and His Friends*, trans. J. Miller. New York: Appleton-Century, 1965.

Pells, Richard. *Modernist America: Art, Music, Movies, and the Globalization of American Culture*. New Haven, CT: Yale University Press, 2011.

Pells, Richard. *Not Like Us: How Europeans Have Loved, Hated, and Transformed American Culture Since World War II*. New York: Basic Books, 1987.

"Percussionist." *Time* 41, no. 8 (February 22, 1943): 68.

Phillips, McCandlish. "Mr. Hulot Stalks into Town for *Trafic*." *New York Times*, December 15, 1972.

Picabia, Francis. "Instantanism." In *I Am a Beautiful Monster: Poetry, Prose, and Provocation*, trans. Marc Lowenthal, 317–18. Cambridge, MA: MIT Press, 2007.

Pym, John "*Parade*." *Monthly Film Bulletin* 51, no. 600 (January 1984): 20.

Rancière, Jacques. *The Emancipated Spectator*, trans. Gregory Elliott. London: Verso, 2009.

Reff, Theodore. "Harlequins, Saltimbanques, Clowns, and Fools." *Artforum* 10, no. 2 (October 1971): 31–43.

Ritter, Naomi. *Art as Spectacle: Images of the Entertainer Since Romanticism*. Columbia: University of Missouri Press, 1989.

Robinson, Joanna. "Did *Twin Peaks* Star Naomi Watts Just Hint That We'll Never See Agent Cooper Again?" *Vanity Fair Hollywood*, July 21, 2017. https://www.vanityfair.com/hollywood/2017/07/twin -peaks-comic-con-naomi-watts-agent-cooper-never-waking-up.

Rosenbaum, Jonathan. "The Death of Hulot." *Sight and Sound* 52, no. 2 (Spring 1983): 94–97.

Rosenbaum, Jonathan. "*PlayTime*." *Jonathan Rosenbaum* (blog), July 10, 2018. https://www.jonathanrosenbaum .net/2018/07/playtime-2/.

Rosenbaum, Jonathan. "Tati's Democracy." *Film Comment* 9, no. 3 (May–June 1973): 36–41.

Rosenbaum, Jonathan. "The World as a Circus: Tati's *Parade*." In *Goodbye Cinema, Hello Cinephilia: Film Culture in Transition*, 152–59. Chicago: University of Chicago Press, 2010.

Ross, Kristin. *Fast Cars, Clean Bodies: Decolonization and the Reordering of French Culture*. Cambridge, MA: MIT Press, 1995.

Seidman, Steve. *Comedian Comedy: A Tradition in Hollywood Film*. Ann Arbor, MI: UMI Research Press, 1981.

Shattuck, Roger. *The Banquet Years: The Origins of the Avant-Garde in France, 1885 to World War I*. New York: Vintage, 1968.

Sherman, Daniel J. *French Primitivism and the Ends of Empire, 1945–1975*. Chicago: University of Chicago Press, 2011.

Shklovsky, Viktor. "Literature and Cinema" (extract). In *The Film Factory: Russian and Soviet Cinema in Documents 1896–1939*, ed. Richard Taylor and Ian Christie, 98–99. London: Routledge, 1988.

Sichère, Marie-Anne. "Jacques Tati: Où est l'architecte?" *Monuments Historiques* 137 (1985): 85–90.

Simmons, Sherwin. "Chaplin Smiles on the Wall: Berlin Dada and Wish-Images of Popular Culture." *New German Critique* 84 (Autumn 2001): 3–34

Sitney, P. Adams. *Modernist Montage: The Obscurity of Vision in Cinema and Literature*. New York: Columbia University Press, 1990.

Solomon, William. *Slapstick Modernism: Chaplin to Kerouac to Iggy Pop*. Urbana: University of Illinois Press, 2016.

Starobinski, Jean. "The Grimacing Double." In *The Great Parade: Portrait of the Artist as Clown*, ed. Gerard Regnier (Jean Clair), 16–17. New Haven, CT: Yale University Press, 2004.

Storey, Robert. *Pierrots on the Stage of Desire: Nineteenth-Century French Literary Artists and the Comic Pantomime*. Princeton, NJ: Princeton University Press, 1985.

The Surrealist Group. "Hands off Love." In *The Shadow and Its Shadow: Surrealist Writings on the Cinema*, 3rd edition, ed. and trans. Paul Hammond, 173–80. San Francisco: City Lights, 2000.

Sutcliffe, Anthony. *Paris: An Architectural History*. New Haven, CT: Yale University Press, 1993.

Taylor, Charles. *Sources of the Self: The Making of the Modern Identity*. Cambridge, MA: Harvard University, 1989.

Thiraud, Paul-Louis. "*Parade*." *Positif* 166 (February 1975): 70.

Thomas, Kevin. "Jacques Tati: Silent Comedy's Heir." *Los Angeles Times*, November 24, 1972.

Thompson, Kristin. "Boredom on the Beach." In *Breaking the Glass Armor: Neoformalist Film Analysis*, 89–109. Princeton, NJ: Princeton University Press, 1988.

Thompson, Kristin. "*Parade*: A Review of an Unreleased Film." *The Velvet Light Trap* 22 (January 1986): 75–83.

Thompson, Kristin. "*Play Time*: Comedy on the Edge of Perception." In *Breaking the Glass Armor: Neoformalist Film Analysis*, 247–62. Princeton, NJ: Princeton University Press, 1988.

Thompson, Kristin. "Where in the World is M. Hulot?" *Observations on Film Art*, July 22, 2009, http:// www.davidbordwell.net/blog/2009/07/22/where-in-the-world-is-m-hulot/.

Toffler, Alvin. *Future Shock*. New York: Bantam Books, 1971.

Truffaut, François. "A Certain Tendency of the French Film Industry." In *Movies and Methods*, vol. 1, ed. Bill Nichols, 224–36. Berkeley: University of California Press, 1976.

Tsivian, Yuri. "Charlie Chaplin and His Shadows: On Laws of Fortuity in Art." *Critical Inquiry* 40, no. 3 (Spring 2014): 71–84.

Turner, Fred. *The Democratic Surround: Multimedia and American Liberalism from World War II to the Psychedelic Sixties*. Chicago: University of Chicago Press, 2013.

Turvey, Malcolm. *Doubting Vision: Film and the Revelationist Tradition*. Oxford: Oxford University Press, 2008.

Turvey, Malcolm. *The Filming of Modern Life: European Avant-Garde Film of the 1920s*. Cambridge, MA: MIT Press, 2011.

Weiss, Jeffrey. *The Popular Culture of Modern Art: Picasso, Duchamp, and Avant-Gardism*. New Haven, CT: Yale University Press, 1994.

Welchman, John C., ed. *Black Sphinx: On the Comedic in Modern Art*. Zurich: JRP Ringier, 2010.

Wild, Jennifer. "The Automatic Chance of the Modern Tramp: Chaplin and the Parisian Avant-Garde." *Early Popular Visual Culture* 8, no. 3 (August 2010): 263–83.

Wild, Jennifer. "What Léger Saw: The Cinematic Spectacle and the Meteor of the Machine Age." In *Léger: Modern Art and the Metropolis*, ed. Anna Vallye, 145–50. Philadelphia: Philadelphia Museum of Art, 2013.

Woodside, Harold G. "Tati Speaks." *Take One* 2, no. 6 (July–August 1969): 6–8.

INDEX

4′33″ (1952, Cage), 100

FILM AND CULTURE

A series of Columbia University Press

Edited by John Belton